Dhyan Manik

Learning Thai
with
Original Thai Words

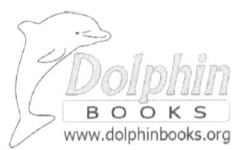

Learning Thai Quickly and Easily

Copyright © Dhyan Manik 2019

Cover design and layout: by Uri Hautamäki / Data Graphics
Pictures: by Tone Artist

Audio spoken in MP3 format by native speakers can be loaded from the following address:

www.thaibooks.net

Thai voices: Ms. Duangmon Loprakhong
                Ms. Waree Singhanart
                Mr. Watit Pumyoo

English voice: Ms. Jiraporn Buasuk

Publisher:
Dolphin Books
info@dolphinbooks.org
www.dolphinbooks.org

ISBN 978-952-6651-43-9

Acknowledgement

I would like to thank the following people for valuable guidance on Thai syntax and grammar, and assistance with editing and proofreading the text to reflect standard spoken Thai:

Ms. Duangmon Loprakhong, Thai Teacher, Duke Language School, Bangkok

Ms. Waree Singhanart, Thai Teacher, Bangkok

Mr. Watit Pumyoo, Chiang Mai University, Chiang Mai

I am also grateful to Mr. Walter Kassela for editing and proofreading the English text.

With the help of the above people, the clarity of the written Thai and English text has been significantly improved.

Special thanks to Duke Language School for kind co-operation.

Table of Contents

Introduction 9

Chapter 1
Simple expressions – coming and going 13
    A. Sentences 14
    B. Vocabulary 15
    C. How the language works 16
    D. New sounds 19
    E. Simple advice 19
    F. Take it further 20

Chapter 2
Using personal pronouns, nouns and adjectives 21
    A. Sentences 22
    B. Vocabulary 24
    C. How the language works 25
    D. New sounds 26
    E. Simple advice 27
    F. Take it further 27

Chapter 3
My name is…, to have, there is, to show possession 29
    A. Sentences 30
    B. Vocabulary 32
    C. How the language works 33
    D. New sounds 35
    E. Simple advice 36
    F. Take it further 37

Chapter 4
At the market and buying things 39
    A. Sentences 40
    B. Vocabulary 42
    C. How the language works 44
    D. New sounds 47
    E. Simple advice 48
    F. Take it further 49

Chapter 5
    Eating and drinking 51
    A. Sentences..52
    B. Vocabulary..54
    C. How the language works 56
    D. New sounds..59
    E. Simple advice 60
    F. Take it further...61

Chapter 6
    Going out – romantic meeting...63
    A. Sentences..64
    B. Vocabulary..66
    C. How the language works 67
    D. New sounds..69
    E. Simple advice 69
    F. Take it further...70

Chapter 7
    Question words 71
    A. Sentences..72
    B. Vocabulary..74
    C. How the language works 75
    D. New sounds..78
    E. Simple advice 78
    F. Take it further...79

Chapter 8
    Colours, tastes and flavours..81
    A. Sentences..82
    B. Vocabulary..84
    C. How the language works 86
    D. New sounds..90
    E. Simple advice 91
    F. Take it further...92

Chapter 9
    At the pharmacy and not being well..93
    A. Sentences..94
    B. Vocabulary..96

    C. How the language works 98
    D. New sounds 101
    E. Simple advice 102
    F. Take it further 103

Chapter 10
    Using prepositions, nouns, adjectives and adverbs 105
    A. Sentences 106
    B. Vocabulary 108
    C. How the language works 111
    D. New sounds 115
    E. Simple advice 116
    F. Take it further 117

Chapter 11
    Using adverbs of frequency – "how often" -words 119
    A. Sentences 120
    B. Vocabulary 122
    C. How the language works 124
    D. New sounds 129
    E. Simple advice 129
    F. Take it further 130

Chapter 12
    Comparisons: *more, less, most, same, equal, as* 131
    A. Sentences 132
    B. Vocabulary 134
    C. How the language works 136
    D. New sounds 140
    E. Simple advice 141
    F. Take it further 142

Chapter 13
    Using hâi ให้ and dâai ได้ – to give and to get 143
    A. Sentences 144
    B. Vocabulary 146
    C. How the language works 148
    D. New sounds 156
    E. Simple advice 157
    F. Take it further 158

Chapter 14
Using เรียน แล้ว and ก่อน ก็ 159
   A. Sentences 160
   B. Vocabulary 163
   C. How the language works 165
   D. New sounds 174
   E. Simple advice 175
   F. Take it further 176

Chapter 15
Expressing Thai tenses 177
   A. Sentences 179
   B. Vocabulary 181
   C. How the language works 183
   D. New Sounds 195
   E. Simple advice 196
   F. Take it further 197

Chapter 16
Thai tenses – duration of time / point of time 199
   A. Sentences 200
   B. Vocabulary 204
   C. How the language works 206
   D. New sounds 212
   E. Simple advice 213
   F. Take it further 214

Chapter 17
Expression of time: clock time, days, months, years... 215
   A. Sentences 216
   B. Vocabulary 220
   C. How the language works 222
   D. New sounds 229
   E. Simple advice 230
   F. Take it further 231

Chapter 18
Using classifiers and numbers 233
   A. Sentences 234
   B. Vocabulary 237

    C. How the language works 239
    D. New Sounds 248
    E. Simple advice 249
    F. Take it further 250

Chapter 19
    Using Thai prefixes to form special meanings 251
    A. Sentences 252
    B. Vocabulary 258
    C. How the language works 262
    D. New sounds 280
    E. Simple advice 281
    F: Take it further 282

Chapter 20
    Connecting words, phrases and sentences 283
    A. Sentences 284
    B. Vocabulary 286
    C. How the language works 288
    D. New sounds 296
    E. Simple advice 297
    F. Take it further 298

Chapter 21
    Tones of the Thai language 299
    A. Tones with short and long vowels 300
    B. Vocabulary 304
    C. How the language works 304
    D. New sounds 307
    E. Simple advice 307
    F. Take it further 308

Introduction

As a learner, you will normally face several obstacles when studying Thai. First, Thai uses a script which is unfamiliar to most of us. Secondly, there is no single transliteration system to write Thai sounds with western letters. So, you need to get used to many different transliteration – sometimes called Romanization – styles, which are not always very accurate and can be difficult to understand. Some of them do not contain any tone marks either. Thirdly, the tonal structure of the Thai language can be a major challenge for a beginner to master. Fourthly, Thai uses a complex system of classifiers, which puts some additional load to your shoulders since you need to learn many special count words in order to express plurals of objects.

We shall point out these challenges in a systematic way. So, you will gain the necessary knowledge and understanding about the Thai language as a whole; this will happen easily without too much effort on your part. We shall also point out what you need to know and what you can leave out in the beginning in order to speak Thai fluently!

In this book, we shall concentrate on the original Thai words which form the basics of the Thai language. It is estimated that the original Thai words constitute less than 50% of the total Thai vocabulary. Concentrating first on the original Thai words makes your language studies easier, and you will learn all the Thai consonant sounds and vowel sounds used today in Thai. The original Thai words are used often, and they play a central role in everyday speaking. They are written with the most common Thai consonants and form a kind of core of the Thai language.

Original Thai words have only one vowel sound in each word. They can be called monosyllables. Hence, they are easier to spell and pronounce since they are spelled with the most common consonants, while borrowed foreign words are often spelled with rare consonants and can have more than one syllable in one word.

The Thai writing system is very complex containing sophisticated tone rules and a vast number of consonants (42 altogether) representing only 20 different consonant sounds. This is due to the fact that many foreign words borrowed from foreign languages such as Pali and Sanskrit use rare consonant symbols for the same common Thai sounds. Note, however, that these borrowed words, spelled with different consonant symbols (called rare consonants), do not add any more sounds to the Thai language. Only the spelling is different.

Therefore, it makes sense in the beginning to concentrate on the original Thai words and sounds. Otherwise, your task could prove to be overwhelming and you may even give up. Learning the Thai script comes later if you wish to do so. That is a totally different game. In order to speak Thai well, you do not need to know the Thai writing system. So, your priority should be to learn simple everyday words, all the sounds of the Thai language, and how the language works; that means how the words are put together. If you have enough time and energy to put some effort into learning to speak Thai, you should be able to acquire sufficient knowledge about the Thai language quite fast; then, you are well prepared to make a decision on how to proceed. However, this process will be different for each learner.

Thai is not as difficult as it sounds . It can be made difficult if you start from the wrong perspective. We will make it simple for you. We teach all the sounds of the Thai language and how words are put together in a sentence. That is the basics of any language. You need to know the sounds well in order to be able to communicate with others. You do not need to know how to read or write in Thai script. Learning to read and write Thai takes considerable effort. Understanding the structure and grammar of the Thai language is very important since it may differ considerably from your own language. When you learn a new language as an adult, your brain wants to understand the process. If you do not have the right skills for the new language, your brain will understand things in its own way based on knowledge from the past. That can be confusing. Therefore, we also have included the section *How the language works* in order to put you on the right track directly at the very beginning.

Many people have friends living in Thailand who have started to learn Thai by themselves or in one of the language schools. Quite a few of them have, however, given up because they have felt that the Thai language is too complicated and difficult. Now, tell your friends that to learn to speak Thai fluently is easy; you will soon see how!

This book is designed in such a way that it can be used by beginners and by those who already have some knowledge about the Thai language. We would recommend that you first read the book quickly in order to gain some overall knowledge about the Thai language. After that you can read the book many more times and go deeper into it by concentrating on those sections and points which are important to you.

How to use this book

Each chapter includes *Sample sentences* spoken by native speakers (Section A). In the *Vocabulary* (Section B), we usually repeat words again and again so that they sink into your subconscious without much effort on you part.

In the *How the language works* (Section C), we explain how the words are put together; it can be called syntax, grammar, word order or the structure of the language. It only means that every language has a unique way to put words together in the sentence.

In the *New sounds* (Section D), we go through each Thai sound so that you will be able to speak Thai fluently and confidently while communicating with Thai people. We would advise you to place much effort on getting sounds correct directly from the beginning.

The *Simple advice* (Section E) is meant to give you clear guidance so you will be able to make intelligent decisions on how to proceed with your Thai studies. You may wish to read this section first in order to gain an overall understanding of the Thai language. This is quite important for learning Thai.

Lastly, in the *Take it further* (Section F), we point out possibilities on how to deepen your understanding about the Thai language and how to proceed with your studies. We have also designed a completely new book Dhyan Manik: *Understanding the Thai Language and Grammar – Take It Further* (ISBN 978-952-6651-46-0) as a supplement to this book. You may also wish to use it alongside with this book in order to facilitate your studies. It can be used with any other Thai learning book as well.

We use a direct method which is easy to comprehend. There is no need to let anything hinder you. When speaking, you don't need to know the complex Thai writing system. However, we also write every sentence in Thai script. You are well advised to ignore that part in the beginning. Later on, if you wish, you may review the Thai script. But in the beginning, it is better to concentrate only on the pronunciation and understanding of the Thai language.

It is quite important to understand the overall complexity of the Thai language. We will guide you through it step by step and introduce the most important features of the Thai language. We recommend that you start listening to audio recordings directly from the beginning. There is no need to understand everything. Just get used to Thai sounds.

We believe that each person has her/his own way to handle information and approach the learning process. So, be creative!

◊

Chapter 1

Simple expressions – coming and going

yùu thîi-nôon
อยู่ ที่ โน่น
It is over there.

Chapter 1

Highlights

pai	ไป	to go
maa	มา	to come
lɛ́ɛu	แล้ว	already

A. Sentences

1 *pai* nǎi ไป ไหน
go where – *Where are you going to?*

2 *pai* nǎi *maa* ไป ไหน มา
go where come – *Where have you been?*

3 tɔ̂ng *pai lɛ́ɛu* ต้อง ไป แล้ว
must go already – *I must go now.*

4 kháu *maa lɛ́ɛu* เขา มา แล้ว
he come already – *He has already come.*

5 kháu *pai lɛ́ɛu* เขา ไป แล้ว
he go already – *He has gone already.*

6 kháu *pai* nǎi เขา ไป ไหน
he go where – *Where did he go?*

7 *yùu* thîi-nǎi อยู่ ที่ ไหน
stay place-where – *Where are you?*

8 *yùu* thîi-níi อยู่ ที่ นี่
stay place-this – *I am here.*

9 yùu thîi-nân อยู่ ที่ นั่น
stay place-that – *It is there.*

10 yùu thîi-nôon อยู่ ที่ โน่น
stay place-that – *It is over there.*

Common expressions
(kham thîi ʧái bɔ̀i-bɔ̀i คำ ที่ ใช้ บ่อยๆ)

Hello!/Hi!/Good bye!

sàwàtdii	สวัสดี	*hello*
sàwàtdii khâ (women say)	สวัสดี ค่ะ	*hello khâ*
sàwàtdii khráp (men say)	สวัสดี ครับ	*hello khráp*

B. Vocabulary

pai năi	ไป ไหน	where are you going to?
pai năi maa	ไป ไหน มา	where have you been?
pai	ไป	to go
maa	มา	to come
tông	ต้อง	must
lέεu	แล้ว	already
thîi-năi	ที่ ไหน	where?
thîi-nân	ที่ นั่น	there
thîi-nôon	ที่ โน่น	there, over there (further)
yùu	อยู่	to stay, to live
thîi-nîi	ที่ นี่	here
thîi	ที่	place, at
năi	ไหน	which?

sàwàtdii khâ	สวัสดี ค่ะ	hello for women
sàwàtdii khráp	สวัสดี ครับ	hello for men
khâ	ค่ะ	polite ending particle for women
khráp	ครับ	polite ending particle for men

C. How the language works

A) Here we want to show that constructing Thai sentences is simple. In Thai, there is no need for any subject in the sentence if it is understood from the context.

> **1** pai năi ไป ไหน
> go where – *Where are you going to?*

- In this sentence, there isn't any subject in Thai since it is understood from the context.
- In English, we need to include the subject (you) for the sentence to be complete.
- In Thai, it is very common to drop the subject.

> **2** tông pai lέεu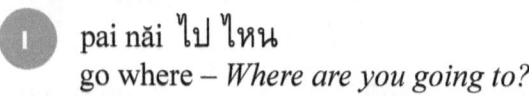
> must go already – *I must go now.*

- In this sentence, there isn't any subject since it is obvious.
- In English, we need to include the subject (I) for the sentence to be complete.
- In Thai, it is very common to drop the subject.
- **tông** ต้อง *must* is a helping verb. **tông pai** ต้อง ไป *must go* is also expressed in a similar manner in English.

> **3** kháu maa *lέεu*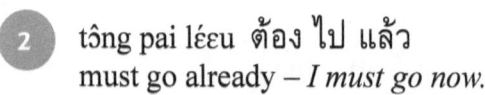
> he come *already* – *He has already come.*

- In this sentence, there is a subject in Thai and in English, **kháu** เขา *he*.
- In Thai, it is fine to include the subject if needed for clarification.
- **lɛ́ɛu** แล้ว *already* is normally placed at the end of the sentence in Thai.

B) Here, there, over there.

> **1** thîi-nîi ที่ นี่
> place-this – *Here.*

- *Here* in Thai is *place-this*.

> **2** thîi-nân ที่ นั่น
> place-that – *There.*

- *There* in Thai is *place-that*.

> **3** thîi-nôon ที่ โน่น
> place-there – *Over there.*

The difference between **thîi-nân** ที่ นั่น *there* and **thîi-nôon** ที่ โน่น *over there* is that the latter is further away from the speaker.

C) Thai people often use simple short expressions; they like to be playful and direct to the point. How the words and phrases are understood depends to a great extent on the context.

For example:
1. **sàwàtdii khâ**   สวัสดี ค่ะ   (women say)
2. **sàwàtdii khráp**   สวัสดี ครับ   (men say)

Depending on the context, this expression can have several different meanings. **sàwàtdii** สวัสดี in the morning means *good morning*, in the evening *good evening*, during the day and when you meet someone *hi* or *hello* and when you depart *goodbye*. It seems that this word cannot be misused. Using it shows some respect on your part. You will hear this expression many times a day.

This word is a loan word from Pali/Sanskrit origin languages. So, we need to say directly in the beginning that in order to learn to speak Thai fluently, we also need to use some loan words. That is because some common loan words are used everyday. Sometimes, there is not any suitable Thai counterpart to replace a loan word either. **sàwàtdii** สวัสดี is one of them. The same goes for the numbers, the names of the days and months, and many technical terms.

D) We must understand that the Thai language is very ancient.

When the original Thai words were used in early days, life was very simple. Counting by numbers was normally used only up to *five* and after that would become *many*. Now, we have computers, cars, banks, ice cream and thousands of other terms which were not used at that time. So, when life has become more complex, Thai has borrowed many words from other languages.

However, original Thai words are very much used today. In this book, you will learn how the Thai language is built around them. Your first priority should be to learn to speak Thai using original Thai words and those loan words which are used often, everyday.

Before we go on, we would like to point out that commonly Thai people don't divide the language into original Thai words and loan words. For them all words are Thai words no matter of their origin. We make a distinction here since it is the best way to get to know the Thai language.

The Thai writing system is very complex, and it takes a long time and much serious effort to master it completely.

D. New sounds

Consonants:
- **p** as in the Thai word **pai** ไป *to go*
  – English sound: s**p**eak, s**p**y, s**p**in (rating: OK, but pay attention)
- **ph** as in the Thai word **phɔɔ** พอ *enough*
  – English sound: **P**eter, **p**aint, **p**assport (rating: good)
- **p** is an unaspirated sound. When you say **p**-sound in Thai, there is not any puff of air coming out your mouth. **ph** is an aspirated sound. When you say **ph**-sound in Thai, there is a clear puff of air coming out your mouth as in English.

Vowels:
- short **a** as in the word kh**â**
  – English sound: b**u**t, n**u**t, fl**oo**d (rating: good)
- long **aa** as in the word m**aa** *to come*
  – English sound: f**ar**, p**a**st, f**a**ther (rating: OK, but without the **r**-sound)

E. Simple advice

When we translate sentences, we give two different translations. First, a *literal word for word* translation in English; in this instance, all the words are in the basic form. We also give the correct English translation of the overall meaning conveyed by the Thai phrase or sentence. Using this method, you will hopefully be able to follow the structure of the Thai language better. It may also help you to learn new words more easily.

Sounds come first. Like in any language, sounds are very important. If you are not able to produce sounds correctly, then you cannot be understood. In Thai, this is even more important because of the tonal nature of the language. In addition, the Thai language has some special sounds which are not familiar to English speakers.

If you are an English speaker, you need some practise to pronounce **p**-sound *unaspirated*, with no puff of air; you are not used to pronounce it like that. In many Asian languages such as Japanese, Chinese, Cambodian, Malaysian, Indonesian etc., this sound is pronounced unaspirated in the same way as in Thai.

As an aid to adjust your pronunciation, just put your hand in front of your mouth and feel. If there is still a puff of air coming out of your mouth, the sound is aspirated and is incorrect. With a little practice you will get it right. First, try **ph** as in the English word **P**eter and note that there is a clear puff of air coming from your mouth. Then learn to say unaspirated **p** ป correctly with no puff of air.

We give a *rating* for each sound that implies how well the Standard British English or General American English sounds can be used while speaking Thai. The rating given here is only an indication and should not be taken as an absolute truth. Note also that the English language is spoken widely and often with different accents. Sounds, particularly the vowel sounds, differ a lot depending on who uses the language and where.

If you are in Thailand, start using Thai words from day one. Don't be afraid. It is a nice game to play to see whether Thais will understand what you are saying. In the beginning, use simple Thai words which are used every day. They are easily understood even if your pronunciation is not perfect. If you are not in Thailand, listen to the audio files and start repeating words you have learned. The key is to practice and use simple words and phrases.

F. Take it further

Refer to the book:

Dhyan Manik: *Understanding the Thai Language and Grammar:*

- More about Thai consonant and vowel sounds can be found in Chapter 1, sections 1.1 and 1.2.
- You may also like to study a list of short term action verbs + **lέεu** แล้ว *already* in Chapter 13, section 13.4.

Chapter 2

Using personal pronouns, nouns and adjectives

phûu-yĭng sŭuai
ผู้ หญิง สวย
Girls are beautiful.

Highlights

tʃán	ฉัน	*I (for women)*
kháu	เขา	*he*
rau	เรา	*we*
phûu-yĭng	ผู้ หญิง	*woman, female*
phûu-tʃaai	ผู้ ชาย	*man, male*
sŭuai	สวย	*to be beautiful*
lɔ̀ɔ	หล่อ	*to be handsome*
kràpău	กระเป๋า	*bag*

A. Sentences

1. tʃán sàbaai *dii* ฉัน สบาย ดี
I fine *good* – *I am good.*

2. piitɔ̂ɔ *sŭung* mâak ปีเตอร์ สูง มาก
peter *tall* very – *Peter is very tall.*

3. kháu *nâa-rák* tsang เขา น่า รัก จัง
she *nâa-love* very – *She is very cute.*

4. rau *dii-tsai* tsing-tsing เรา ดี ใจ จริงๆ
we *good-heart* really-really – *We are really happy.*

5. phûu-yĭng *sŭuai* ผู้ หญิง สวย
person-woman *beautiful* – *Girls are beautiful.*

6. phûu-tʃaai *lɔ̀ɔ* ผู้ ชาย หล่อ
person-man *handsome* – *Men are handsome.*

(7) *dii* lɛ́ɛu ดี แล้ว
good already – *It is already good.*

(8) kràpǎu *nàk* mâak กระเป๋า หนัก มาก
bag *heavy* very – *The bag is very heavy.*

(9) lôok *klom* โลก กลม
world *round* – *The world is round.*

(10) tʃán *yûng* ฉัน ยุ่ง
I *busy* – *I am busy.*

(11) tʃiiang-mài *nâa-yùu* mâak เชียงใหม่ น่า อยู่ มาก
Chiang Mai *nâa-live* very
Chiang Mai is a very pleasant place to live.

(12) fɛɛn tʃán *kèng* แฟน ฉัน เก่ง
boyfriend I *talented* – *My boyfriend is talented.*

(13) wan-níi *nǎau* mâak วัน นี้ หนาว มาก
day-this *cold* very – *Today is very cold.*

Common expressions
(kham thîi tʃái bɔ̀i-bɔ̀i คำ ที่ ใช้ บ่อยๆ)

sàbaai *dii* mái สบาย ดี ไหม
fine *good* "question" – *How are you?*

sàbaai *dii* khâ สบาย ดี ค่ะ
fine *good* khâ – *I am fine, thank you!* (woman)

sàbaai *dii* khráp สบาย ดี ครับ
well *good* khráp – *I am fine, thank you!* (man)

sàbaai-sàbaai สบายๆ
fine-fine – Quite okay.

B. Vocabulary

tʃán	ฉัน	I (women say)
sàbaai	สบาย	to be well
phǒm	ผม	I (men say)
kháu	เขา	she, he
rau	เรา	we
phûu-yǐng	ผู้ หญิง	girl, lady, woman, female
phûu-tʃaai	ผู้ ชาย	boy, man, male
sǔung	สูง	to be tall
nâa-rák	น่า รัก	to be cute, pretty, attractive
tsang	จัง	very, much, really
dii-tsai	ดี ใจ	to be happy
dii	ดี	to be good
tsing-tsing	จริงๆ	really, honestly
sǔuai	สวย	to be beautiful, attractive
lɔ̀ɔ	หล่อ	to be handsome, attractive
lɛ́ɛu	แล้ว	already
kràpǎu	กระเป๋า	bag, wallet
nàk	หนัก	to be heavy
lôok	โลก	world
klom	กลม	to be round
yûng	ยุ่ง	to be busy
nâa-yùu	น่า อยู่	to be pleasant to stay, liveable
yùu	อยู่	to stay, to live
mâak	มาก	very
fɛɛn	แฟน	boyfriend
kèng	เก่ง	to be talented, diligent

wan-níi	วัน นี้	today
năau	หนาว	to be cold
sàbaai dii	สบาย ดี	to feel good
mái	ไหม	basic question word
sàbaai-sàbaai	สบายๆ	to be quite OK
khâ	ค่ะ	polite ending particle for women
kráp	ครับ	polite ending particle for men

C. How the language works

A) One particular feature of the Thai language is that adjectives can play the role of a verb when placed after a subject. Hence, there is no need for any other verb.

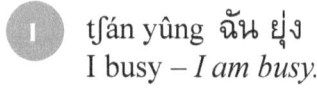

tʃán yûng ฉัน ยุ่ง
I busy – *I am busy.*

- In this sentence, there is not any verb but there is the subject **tʃán** ฉัน *I* and the adjective **yûng** ยุ่ง *to be busy.*
- In English, we need to have a verb (I *am*) for the sentence to be complete.
- In Thai, the verb is understood from the adjective **yûng** ยุ่ง *to be busy.*
- It would be grammatically wrong to add a verb here in Thai.
- If we do add the verb **pen** เป็น *to be* here, then things become a bit more complicated, and we would need to use a different structure. We would need to use a classifier.
- The above sentences 1–13 in the section A are correct; this is the most common way to use adjectives in Thai.

B) The *"question word"* **mái** ไหม is commonly placed at the end of a sentence to form a question in Thai.

① **sàbaai dii *mái*** สบาย ดี ไหม
fine good *"question"* – How are you?

- Here *"question word"* **mái** ไหม is placed at the end of the sentence and after the adjective **dii** ดี *good*.

C) The polite ending particles are commonly used in Thai in order to pay respect and to be polite.

① **sàbaai dii *khâ/khráp*** สบาย ดี ค่ะ/ครับ
fine good *khâ/khráp* – I am fine, thank you!

- Women use **khâ** ค่ะ, and men use **khráp** ครับ.
- These two words cannot really be translated into English. So, we have used here *thank you*.
- In Thai the subject is often dropped when it is understood from the context, here *I*. In English, that is not usually possible.

② ***phŏm* sàbaai dii *khráp*** ผม สบาย ดี ครับ
I fine good *khráp* – I am fine, thank you!

- It is also perfectly fine to include the subject, here **phŏm** ผม *I*.
- Note that in English, when we use the personal pronoun *I*, it doesn't reveal the gender. However, in Thai women use **tʃán** ฉัน *I* and men use **phŏm** ผม *I*.

D. New sounds

Consonants:

- **b** as in the Thai word **bai-máai** ใบ ไม้ *leaf*
  – English sound: **b**lue, **b**ing, **b**ird (rating: good)
- **d** as in the Thai word **dèk** เด็ก *child*
  – English sound: **d**ark, **d**ance, **d**ime (rating: good)

Vowels:
- short **i** as in the word tsing จริง *really*
  – English sound: **i**t, **s**it, **l**ittle (rating: good)
- long **ii** as in the word dii ดี *good*
  – English sound: s**ee**, l**ea**k, b**ea**t (rating: good)

E. Simple advice

We have used spaces between words in the Thai script in a sentence. That is for those who would like to make some effort to learn to read and write Thai. In the Thai script, words and sentences are usually written together without any spaces. We use spaces between Thai words in this book since it will be easier for the learner to identify individual written Thai words.

If your aim is to learn to speak Thai fast and easily, then *ignore the Thai script totally*. We have included it here because it simply makes sense; it would not be correct to write a Thai learning book without the Thai script. Also, there may be someone who wishes to gain some knowledge about the Thai script. Learning to master the Thai writing system and script takes a long time. In order to learn to speak Thai fluently, you do not need that aspect now. It only hinders you in the beginning.

F. Take it further

Refer to the book:

Dhyan Manik: *Understanding the Thai Language and Grammar:*

- More about Thai consonant and vowel sounds can be found in Chapter 1, sections 1.1 and 1.2.
- List of personal pronouns and family relationships can be found in Chapter 3.
- More extensive list of adjectives can be found in Chapter 11.

Chapter 3

My name is…, to have, there is, to show possession

tʃán mii mɔɔtɤ̂ɤsai
ฉัน มี มอเตอร์ไซค์
I have a motorcycle.

> **Highlights**
>
> | | | |
> |---|---|---|
> | mii | มี | to have, there is, there are |
> | tʃŵɯ | ชื่อ | to be named, my name is |
> | khɔ̌ɔng | ของ | of (to show possession) |

A. Sentences

1. tʃán *tʃŵɯ* sìrì ฉัน ชื่อ สิริ
   I *named* Siri – *My name is Siri.*

2. tʃán *mii* taa ฉัน มี ตา
   I *have* eye – *I have eyes.*

3. *mii* hǔu มี หู
   have ear – *I have ears.*

4. *mii* pàak มี ปาก
   have mouth – *I have a mouth.*

5. khun *mii* lûuk mái คุณ มี ลูก ไหม
   you *have* child "question" – *Do you have children?*

6. *mii* khâ มี ค่ะ
   have khâ – *Yes, I have.*

7. tʃán *mii* lûuk ฉัน มี ลูก
   I *have* child – *I have children.*

8. tʃán *mii* mɔɔtɔ̂ɔsai ฉัน มี มอเตอร์ไซค์
   I *have* motorcycle – *I have a motorcycle.*

(9) *mii* khon yɔ́ มี คน เยอะ
have person many – *There are many people.*

(10) thîi-nîi *rɔ́ɔn* mâak ที่ นี่ ร้อน มาก
place-this *hot* very – *It is very hot here.*

(11) an-níi mɯɯ-thɯ̌ɯ *khɔ̌ɔng tʃán* อัน นี้ มือ ถือ ของ ฉัน
piece-this hand-hold *of I* – *This is my mobile phone.*

(12) an-nán rót *khun* อัน นั้น รถ คุณ
piece-that car *you* – *That is your car.*

(13) phǒm *khun* yaau ผม คุณ ยาว
hair *you* long – *Your hair is long.*

Common expressions
(kham thîi tʃái bɔ̀i-bɔ̀i คำ ที่ ใช้ บ่อยๆ)

mâi mii weelaa ไม่ มี เวลา
no have time – *I do not have time.*

rɔɔ sàk-khrûu รอ สัก ครู่
wait just-moment – *Wait a little!*

pép-nɯ̀ng แป๊บ นึง
just moment-one – *Just a moment!*

ìik sàk-khrûu อีก สัก ครู่
more just-moment – *In a little while.*

B. Vocabulary

tʃán	ฉัน	I (women say)
tʃûɯ	ชื่อ	to be named, name
sìrì	สิริ	name of the girl
taa	ตา	eye, eyes
hŭu	หู	ear, ears
pàak	ปาก	mouth
khun	คุณ	you
mii	มี	to have, there is, there are
mái	ไหม	basic question word
lûuk	ลูก	child
dûuai	ด้วย	also
mɔɔtɔ̂əsai	มอเตอร์ไซค์	motorcycle
khon yə́	คน เยอะ	a lot of people, many people
khon	คน	a person
yə́	เยอะ	much, many, a lot
thîi-nîi	ที่ นี่	here
rɔ́ɔn	ร้อน	hot
mâak	มาก	very
an-níi	อัน นี้	this, this one
mɯɯ-thɯ̆ɯ	มือ ถือ	mobile phone
an-nán	อัน นั้น	that, that one
rót	รถ	car
phǒm	ผม	hair, I (men say)
khɔ̌ɔng	ของ	of, to show possession
yaau	ยาว	to be long
mâi	ไม่	no

Chapter 3   33

weelaa	เวลา	time
rɔɔ-sàk-khrûu	รอ สัก ครู่	wait a moment
rɔɔ	รอ	to wait
pɛ́p-nùng	แป๊บ นึง	just a moment, just a second
ìik sàk-khrûu	อีก สัก ครู่	in a little while
ìik	อีก	more
sàk-khrûu	สัก ครู่	a while

C. How the language works

A) The Thai verb **mii** มี *to have* has two distinct meanings in English.

> **1** **mii** มี *to have*
> tʃǎn *mii* taa   ฉัน มี ตา
> I *have* eye – *I have eyes.*

- Here the verb **mii** มี *to have* is used in a similar way as the English verb *to have*.
- The word order is the same as in English, subject **tʃǎn** ฉัน *I* → verb **mii** มี *to have* → object **taa** ตา *eye*.
- All the words in Thai are always in the basic form. For example **taa** ตา *eye* can also mean *eyes*.

> **2** **mii** มี *there is*
> *mii* khon yɔ́   มี คน เยอะ
> *have* person many – *There are many people.*

- Here the verb **mii** มี is used in a similar way as the English verb *there is, there are*.
- So, the verb **mii** มี has two meanings, *to have* and *there is, there are*.

B) The *"question word"* **mái** ไหม comes at the end of the sentence.

> **1** khun mii lûuk *mái* คุณ มี ลูก ไหม
> you have child *"question"* – Do you have children?

- The *"question word"* **mái** ไหม is commonly placed at the end of a sentence to form a question in Thai.
- Here *"question word"* **mái** ไหม is placed at the end of the sentence and after the noun **lûuk** ลูก *child*.

C) **tʃûɯ** ชื่อ *to be named, name* can be either a verb or a noun. Hence, there are three ways to say: *My name is Siri*.

> **1** tʃán *tʃûɯ* sìrì ฉัน ชื่อ สิริ
> I *named* Siri – *My name is Siri*.

- Here **tʃûɯ** ชื่อ *to be named* is used as a verb. This is quite a common expression in Thai. It is normally used in speaking.

> **2** *tʃûɯ khɔ̌ɔng* tʃán khɯɯ sìrì ชื่อ ของ ฉัน คือ สิริ
> *name of* I be Siri – *My name is Siri*.

- Here **tʃûɯ** ชื่อ *name* is used as a noun. We use the long possessive form **khɔ̌ɔng** ของ *of*. It is placed before the personal pronoun **tʃán** ฉัน *I*.

> **3** *tʃûɯ* tʃán khɯɯ sìrì ชื่อ ฉัน คือ สิริ
> *name* I be Siri – *My name is Siri*.

- **khɔ̌ɔng** ของ *of* is dropped here. **tʃûɯ** ชื่อ *name* is still used as a noun. It is placed before the personal pronoun **tʃán** ฉัน *I*.

Chapter 3

D) The possessive form can be expressed in two ways in Thai.

> **1** an-nán rót *khɔ̌ɔng khun* อัน นั้น รถ ของ คุณ
> piece-that car *of you* – *That is your car.*

- This sentence is expressed with **khɔ̌ɔng** ของ *of*.
- **khɔ̌ɔng** ของ *of* is placed before the possessor **khun** คุณ *you*.

> **2** an-nán *rót khun* อัน นั้น รถ คุณ
> piece-that *car you* – *That is your car.*

- In the short form **khɔ̌ɔng** ของ *of* can also be dropped, and the meaning is the same.
- The possessor **khun** คุณ *you* follows directly after the noun in question, here **rót** รถ *car*.

D. New sounds

Consonants:

- **t** as in the Thai word **tàu** เต่า *turtle*
  – English sound: **s**take, **s**tink, **s**table (rating: OK, but pay attention)
- **th** as in the Thai word **th**áhǎan ทหาร *soldier*
  English sound: **t**ime, **t**ell, **t**ask (rating: good)
- **t** is an unaspirated sound. When you say **t**-sound in Thai, there is not any puff of air coming out your mouth. **th** is an aspirated sound. When you say **th**-sound in Thai, there is a clear puff of air coming out your mouth as in English.

Vowels:

- short **u** as in the word khun *you*
  – English sound: p**u**t, l**oo**k, f**oo**t (rating: good)

- long **uu** as in the word l**ûu**k *child*
  – English sound: s**oo**n, s**ou**p, d**o** (rating: good)
- Vowels in Thai are always clearly pronounced either long or short.

E. Simple advice

Some of you may already have realized that it is almost impossible to write a complete Thai learning book with original Thai words only. Many words, which are borrowed from Chinese, English, Khmer or Pali/Sanskrit, are used in everyday conversation and are not regarded as foreign words by Thais. However, a closer look would reveal that they are actually borrowed into Thai from other languages.

In this book, we will concentrate on original Thai words as much as possible; they form the basis for the Thai language. Normally, it is not possible to write meaningful and correct sentences in Thai without original Thai words since they constitute the major part of the Thai grammar.

Thai people do not normally know which word is an original Thai word and which word is borrowed from other foreign languages. They are born into the habit of using the Thai language as it is spoken today. Therefore, it does not make sense to ask your Thai friends about it. However, it is good for us foreigners to understand the difference. It makes it easier for us to understand the overall complexity of the Thai language.

Don't worry too much about the tones at the beginning even though they are an essential part of the Thai language. Before you can master tones, you need to know how words are pronounced without including the correct tones to them.

Note that Thai people do not separate the pronunciation and the tone of the word. Hence, if you ask a Thai person which of the two you are mispronouncing, they will have some difficulty to answer. For them the tone is very much built into the pronunciation.

However, if your pronunciation is correct, but the tone is wrong, you may be understood if you are using the correct word in the right context. Thais tend to understand meaning very much from the context. On the other hand, if your pronunciation is not correct even though the tone is quite right, Thais would certainly have difficulties to understand the meaning.

All the words in Thai are in basic form; hence, the word order becomes very important.

While learning Thai, it would be good if you could forget the English way of spelling sounds altogether and learn a new phonetic way as shown in this book. That way, you will more quickly learn to pronounce Thai words and sounds accurately and correctly.

F. Take it further

Refer to the book:

Dhyan Manik: *Understanding the Thai Language and Grammar:*

- More about Thai consonant and vowel sounds can be found in Chapter 1, sections 1.1 and 1.2.
- More extensive list of body parts can be found in Chapter 3, section 3.3.
- More extensive list of adjectives can be found in Chapter 11.

Chapter 4

At the market and buying things

au khɔ̌ɔng lên
เอา ของ เล่น
I want some toys.

Chapter 4

Highlights

tàlàat	ตลาด	market
thîi tàlàat	ที่ ตลาด	at the market
thîi	ที่	at, to
súu	ซื้อ	to buy
khɔ̌ɔng	ของ	things
khɔ̌ɔ duu nɔ̀i	ขอ ดู หน่อย	may I have a look?
thâu-rai	เท่า ไร	how much?

A. Sentences

1. sàwàtdii khâ   สวัสดี ค่ะ
   hello khâ – *Hello!*

2. pai năi khá   ไป ไหน คะ
   go where khá – *Where are you going?*

3. pai tàlàat *súu* khɔ̌ɔng khâ   ไป ตลาด ซื้อ ของ ค่ะ
   go *buy* thing khâ – *I go to the market to buy some things.*

4. *au* khɔ̌ɔng lên   เอา ของ เล่น
   take thing play – *I want some toys.*

5. khun *mii* keem arai mái   คุณ มี เกม อะไร ไหม
   you *have* game what "question"
   Do you have any games?

6. tʃán *yàak-dâai* keem sămràp dèk
   ฉัน อยาก ได้ เกม สำหรับ เด็ก
   I *want-get* game for child
   I would like to have children's games.

7. t͡ʃán *tông-kaan* keem khɔɔmphíutəə ฉัน ต้อง การ เกม คอมพิวเตอร์
I *need-task* game computer – *I need computer games.*

8. pai thîi ráan *khăai* sûɯa-phâa ไป ที่ ร้าน ขาย เสื้อ ผ้า
go to shop *sell* shirt-cloth
Going to the shop that sells clothing.

9. *mii* sûɯa-yûɯt mái มี เสื้อ ยืด ไหม
have shirt-stretch "question" – *Do you have T-shirts?*

10. *khɔ̆ɔ duu* nɔ̀i ขอ ดู หน่อย
ask see little – *May I have a look?*

11. *khɔ̆ɔ lɔɔng* nɔ̀i ขอ ลอง หน่อย
ask try little – *Could I try it?*

12. *yài* tsang ใหญ่ จัง
big much – *This is very big.*

13. *lék* kəən-pai เล็ก เกิน ไป
small excess-go – *This is too small.*

14. khít duu kɔ̀ɔn คิด ดู ก่อน
think see first – *I'll think about it.*

Common expressions
(kham thîi t͡ʃái bɔ̀i-bɔ̀i คำ ที่ ใช้ บ่อยๆ)

an-níi thâu-rai อัน นี้ เท่า ไร
piece-this equal-something – *How much is this?*

phɛɛng mâak แพง มาก
expensive very – *Very expensive!*

> phɛɛng nít-nɔ̀i แพง นิด หน่อย
> expensive bit-little – *A little expensive!*
>
> mâi phɛɛng rɔ̀ɔk ไม่ แพง หรอก
> no expensive at-all – *Not at all expensive.*

B. Vocabulary

thîi	ที่	at, which, that
tàlàat	ตลาด	market
sàwàtdii	สวัสดี	hello, good afternoon etc.
pai	ไป	to go
năi	ไหน	where
khá	คะ	polite particle for women
súu	ซื้อ	to buy
khɔ̆ɔng	ของ	things, of (to show possession)
au	เอา	to take, to want
khɔ̆ɔng lên	ของ เล่น	toys
lên	เล่น	to play
khun	คุณ	you
mii	มี	to have, there is, there are
keem	เกม	game
sămràp	สำหรับ	for
dèk	เด็ก	child
arai	อะไร	what?
tʃán	ฉัน	I (women)
yàak-dâai	อยาก ได้	to want

tông-kaan	ต้อง การ	to want, to need
khɔɔmphíutə̂ə	คอมพิวเตอร์	computer
ráan	ร้าน	shop, store
khăai	ขาย	to sell
sûɯa-phâa	เสื้อ ผ้า	clothes
sûɯa	เสื้อ	shirt, blouse
phâa	ผ้า	cloth, fabric, textile
sûɯa-yûɯt	เสื้อ ยืด	T-shirt
mái	ไหม	basic question word
khɔ̌ɔ	ขอ	to ask (for something)
duu	ดู	to see
nɔ̀i	หน่อย	a little
lɔɔng	ลอง	to try
yài	ใหญ่	to be big
tsang	จัง	very, much
lék	เล็ก	to be small
kəən-pai	เกิน ไป	too much, excessively
kəən	เกิน	to exceed
pai	ไป	to go
lék kəən-pai	เล็ก เกิน ไป	to be too small
khít	คิด	to think
duu	ดู	to see
kɔ̀ɔn	ก่อน	first
thâu-rai	เท่า ไร	how much?
phɛɛng	แพง	to be expensive
nít-nɔ̀i	นิด หน่อย	a little bit, just a little
mâi	ไม่	no
rɔ̀ɔk	หรอก	at all

C. How the language works

A) The word for *things, stuff, goods* is **khɔ̌ɔng** ของ

> **1** pai súu *khɔ̌ɔng* ไป ซื้อ ของ go
> to buy *thing* – *I go to buy some things.*

- Here in Thai, we have dropped the subject *I* since it is understood from the context.
- **pai súu khɔ̌ɔng** ไป ซื้อ ของ is a complete sentence in Thai. It has only three words. In English, we must use many more words here.

B) The possessive form in Thai is also expressed by the word **khɔ̌ɔng** ของ. It is normally placed before the personal pronoun.

> **1** an-níi *khɔ̌ɔng* tʃán อัน นี้ ของ ฉัน
> piece-this *of* I – *This is mine.*

- So, **khɔ̌ɔng** ของ has two meanings, stuff and a possessive form *of*. As a possessive form, it is used in the same way as *of* in English.

> **2** an-níi rót tʃán อัน นี้ รถ ฉัน
> piece-this car I – *This is my car.*

- The possessive form **khɔ̌ɔng** ของ *of* can also be dropped. It is quite common to drop **khɔ̌ɔng** ของ *of* in speaking.

> **3** an-níi *khɔ̌ɔng khɔ̌ɔng* tʃán อัน นี้ ของ ของ ฉัน
> piece-this *thing of* I – *These are my things.*

- In Thai, it is also possible to say, **khɔ̌ɔng khɔ̌ɔng tʃán** ของ ของ ฉัน *my things, my stuff.*
- In this sentence **khɔ̌ɔng** ของ has two meanings, stuff and *of*.

Chapter 4

- See also Chapter 3, Section C for the possessive form **khɔ̌ɔng** ของ *of*.

C) There are four ways to say *I want* in Thai

> **1** *au* khâau เอา ข้าว
> *take* rice – *I want some rice.*

- **au** เอา *to take* is often translated into English as *to want*.
- One particular feature of **au** เอา *to take* is that it can be placed before *nouns* only.
- So, it is not grammatically correct to say **au pai** *I want to go*.
- Many foreigners make a mistake and place this word also before verbs. Thais would understand the meaning but they would feel that you make a common mistake which natives never do.

> **2** tʃán *yàak-dâai* khâau ฉัน อยาก ได้ ข้าว
> I *want-get* rice – *I would like to have some rice.*

- Another way to say the similar meaning as **au** เอา *to take, to want* is to use the verb combination **yàak-dâai** อยาก ได้ *to want, to want to get, would like to have*.
- **yàak-dâai** อยาก ได้ is commonly placed before *nouns* only.

> **3** tʃán *tɔ̂ng-kaan* khâau ฉัน ต้อง การ ข้าว
> I *need-task* rice – *I want some rice.*

- The third way to say the similar meaning as in the above two sentences is to use the construction **tɔ̂ng-kaan** ต้อง การ *to need, to want, would like to have etc.*
- **tɔ̂ng-kaan** ต้อง การ is normally used in formal situations only.

tʃán *tôŋ-kaan* kin-khâau ฉัน ต้อง การ กิน ข้าว
I *need-task* eat-rice – *I want to eat rice.*

- One particular feature of **tôŋ-kaan** ต้อง การ is that it can be placed before *nouns* and also before *verbs*.
- **tôŋ-kaan** ต้อง การ is quite an official way to express *wanting* and is not used much in everyday informal speaking. However, you will see this word in many other Thai learning books.

 tʃán *yàak* kin-khâau ฉัน อยาก กิน ข้าว
I *want* eat-rice – *I want to eat rice.*

- The fourth way to say " I want" is to place **yàak** อยาก *to want* before the verb, here **kin** กิน *to eat.*
- Instead of **tôŋ-kaan** ต้อง การ *to need, to want* we may use **yàak** อยาก *to want.*
- **yàak** อยาก is commonly placed before *verbs* only.
- This expression is used commonly in speaking.

D) Four commonly used expressions

 khɔ̌ɔ duu *nɔ̀i* ขอ ดู หน่อย
ask see *little* – *May I have a look?*

- **nɔ̀i** หน่อย *a little, a little bit* is a nice expression in Thai.
- **nɔ̀i** หน่อย is often used to make a request softer in Thai. It is usually placed at the end of the sentence.
- **nɔ̀i** หน่อย is also often used together with **nít** นิด *small.*
- **nít-nɔ̀i** นิด หน่อย *a little bit, just a little.*

> **2** lék *kəən-pai* เล็ก เกิน ไป
> small exceed-go – *It is too small.*

kəən-pai เกิน ไป *too* is used to express meanings like *too small, too big* etc. It is usually placed at the end of the sentence.

> **3** lék *pai* เล็ก ไป
> small go – *It is too small.*

- Sometimes, **kəən** เกิน *excess* is dropped, and only **pai** ไป *to go* is used. The meaning is the same, however.

> **4** *khít duu kɔ̀ɔn* คิด ดู ก่อน
> think see first – *I'll think about it.*

khít duu kɔ̀ɔn คิด ดู ก่อน *I'll think about it* can be understood as a polite way to say *no*. Things are left open.

E) **mâi** ไม่ before a verb or an adjective means *no*

> **1** tʃán *mâi* sàbaai ฉัน ไม่ สบาย
> I *no* fine – *I am not feeling good.*

- Here **mâi** ไม่ is placed before the verb **sàbaai** สบาย *to be well, to be fine*. The meaning becomes *not to be fine*.

D. New sounds

Consonants:

- **k** as in the Thai word **kài** ไก่ *chicken*
  – English sound: **sk**in, **sk**ate, **sk**y (rating: OK, but pay attention)

- **kh** as in the Thai word **kh**waai ควาย *water buffalo*
  – English sound: **k**eep, **k**ind, **k**ey (rating: good)
- **k** is an unaspirated sound. When you say **k**-sound in Thai, there is not any puff of air coming out your mouth. **kh** is an aspirated sound. When you say **kh**-sound in Thai, there is a clear puff of air coming out of your mouth as in English.

Vowels:
- short **e** as in the word l**é**k เล็ก *small*
  – English sound: br**e**ad, s**e**t, p**e**t (rating: good)
- long **ee** as in the word n**é**en เน้น *to emphasize*
  – English sound: g**a**me, l**a**te, s**a**me (rating: not very good)
- Vowels in Thai are always clearly pronounced either short or long.

E. Simple advice

If you need to learn only two words for *wanting*, then use **au** เอา *to take, to want* before the nouns and **yàak** อยาก *to want* before the verbs.

Everything becomes much easier in Thailand if you are able to express yourself politely. In fact, it is almost impossible to be too polite in Thailand. To be simple and humble is regarded as having good manners.

In Thai, you should respect everyone and be polite regardless of their position or status. This is true in every country, but in Thailand being polite is built into the language more than in many other languages.

Therefore, it is important to use polite request particles like **khâ** ค่ะ and **khráp** ครับ when you request something.

Also, **nɔ̀i** หน่อย *a little* is also commonly employed in Thai to make a request sound like it is not a big deal.

sàwàtdii สวัสดี is a very handy expression to be polite. It can be used all the time. It can be translated into English as *Hello! Goodbye! Good* *morning! Good afternoon! Good evening!* and so on. **sàwàtdii** สวัสดี is a Pali/Sanskrit origin word.

In order to speak Thai, it is not necessary to understand the Thai writing system with three different consonant classes, with five different tones, with the number of rare consonants (Bali/Sanskrit), with special spellings (English, Khmer etc.). The Thai writing system is quite complex. To master it well can be very challenging and time consuming. In this book, we have deliberately left all that out.

However, if you do want to understand the Thai writing system, then you may wish to read the book:

22 Secrets of Learning Thai
– Complete Guide to Sounds, Tones and Thai Writing System (+ 2CD)
ISBN 978-952-5572-85-8

F. Take it further

Refer to the book:

Dhyan Manik: *Understanding the Thai Language and Grammar:*

- More about Thai consonant and vowel sounds can be found in Chapter 1, sections 1.1 and 1.2.

    Original Thai words or borrowed words? Examples of original Thai words and loanwords can be found in Chapter 2.

Chapter 5

Eating and drinking

phŏm hĭu mâak
ผม หิว มาก
I am very hungry.

Highlights

ráan-aahăan	ร้าน อาหาร	*restaurant*
thîi ráan-aahăan	ที่ ร้าน อาหาร	*at the restaurant*
kin-khâau	กิน ข้าว	*to eat*
dùɯm	ดื่ม	*to drink*
nɯ́ɯa	เนื้อ	*meat*
plaa	ปลา	*fish*
phèt	เผ็ด	*to be spicy*
nám-sôm	น้ำ ส้ม	*orange juice*
kin-tsee	กิน เจ	*to be a vegetarian*

A. Sentences

1. *kin-khâau rɯ́-yang* กิน ข้าว รึ ยัง
   eat-rice or-not – *Have you already eaten?*

2. *tʃǎn hǐu* mâak ฉัน หิว มาก
   I hungry very – *I am very hungry.*

3. ráan-aahăan *yùu* năi ร้าน อาหาร อยู่ ไหน
   shop-food *stay* where – *Where is the restaurant?*

4. mii arai *né-nam* bâang มี อะไร แนะ นำ บ้าง
   have what *recommend* some – *What do you recommend?*

5. *thaang níi* khâ ทาง นี้ ค่ะ
   way this khâ – *This way, please!*

6. khun yàak *thaan* arai khá คุณ อยาก ทาน อะไร คะ
   you want *eat* what khá – *What would you like to eat?*

7 mâi au nɯ́ɯa-sàt khâ ไม่ เอา เนื้อ สัตว์ ค่ะ
no take meat-animal khâ – *I don't want any meat.*

8 mâi au mǔu khâ ไม่ เอา หมู ค่ะ
no take pork khâ – *I don't want pork.*

9 mâi au kài khâ ไม่ เอา ไก่ ค่ะ
no take chicken khâ – *I don't want chicken.*

10 tʃán *kin-tsee* khâ ฉัน กิน เจ ค่ะ
I *eat-vegetarian* khâ – *I am a vegetarian.*

11 phàk *dii* ผัก ดี
vegetable *good* – *Vegetables are good.*

12 plaa *kɔ̂ɔ dii* khâ ปลา ก็ ดี ค่ะ
fish *also good* khâ – *Fish is also fine.*

13 tôm-yam-kûng *kɔ̂ɔ arɔ̀i* khâ ต้ม ยำ กุ้ง ก็ อร่อย ค่ะ
"tôm-yam-kûng" *also delicious* khâ
"Tôm-yam-kûng" is also delicious.

14 tʃán *tʃɔ̂ɔp* sômtam ฉัน ชอบ ส้มตำ
I *like* "sômtam" – *I like "sômtam".*

15 aahǎan thai *phèt* nít-nɔ̀i อาหาร ไทย เผ็ด นิด หน่อย
food Thai *spicy* bit-little – *Thai food is a little spicy.*

16 *mii* phǒnlámáai *mái* khá มี ผลไม้ ไหม คะ
have fruit *"question"* khá – *Do you have any fruits?*

17 *yàak dɯ̀ɯm* arai khá อยาก ดื่ม อะไร คะ
want drink what khá – *What would you like to drink?*

18 *au* nám-sôm khâ   เอา น้ำ ส้ม ค่ะ
take liquid-orange khâ
I would like to have orange juice.

19 *au* nám-plaàu khâ   เอา น้ำ เปล่า ค่ะ
take water-fresh khâ
I would like to have drinking water, please.

Common expressions
(kham thîi ʧái bɔ̀i-bɔ̀i คำ ที่ ใช้ ป่อยๆ)

khun khá/khráp kèp-tang dûuai khâ/khráp
คุณ คะ/ครับ เก็บ ตังค์ ด้วย ค่ะ/ครับ
you khá/khráp collect-money also khâ/khráp
Waiter, may I pay?

sɔ̌ɔng-rɔ́ɔi sǎam-sìp khâ/khráp   สอง ร้อย สาม สิบ ค่ะ/ครับ
two-hundred three-ten khâ/khráp
It is two hundred and thirty.

khɔ̀ɔp khun mâak   ขอบ คุณ มาก
thank you very – *Thank you very much!*

oogàat-nâa ʧɔǝn mài ná khá/khráp
โอกาส หน้า เชิญ ใหม่ นะ คะ/ครับ
occasion-next invite again ná khá/khráp – *Please, come again!*

B. Vocabulary

né-nam	แนะ นำ	to recommend, to introduce
bâang	บ้าง	some, any
arai	อะไร	what?
kin	กิน	to eat, to drink

khâau	ข้าว	rice
kin-khâau	กิน ข้าว	to eat
hĭu	หิว	to be hungry, thirsty
hĭu-khâau	หิว ข้าว	to be hungry
náam	น้ำ	water, liquid
hĭu-náam	หิว น้ำ	to be thirsty
yàak	อยาก	to want
au	เอา	to take, to want
kɔ̂ɔ	ก็	also
sôm	ส้ม	orange
nám-sôm	น้ำ ส้ม	orange juice
thaang	ทาง	way
thaang-níi	ทาง นี้	this way
arai	อะไร	what?
dɯ̀ɯm	ดื่ม	to drink
mâi	ไม่	no
mâi au	ไม่ เอา	I don't want
nɯ́ɯa-sàt	เนื้อ สัตว์	meat
nɯ́ɯa	เนื้อ	beef, meat
kài	ไก่	chicken
thaan	ทาน	to eat
plaa	ปลา	fish
tôm-yam-kûng	ต้ม ยำ กุ้ง	a kind of spicy crayfish soup
tʃɔ̂ɔp	ชอบ	to like
sômtam	ส้มตำ	a kind of spicy papaya salad from Isaan
aahăan	อาหาร	food
phrík	พริก	chilli

phrík-nám-plaa	พริก น้ำ ปลา	fish source with chilli
aahăan	อาหาร	food
thai	ไทย	Thai
phèt	เผ็ด	to be spicy
nít-nòi	นิด หน่อย	a little bit
khɔ̆ɔ	ขอ	to ask
nám-plaàu	น้ำ เปล่า	drinking water, fresh water
kèp-tang	เก็บ ตังค์	bill
sɔ̌ɔng-rɔ́ɔi sǎam-sìp	สอง ร้อย สาม สิบ	two hundred and thirty
oogàat	โอกาส	opportunity
nâa	หน้า	next
oogàat-nâa	โอกาส หน้า	next time, in the future
tʃəən	เชิญ	to invite
mài	ใหม่	to be new, again
ná	นะ	ná (polite particle)

C. How the language works

A) Rice has been a basic food in Thailand for ages. Therefore, it is associated with being hungry and eating.

Eating and drinking is expressed in Thai somewhat differently compared to English.

- **hǐu-khâau** หิว ข้าว *to be hungry* (literally hungry-rice).
- **kin-khâau** กิน ข้าว *to eat* (literally to eat-rice).
- **kin-khâau rú-yang** กิน ข้าว รึ ยัง *Have you eaten?*
- **thaan** ทาน *to eat* is another word for eating. It is a bit more formal and is usually used in formal situations like being polite in the restaurant.

Chapter 5

- **hǐu-náam** หิว น้ำ *to be thirsty* (literally hungry-water).
- **dùum** ดื่ม means *to drink*.
- **dùum-náam** ดื่ม น้ำ *to drink water*.
- **kin-náam** กิน น้ำ *to eat water* is an informal way to say the same, *to drink water*. This expression is commonly used with friends and informal situations.

B) Everyday language with **rú-yang** รึ ยัง *or not* -question?

> **1** kin-khâau *rú-yang* กิน ข้าว รึ ยัง
> eat-rice *or-not* – *Have you eaten already?*

- This expression in Thai is commonly used as an introduction when you meet someone. Like in the west, it is always safe to start the discussion with the phrase "Looks like it is going to rain".
- When someone asks you **kin-khâau rú-yang** กิน ข้าว รึ ยัง *have you eaten or not,* it only means that she/he wants you to say something which may also be understood as *hello!* This phrase is also often used when someone doesn't know how to start a conversation. It is very common in Thai.

> **2** sàng *lɛ́ɛu rú-yang* สั่ง แล้ว รึ ยัง
> order *already or-not* – *Have you ordered?*

- This expression is commonly used in a restaurant by a waiter when asking *have you been served*.

Reply:

> **2.1** yang ยัง
> not – *Not yet!*

Reply:

> **2.2** sàng *lέεu* สั่ง แล้ว
> order *already* – *Yes, I have.*

C) **mâi au** ไม่ เอา *not to want*

> **1** *mâi au* nɯ́ɯa khâ ไม่ เอา เนื้อ ค่ะ
> *no take* beef khâ – *I don't want any beef.*

- If you need to use the negative term **mâi au** ไม่ เอา, do not forget to use **khâ/khráp** ค่ะ/ครับ at the end of the statement. It is very important in Thai.

D) The Thai way is to be polite when interacting with people.

> **1** khun khá/khráp kèp-tang dûuai khâ/khráp
> คุณ คะ/ครับ เก็บ ตังค์ ด้วย ค่ะ/ครับ
> you khá/khráp collect-money also khâ/khráp
> *Waiter, may I pay?*

- To call a person by **khun** คุณ *you* is very polite in Thai.
- It can also be placed before the first name to show respect, **khun** คุณ Peter.
- **khun** คุณ *you* is a Pali/Sanskrit origin word.

> **2** aahăan *arɔ̀i* mâak อาหาร อร่อย มาก
> food *delicious* very – *The food was very delicious.*

- If you have liked the food, it is common to say to the waiter, **aahăan arɔ̀i mâak** อาหาร อร่อย มาก *the food was very delicious.*

Chapter 5

 khɔ̀ɔp-khun mâak *khâ/khráp* ขอบ คุณ มาก ค่ะ/ครับ
thank-you much *khâ/khráp* – *Thank you very much!*

- The polite ending particles **khâ/khráp** ค่ะ/ครับ at the end of the statement are commonly used when making a request or when thanking.
- **khâ** ค่ะ is used by women and **khráp** ครับ is used by men.

D. New sounds

Consonants:

- **f** as in the Thai word **f**an ฟัน *teeth*
  – English sound: **f**un, **f**ake, **f**eel (rating: good)
- **s** as in the Thai word **s**ôo โซ่ *chain*
  – English sound: **s**even, **s**imple, **s**ink (rating: good)

Vowels:

- short ɛ as in the word nɛ́-nam แนะ นำ *to introduce*
  – English sound: c**a**t, l**a**ptop, r**a**t (rating: good)
- long ɛɛ as in the word lɛ́ɛu แล้ว *already*
  – English sound: s**a**d, m**a**d, S**a**m
  (rating: quite good, but pay attention)
- Vowels in Thai are always clearly pronounced either short or long. ɛɛ-sound in Thai is clearly long, perhaps longer than in the English word s**a**d.

E. Simple advice

We have previously learned the following words.

mài	ใหม่	*new, again* (low tone)
mâi	ไม่	*no* (falling tone)
mái	ไหม	*"question"* (high tone)

For us foreigners, these three words are pronounced in the same way but with different tones. But if you ask Thai people, they would say that these words are not pronounced in the same way since for the Thai people a different tone denotes a different meaning and different pronunciation.

Let's try to make it easier for you to understand. Say, you pronounce all the above three words with a middle tone, sometimes also called a common tone. That is to say that there is not any extra emphasis, no tone. Then, you would say **mai**. There is not any tone mark; that means the tone is the middle tone. That would perhaps be your natural way to speak since you do not speak your own language with Thai tones.

Since there are not many words in Thai which are pronounced that way, Thais would try to understand the meaning from the context. It could be any of the three meanings. When making mistakes with tones, which is common with foreigners, there is a good chance that you will be understood anyway if you are able to use correct words in the given context and pronounce them correctly. However, if your pronunciation is so-so and the tone is wrong, the chances to be understood are very slight.

So, the conclusion here is that it is best to make sure that you know how to pronounce words correctly in Thai. After that you will slowly, slowly learn to use correct tones naturally.

Sounds come first and after you know Thai sounds, it is easier to learn the correct tones. In order to speak, you need not know how to write or spell words. This is the way you have learned your own language as a child.

Also, knowing how to write words in Thai script doesn't tell anything about the actual sound in Thai. It doesn't matter what symbols – Thai or foreign or any international phonetic symbol – you use. Writing tells us only that sounds or words are spelled that way. Sometimes, the sound is the same but spelling and meaning are different. Writing can give you only some indication how to pronounce a certain sound. You need to make the correct sound in your mouth in such a way that others will understand what you are saying. Therefore, we talk a lot about sounds and how to pronounce them.

For the majority of Thai learners, at least in the beginning, speaking is more important than writing. With this simple method you can learn relatively quickly to express yourself orally in Thai. Learning to read and write Thai takes much longer. That is a totally different project.

F. Take it further

Refer to the book:

Dhyan Manik: *Understanding the Thai Language and Grammar:*

- More about Thai consonant and vowel sounds can be found in Chapter 1, sections 1.1 and 1.2.
- There is a comprehensive list of different types of Thai foods, vegetables, fruits, drinks, spices etc. in Chapter 9.

Chapter 6

Going out – romantic meeting

phŏm rák khun
ผม รัก คุณ
I love you.

Chapter 6

Highlights

pai thîiau	ไป เที่ยว	to go out, to have a date
sànùk	สนุก	to be fun
rúu-tsàk	รู้ จัก	to know someone
fɛɛn	แฟน	girlfriend, boyfriend
sǔuai	สวย	to be beautiful
khít-thǔng	คิด ถึง	to miss
wǎan-tsai	หวาน ใจ	sweetheart

A. Sentences

1. *yùu kàp* khun sànùk อยู่ กับ คุณ สนุก
   stay with you fun – *Being with you is fun!*

2. *yàak rúu-tsàk* khun อยาก รู้ จัก คุณ
   want know-will you – *I would like to get to know you.*

3. *pai thîiau kan* mái ไป เที่ยว กัน ไหม
   go tour together "question"
   Can we go out / Let's have a date!

4. *pai dûuai kan* mái ไป ด้วย กัน ไหม
   go also with "question"
   Do you want to go out with me?

5. *phrûng-níi dii mái* khá/khráp พรุ่ง นี้ ดี ไหม คะ/ครับ
   tomorrow good "question" khá/khráp
   How about tomorrow?

6. khun *sŭuai* tsing-tsing คุณ สวย จริงๆ
you *beautiful* really-really – *You are really beautiful.*

7. khun *mii fɛɛn* mái คุณ มี แฟน ไหม
you *have boyfriend* "question"
Do you have a boyfriend?

8. tsà *khít-thŭng* khun mâak-mâak จะ คิด ถึง คุณ มากๆ
will *think-of* you much-much – *I will miss you a lot.*

9. tsà *thoo-hăa* khun จะ โทร หา คุณ
will *phone-search* you – *I will give you a call.*

10. khun mii *iimeeu* mái คุณ มี อีเมล ไหม
you have *email* "question" – *Do you have an email?*

11. phŏm *rák* khun ผม รัก คุณ
I *love* you – *I love you.*

12. *thîi-rák* ที่ รัก
that-love – *Darling.*

13. *wăan-tsai* หวาน ใจ
sweet-heart – *Sweetheart.*

14. *yàa luɯm* phŏm ná อย่า ลืม ผม นะ
don't forget I ná – *Don't forget me.*

Common expressions
(kham thîi ʧái bɔ̀i-bɔ̀i คำ ที่ ใช้ บ่อยๆ)

khun ʧɯ̂ɯ arai คุณ ชื่อ อะไร
you name what – *What is your name?*

tsing-tsing จริงๆ
really-really – *Really!*

> maa nîi nòi khá / khráp มา นี่ หน่อย ค่ะ / ครับ
> come this little khá / khráp – *Please, come here!*
>
> yàak khui kàp khun nòi อยาก คุย กับ คุณ หน่อย
> want chat with you little – *I would like to chat with you a little.*

B. Vocabulary

yùu	อยู่	to stay, to live
kàp	กับ	with
sànùk	สนุก	to be fun, enjoyable
yàak	อยาก	to want
rúu-tsàk	รู้จัก	to get to know, to know
rúu	รู้	to know
pai thîiau	ไป เที่ยว	to go out, to have a date
dûuai	ด้วย	with
kan	กัน	together, jointly
mái	ไหม	basic question word
phrûng-níi	พรุ่ง นี้	tomorrow
dii	ดี	to be good
sŭuai	สวย	to be beautiful
tsing	จริง	to be real, true
tsing-tsing	จริงๆ	really, truly
fɛɛn	แฟน	girlfriend/boyfriend, wife/husband, partner, lover
tsà	จะ	will (future tense marker)
khít-thŭng	คิด ถึง	to miss, to think about
khít	คิด	to think

thǔng	ถึง	about, of, to arrive
mâak-mâak	มากๆ	very much
thoo-hǎa	โทร หา	to telephone to someone
thoo	โทร	to phone
hǎa	หา	to look for
iimeeu	อีเมล	email
phǒm	ผม	I (male)
rák	รัก	to love
thîi-rák	ที่ รัก	darling
wǎan-tsai	หวาน ใจ	sweetheart
yàa	อย่า	don't
lɯɯm	ลืม	to forget
ná	นะ	polite request particle
tʃɯ̂ɯ	ชื่อ	to be named
yàak	อยาก	to want
khui	คุย	to chat, to speak
thǔng	ถึง	to reach, to arrive
weelaa	เวลา	time
lɛ́ɛu	แล้ว	already
tɛ̀ɛ	แต่	but

C. How the language works

Generally, the word order in Thai is the same as in English, *subject* → *verb* → *object*. However, in Thai the subject or the verb is often dropped.

 khun mii iimeeu *mái* คุณ มี อีเมล ไหม
you have email *"question"* – Do you have an email?

- This sentence follows the word order (**khun** คุณ) subject → (**mii** มี) verb → (**iimeeu** อีเมล) object.
- The *"question"* **mái** ไหม comes always at the end of the sentence.

> **2**   *yàak* rúu-tsàk khun อยาก รู้ จัก คุณ
> want know-will you – *I would like to get to know you.*

- In this sentence, the subject *I* is dropped; it is understood from the context.
- **yàak** อยาก *to want* can be placed before verbs only. Here it is placed before the verb **rúu-tsàk** รู้ จัก *to get to know.*
- In Thai, it is fine to say *I want to know you,* but in English it is more polite to say *I would like to know you.*

> **3**   pai dûuai kan *mái* ไป ด้วย กัน ไหม
> go also with *"question"*
> *Do you want to go out with me?*

- In this sentence, the subject *you* is dropped; it is understood from the context.
- The *"question"* **mái** ไหม always comes at the end of the sentence.

> **4**   phrûng-níi *dii mái* khá พรุ่ง นี้ ดี ไหม คะ
> tomorrow *good "question"* khá – *Is tomorrow fine?*

- In this sentence there doesn't seem to be any verb.
- The adjective **dii** ดี *good* also plays the role of the verb.
- The *"question"* **mái** ไหม comes always at the end of the sentence. However, it cannot be placed after the polite ending particle **khá** คะ.

D. New sounds

Consonants:

- **ts** as in the Thai word **ts**aan จาน *plate*
  – English sound: **j**ob, **J**ohn, **J**une, **ts**unami
  (rating: OK, but pay attention)
- **tʃ** as in the Thai word **tʃ**áang ช้าง *elephant*
  – English sound: **ch**ild, **ch**oice, **ch**eck (rating: good)
- **ts** is an unaspirated sound. When you say **ts**-sound in Thai, there is not any puff of air coming out of your mouth. The English consonant **j** is voiced, but the Thai sound **ts** is unvoiced. **tʃ** is an aspirated sound. When you say **tʃ**-sound in Thai, there is a clear puff of air coming out of your mouth as in English. The sound **ts** is often transliterated as **j** and the sound **tʃ** as **ch**.

Vowels:

- short **o** as in the word sòng ส่ง *to send*
  – English sound: f**o**lk, r**o**ll, b**o**lt (rating: not very good)
- long **oo** as in the word thoo โทร *to call, to phone*
  – English sound: n**o**, g**o**, s**o** (rating: not very good)
- Vowels in Thai are always clearly pronounced either short or long.

E. Simple advice

Thai people are fun, and they love to flirt. Start using simple words with a wink of the eye and a smile on your lips. Don't be too serious.

See if you can remember the following words and expressions.

sàwàtdii สวัสดี is a very handy expression. It can be used all the time. It can be translated into English as *Hello!, Goodbye!, Good morning!, Good afternoon!, Good evening!* and so on.

sàbaai dii mái	สบาย ดี ไหม	*How are you?*
phŏm/tʃán sàbaai dii khráp/khâ		
ผม/ฉัน สบาย ดี ครับ/ค่ะ		*I am fine. Thank you!*
wan-níi rɔ́ɔn mâak	วัน นี้ ร้อน มาก	*It is very warm today.*
kin-khâau rŭu-yang	กิน ข้าว หรือ ยัง	*Have you eaten?*
khun ʧûu arai	คุณ ชื่อ อะไร	*What is your name?*
tsing-tsing	จริงๆ	*Really?*

Your challenge is to learn to communicate with Thai people in a simple, relaxed and fun way. Keep it simple. Be confident and play! A few words first in Thai before you switch into English may do wonders.

F. Take it further

Refer to the book:

Dhyan Manik: *Understanding the Thai Language and Grammar:*

- More about Thai consonant and vowel sounds can be found in Chapter 1, sections 1.1 and 1.2.
- Being "sweet" and expressing feelings:

a) **nâa-rák** น่า รัก *to be cute, pretty, attractive* – a list of adjectives, normally related to people and feelings, can be found in Chapter 11, section 11.2.

b) **wan-tsai** หวาน ใจ *sweetheart* – **tsai** ใจ *heart, mind* – is one of the most important words in Thai. Study the list of **tsai** ใจ -words in Chapter 20, then you will understand the Thai way.

Chapter 7

Question words

an-níi thâu-rai
อัน นี้ เท่า ไร
How much is this?

Chapter 7

Highlights

mûɯa-rai	เมื่อ ไร	when?
khɔ̌ɔ	ขอ	to ask for something
thammai	ทำไม	why?
arai	อะไร	what?
kìi	กี่	how many? how much?
khrai	ใคร	who?

A. Sentences

1. khɔ̌ɔng phɛɛng *mái* khá ของ แพง ไหม คะ
   thing expensive "*question*" khá
   Are these goods expensive?

2. *khɔ̌ɔ* duu nɔ̀i ขอ ดู หน่อย
   ask see little – *May I have a look?*

3. sɯ́ɯ *arai* khá ซื้อ อะไร คะ
   buy *what* khá – *What are you going to buy?*

4. sɯ́ɯ *mûɯa-rai* khá ซื้อ เมื่อ ไร คะ
   buy *when* khá – *When are you going to buy it?*

5. tʃûuai nɔ̀i *dâai-mái* khá ช่วย หน่อย ได้ ไหม คะ
   help little *can-question* khá – *Could you help me a little?*

6. tham *yang-ngai* khá ทำ ยังไง คะ
   do *how* khá – *How shall I do it?*

7. bɛ̀ɛp-níi ookee *rɯ́-plàu* แบบ นี้ โอเค รึ เปล่า
   way-this OK *or-not* – *Is like this OK or not?*

⑧ pai *thîi-nǎi* khá ไป ที่ ไหน คะ
go *place-where* khá – *Where are you going?*

⑨ káu pai *thammai* เขา ไป ทำไม
he go *why* – *Why did he go?*

⑩ tʃán pai *dâai-mái* khá ฉัน ไป ได้ ไหม คะ
I go *can-question* khá – *Can I go?*

⑪ *khrai* tsà pai bâang ใคร จะ ไป บ้าง
who will go any – *Who is going?*

⑫ tsà maa *kìi* khon จะ มา กี่ คน
will come *how-many* people
How many people are coming?

⑬ rîip nɔ̀i *dâai-rɯ́-plàu* รีบ หน่อย ได้ รึ เปล่า
hurry-little *can-or-not* – *Can you hurry up a little or not?*

⑭ pen phɯ̂an kan *dâai-mái* เป็น เพื่อน กัน ได้ ไหม
be friend *can-question* – *Can we be friends?*

⑮ yím *thammai* ยิ้ม ทำไม
smile *why* – *Why do you smile?*

Common expressions
(kham thîi tʃái bɔ̀i-bɔ̀i คำ ที่ ใช้ บ่อยๆ)

an-níi *arai* อัน นี้ อะไร
piece-this *what* – *What is this?*

an-níi *thâu-rai* อัน นี้ เท่า ไร
piece-this *equal-something* – *How much is this?*

dii *mái* ดี ไหม
good *"question"* – *Is it good?*

> dii mâak ดี มาก
> good very – *Very good!*

B. Vocabulary

khɔ̌ɔng	ของ	things, goods, of
phɛɛng	แพง	to be expensive
mái	ไหม	basic question word
khɔ̌ɔ	ขอ	to ask for something
sɯ́ɯ	ซื้อ	to buy
arai	อะไร	what?
mûɯa-rai	เมื่อ ไร	when?
tʃûuai	ช่วย	to help
dâai-mái	ได้ ไหม	could you?
nɔ̀i	หน่อย	a little
tham	ทำ	to do
yang-ngai	ยังไง	how?
bɛ̀ɛp-níi	แบบ นี้	like this
ookee	โอเค	OK
rɯ́-plàu	รึ เปล่า	or not?
káu	เขา	she, he
pai	ไป	to go
thammai	ทำไม	why?
thîi-nǎi	ที่ ไหน	where?
kìi	กี่	how many?
khrai	ใคร	who?
tsà	จะ	future tense marker

maa	มา	to come
rîip	รีบ	to hurry up
dâai-rú-plàu	ได้ รึ เปล่า	can or not?
pen	เป็น	to be
phûuan	เพื่อน	friend
kan	กัน	with, together
dâai-mái	ได้ ไหม	can we?
yím	ยิ้ม	to smile
an-níi	อัน นี้	this
arai	อะไร	what?
thâu-rai	เท่า ไร	how much?
dii	ดี	to be good
mâak	มาก	very

C. How the language works

A) Generally, question words in Thai are placed at the end of the sentence.

> an-níi *thâu-rai* อัน นี้ เท่า ไร
> piece-this *equal-something* – How much is this?

- **thâu-rai** เท่า ไร *how many, how much* is often used when asking questions like: *How much is this?*

B) For different emphasis *some question words* can be placed either at the end of the sentence or at the beginning of the sentence.

> tsà súu *mûua-rai* khá จะ ซื้อ เมื่อ ไร คะ
> will buy *when* khá – *When are you going to buy it?*

- Here the emphasis is on *buying*, and we placed **mûua-rai** เมื่อ ไร *when* at the end of the sentence.

> 2 *mûua-rai* tsà súu khá เมื่อ ไร จะ ซื้อ คะ
> *when* will buy khá – *When are you going to buy it?*

- Here the emphasis is on *when*, and we placed **mûua-rai** เมื่อ ไร *when* at the beginning of the sentence.

C) A few question words are placed at the beginning of the sentence only.

> 1 *khɔ̌ɔ* duu nɔ̀i ขอ ดู หน่อย
> *ask* see little – *May I have a look?*

- **khɔ̌ɔ** ขอ is a polite way *to ask for something*. It is always placed at the beginning of the sentence.

> 2 *khrai* tsà maa bâang ใคร จะ มา บ้าง
> *who* will come any – *Who will come?*

- **khrai** ใคร *who* is commonly placed at the beginning of the sentence in the same way as in English.

> 3 khun pen *khrai* คุณ เป็น ใคร
> you be *who* – *Who are you?*

- In some cases, **khrai** ใคร *who* can be placed at the end of the sentence, but the meaning is different.

D) Place **dâai** ได้ *can, to be able to* before the question word **mái** ไหม to transform a direct question into a softer form of request. That is an easy way to express politeness and gratitude in Thai.

> **I** tʃûuai nɔ̀i *dâai-mái* khá ช่วย หน่อย ได้ ไหม คะ
> help little *can-question* khá – *Could you help me a little?*

- **dâai-mái** ได้ ไหม *could you* "question" is normally placed at the end of the sentence in order to make a request sound soft and polite.
- Polite request particles **khá** คะ or **kráp** ครับ at the end of the statement are frequently used by Thais to soften a request or a command.
- In addition, **nɔ̀i** หน่อย *a little* can also be employed in Thai to make the request sound like *it is not a big deal*.

E) **dâai** ได้ *can, to be able to* can be placed before many question words.

dâai-mái	ได้ ไหม	*may I, can I, could I?*
dâai-rú-plàu	ได้ รึ เปล่า	*may I or not, can I or not, could I or not?*
dâai-thîi-nǎi	ได้ ที่ ไหน	*where is it possible?*
dâai-yang-ngai	ได้ ยังไง	*how can I? how is it possible?*
dâai-mûua-rai	ได้ เมื่อ ไร	*when can I? when is it possible?*

Any question word that includes **dâai** ได้ is commonly placed at the end of the sentence.

F) **kìi** กี่ *how many?*

kìi กี่ *how many* behaves somewhat differently compared to other question words. It is commonly placed before nouns (classifiers).

> **I** tsà maa *kìi khon* จะ มา กี่ คน
> will come *how-many people*
> *How many people are coming?*

- In this sentence the question word **kìi** กี่ means *how many*.

- It is placed before the noun (classifier) **khon** คน *people*.

> **2** tsà pai *kìi-moong* จะ ไป กี่ โมง
> will go *how-many hour* – *What time are we going?*

- In this context **kìi** กี่ *how many* is best translated into English as *what*.
- Here we have placed **kìi** กี่ before the noun **moong** โมง *hour*.

D. New sounds

Consonants:

- **m** as in the Thai word **máa** ม้า *horse*
  – English sound: **m**uch, **m**ake, **m**ind (rating: good)
- **n** as in the Thai word **nŭu** หนู *mouse*
  – English sound: **n**ine, **n**oise, **n**umber (rating: good)

Vowels:

- short **ɔ** as in the word **nɔ̀i** หน่อย *a little*
  – English sound: n**o**t, h**o**t, l**o**ts (rating: quite good)
- long **ɔɔ** as in the word **khɔ̌ɔng** ของ *of, things*
  – English sound: **a**ll, c**a**ll, l**a**w (rating: quite good)
- Vowels in Thai are always clearly pronounced either short or long.

E. Simple advice

To be able to make questions or requests politely is very important in Thai. Politeness is an important aspect in the Thai language. Learn to use two handy expressions **dâai-mái** ได้ ไหม *may I, can I, could I* and **nɔ̀i** หน่อย *a little, it is not a big deal* well.

It is also almost a standard rule that the polite request particles, **khá** คะ or **kráp** ครับ, are used in every form of request. Practise your Thai by being polite! That is a good starting point when learning Thai. Note that **khá** คะ has two pronunciations. In a question, it is pronounced as **khá** คะ (high tone) but in a statement it is pronounced as **khâ** ค่ะ (falling tone). **kráp** ครับ is always pronounced with the high tone.

Build up your confidence gradually and start by using everyday words. They are generally easily understood even if your pronunciation is not exactly right. Learn to choose the right word in the right situation. That is the Thai way.

Since all the words are in basic form in Thai, the choice of words becomes crucial. That means that in Thai there are no articles, no plurals, no genders, no tenses (verbs are not conjugated) etc. However, Thai is a very expressive language; you just need to learn a new way to play with words. You may call it grammar, syntax or the structure of the language; it does not matter. Hence, we talk much about how words are put together or how the language works.

F. Take it further

Refer to the book:

Dhyan Manik: *Understanding the Thai Language and Grammar:*

- More about Thai consonant and vowel sounds can be found in Chapter 1, sections 1.1 and 1.2.
- A comprehensive list of Thai question words can be found in Chapter 14.

Chapter 8

Colours, tastes and flavours

au ìik mái
เอา อีก ไหม
Do you want some more?

Chapter 8

Highlights

sǐi-sôm	สี ส้ม	orange (colour)
sǐi-dam	สี ดำ	to be black
sǐi-dɛɛng	สี แดง	to be red
wǎan	หวาน	to be sweet
prîiau	เปรี้ยว	to be sour
àrɔ̀i	อร่อย	to be delicious

A. Sentences

Colours

1. khun tʃɔ̂ɔp *sǐi* arai คุณ ชอบ สี อะไร
   you like *colour* what – *What colour do you like?*

2. *sǐi-dam* sǔuai mái สี ดำ สวย ไหม
   colour-black beautiful "question" – *Is black beautiful?*

3. tʃán tʃɔ̂ɔp *sǐi-sôm* ฉัน ชอบ สี ส้ม
   I like *colour-orange* – *I like orange colour.*

4. klûuai *sǐi-lǔang* กล้วย สี เหลือง
   banana *colour-yellow* – *Bananas are yellow.*

5. thùua *sǐi-nám-taan* ถั่ว สี น้ำ ตาล
   bean *colour-sugar* – *Beans are brown.*

6. mákhɯ̌a-thêet *sǐi-dɛɛng* มะเขือ เทศ สี แดง
   eggplant-foreign *colour-red* – *Tomatoes are red.*

7. tɛɛngmoo *sĭi-khĭau* แตงโม สี เขียว
watermelon *colour-green* – *Watermelons are green.*

Tastes and flavours

8. khun tʃɔ̂ɔp *rót-tʃâat* arai คุณ ชอบ รส ชาติ อะไร
you like *flavour-nature* what – *What flavour do you like?*

9. plaa *khem* arɔ̀i mái ปลา เค็ม อร่อย ไหม
fish *salt* delicious "question" – *Is salted fish delicious?*

10. sômtam *rót-tʃâat khêm* ส้มตำ รส ชาติ เข้ม
papaya salad *flavour-nature rich*
"Somtam" is rich in flavour.

11. nám-taan *wăan* น้ำ ตาล หวาน
water-sugar *sweet* – *Sugar is sweet.*

12. nám-plàu mâi mii *rót-tʃâat* น้ำ เปล่า ไม่ มี รส ชาติ
water-blank no have *flavour-nature*
Plain water doesn't have any flavour.

13. aahăan fàràng *rót-tsɯ̀ɯt* อาหาร ฝรั่ง รส จืด
food western *flavour-bland* – *Western food is tasteless.*

14. nám-sôm *prîiau* น้ำ ส้ม เปรี้ยว
water-orange *sour* – *Orange juice is sour.*

15. phrík nám-plaa *phèt* พริก น้ำ ปลา เผ็ด
chilli water-fish *spicy* – *Chilli sauce is spicy (hot).*

16. khun khəəi *tʃim* thúriian mái คุณ เคย ชิม ทุเรียน ไหม
you once *taste* durian "question"
Have you ever tasted durian?

17 lɔɔng tʃim duu thə̀ ลอง ชิม ดู เถอะ
try *taste* see thə̀ (thə̀ = suggesting particle) – *Try it!*

18 kin wai-wai กิน ไวๆ
eat quickly-quickly – *Eat fast!*

Common expressions
(kham thîi tʃái bɔ̀i-bɔ̀i คำ ที่ ใช้ ป่อยๆ)

aahăan *àrɔ̀i* mâak อาหาร อร่อย มาก
food *delicious* very – *Food is very delicious.*

phèt mâak เผ็ด มาก
spicy very – *Very spicy!*

au ìik mái เอา อีก ไหม
take more "question" – *Do you want some more?*

tʃék-bin dûuai เช็ค บิล ด้วย
check-bill also – *Can I get the bill, please!*

B. Vocabulary

tʃɔ̂ɔp	ชอบ	to like
sĭi	สี	colour
arai	อะไร	what?
sĭi-dam	สี ดำ	to be black
sŭuai	สวย	to be beautiful
mái	ไหม	basic question word
sĭi-sôm	สี ส้ม	to be orange (colour)
sôm	ส้ม	orange (fruit)
klûuai	กล้วย	banana, bananas

sǐi-lǔang	สี เหลือง	to be yellow
thùua	ถั่ว	bean, beans, nut, nuts
sǐi-nám-taan	สี น้ำ ตาล	to be brown
mákhǔua-thêet	มะเขือ เทศ	tomato, tomatoes
sǐi-dɛɛng	สี แดง	to be red
tɛɛngmoo	แตงโม	watermelon, watermelons
sǐi-khǐau	สี เขียว	to be green
rót-tʃâat	รส ชาติ	flavour, taste
rót	รส	flavour, taste
plaa	ปลา	fish
khem	เค็ม	to be salty
arɔ̀i	อร่อย	to be delicious
sômtam	ส้มตำ	papaya salad
khêm	เข้ม	to be rich in flavour
nám-taan	น้ำ ตาล	sugar
wǎan	หวาน	to be sweet
nám-plàu	น้ำ เปล่า	fresh water, drinking water
plàu	เปล่า	to be blank, vacant
mâi	ไม่	no
mii	มี	have
nám-khěng	น้ำ แข็ง	ice
khěng	แข็ง	to be hard, solid, strong
rót-tsɯ̀ɯt	รส จืด	to be bland, tasteless
nám-sôm	น้ำ ส้ม	orange juice
prîiau	เปรี้ยว	to be sour
phrík nám-plaa	พริก น้ำ ปลา	chilli sauce
phrík	พริก	chilli
nám-plaa	น้ำ ปลา	fish sauce

khəəi	เคย	once, ever
tʃim	ชิม	taste
thúriian	ทุเรียน	durian
lɔɔng	ลอง	to try
thə̀	เถอะ	suggesting particle (let us...)
tammai	ทำไม	why?
kin	กิน	to eat
wai-wai	ไวๆ	fast, quickly
aahǎan	อาหาร	food
àrɔ̀i	อร่อย	to be delicious
mâak	มาก	very
phèt	เผ็ด	to be spicy
au	เอา	to want, to take
ìik	อีก	more
mái	ไหม	basic question word
tʃék	เช็ค	check
bin	บิล	bill
dûuai	ด้วย	also

C. How the language works

A) The word **sǐi** สี *colour* is usually placed before the name of the actual colour. Hence, *red* becomes **sǐi-dɛɛng** สี แดง *colour-red* and *blue* becomes **sǐi-fáa** สี ฟ้า *colour-sky*.

B) **náam** น้ำ *water* is often placed in front of other words when referring to specific drinks and beverages.

náam	น้ำ	*water, liquid, fluid*
nám-dùum	น้ำ ดื่ม	*drinking water*

nám-plàu	น้ำ เปล่า	*fresh* or *plain water*
nám-sôm	น้ำ ส้ม	*orange juice*
nám-ɛ̀ɛppɔ̂ən	น้ำ แอปเปิ้ล	*apple juice*
nám-tʃaa	น้ำ ชา	*tea*

- **náam** น้ำ *water* is pronounced with long **aa**-sound.
- However, at the beginning of sentence and together with other words, it is usually shortened to a short **a** as in **nám-khĕng** น้ำ แข็ง *ice*.

C) **náam** น้ำ *water, fluid, liquid* is also used with many other words to form new meanings:

nám-khĕng	น้ำ แข็ง	*ice*
nám-man	น้ำ มัน	*oil*
nám-taan	น้ำ ตาล	*sugar*
sĭi-nám-taan	สี น้ำ ตาล	*brown (colour)*
nám-tòk	น้ำ ตก	*waterfall*
mɛ̂ɛ-náam	แม่ น้ำ	*river*
hɔ̂ng-náam	ห้อง น้ำ	*bathroom, washroom*
nám-nàk	น้ำ หนัก	*weight*

- So, we can conclude that the word **náam** น้ำ *water, fluid, liquid* is a very important word in Thai. It is very much related to the traditional Thai way of living.

D) Tastes and flavours

1. When **khem** เค็ม *salty* is pronounced with a different tone, the meaning becomes as follows:

khem	เค็ม	*to be salty*
khêm	เข้ม	*dark in colour, rich-flavoured*
khĕm	เข็ม	*needle*

- Note that **kluua** เกลือ is *salt* and **khem** เค็ม is *salty*.

2. **rót-tʃâat** รสชาติ *flavour, taste* is often expressed with two words.

rót	รส	*flavour, taste*
tʃâat	ชาติ	*nature*

- There is another commonly used word which is pronounced exactly the same; it is **rót** รถ *car*.
- As you can see the pronunciation and the tone of **rót** รถ *car* and **rót** รส *flavour, taste* is the same even though writing them in Thai script is different.
- So, while speaking, you need to understand the meaning from the context. It is not likely that these two words will create any confusion since they would be used in a totally different context.

> **3** **phèt** เผ็ด *to be spicy*
> mâi au *phèt* khâ/khráp ไม่ เอา เผ็ด ค่ะ/ครับ
> no take *spicy* khâ/khráp – *I don't want spicy food.*

- It is good to know how to say in Thai "I don't want spicy food".
- The object *food* is dropped here since it is understood from the context.

E) Here are some more examples where pronunciation is similar.

pèt	เป็ด	*duck*
phèt	เผ็ด	*to be spicy, hot*
phét	เพชร	*diamond*
pìt	ปิด	*to close*
phìt	ผิด	*to be wrong, incorrect*
phít	พิษ	*poison*

Chapter 8

- The pronunciation in these six words is quite similar. Here your task would be to pronounce the words written with only **p** *without the puff of air* (unaspirated) and the words written with **ph** *with the puff of air* (aspirated).

- Note also that the **e**-sound in Thai is pronounced as in the English word n**e**t and the **i**-sound in Thai as in the English word s**i**t. In addition, if you are able to pronounce the right tone and use each word in the right context, you are on the way to speaking Thai fluently.

- **F)** When you want to pay in a restaurant there are mainly two ways to ask for a bill. You may address the waiter with the phrase **khun khráp** คุณ ครับ (men say) or **khun khá** คุณ คะ (women say). **khun** คุณ *you* is considered to be a polite way to approach anyone in Thailand, while the same type of expression in English (*hey you!*) would not be polite at all.

> **1** *tʃék-bin* dûuai เช็ค บิล ด้วย
> *check-bill* also – *Can I get the bill, please?*

- Here we use two loan words from English **tʃék** เช็ค *check* and **bin** บิล *bill*.

- **dûuai** ด้วย *also, as well* at the end of the sentence is considered to be a polite expression when making a request.

> **2** *kèp-tang* khráp เก็บ ตังค์ ครับ
> *collect-money* khráp – *May I pay?*

- This is almost like an idiomatic expression when asking for a bill; literal meaning is *collect money*. **tang** ตังค์ *money* is borrowed from Sanskrit.

- Sometimes, **tang** ตังค์ *money* is used instead of **ngən** เงิน *money* which is borrowed from Chinese. When asking for a bill, **tang** ตังค์ *money* is normally used.

> **3** mâi tông *thɔɔn* khráp ไม่ ต้อง ทอน ครับ
> no need *reduce/cut* khráp – *Keep the change!*

- The expression **thɔɔn ngən** ทอน เงิน (literally: *cut money*) in English means *to give the change.*
- When you pay, you may simply say **mâi tông thɔɔn khráp** ไม่ ต้อง ทอน ครับ if you would like to give the change as a tip.
- The meaning is understood from the context, *no need to return the change/keep the change.* This is a very handy way to be polite.

D. New sounds

Consonants:

- **y** as in the Thai word **yák** ยักษ์ *giant*
  – English sound: **y**ellow, **y**es, **y**ear (rating: good)
- **w** as in the Thai word **wɛ̌ɛn** แหวน *ring*
  – English sound: **w**eek, **w**ant, **w**inter (rating: good)

Vowels:

- short **ə** as in the word **thə̀** เถอะ *particle adding emphasis to the sentence*
  – English sound: **a**bout, **a**musing, **a**round (rating: good)
- long **əə** as in the word **khəəi** เคย *once, used to*
  – English sound: h**er**, t**ur**n, d**ir**ty (rating: quite good but pay attention). The **əə**-sound is pronounced without **r**-sound.
- Vowels in Thai are always clearly pronounced either long or short.

E. Simple advice

You may have wondered about the tone marks in transliterations. These tone marks are used in transliterations only; they are not used in the Thai script. As you know, the Thai language has five tones. In order to speak Thai fluently, you need to have some knowledge of tones. However, in the beginning, we are placing more emphasis on the correct pronunciation than the tones. In the last Chapter 21, we give you a tone exercise which will help you understand Thai tones better.

Here are the tone marks commonly used in transliterations. Note that the tone marks in transliterations are always placed above vowels.

Examples:

1. *Middle tone*, no tone mark

| pai | ไป | *to go* |
| maa | มา | *to come* |

2. *Low tone*, tone mark pointing downwards

| nòi | หน่อย | *a little* |
| bὲɛp | แบบ | *style, like* |

3. *Falling tone*, tone mark is like a hat

| dâai | ได้ | *can, to get* |
| rîip | รีบ | *to hurry up* |

4. *High tone*, tone mark pointing upwards

| súɯ | ซื้อ | *to buy* |
| yím | ยิ้ม | *to smile* |

5. *Rising tone*, like a hat but upside down

| khɔ̌ɔng | ของ | *things, goods, of* |
| khɔ̌ɔ | ขอ | *to ask* |

For example, when **sii** สี *colour* is pronounced with a different tone, the meaning becomes different as follows:

sìi	สี่	*four* (low tone)
sîi	สี้	*classifier for tooth* (falling tone)
síi	สี้	*to be intimate with someone* (high tone)
sǐi	สี	*colour* (rising tone)

Now, if you use the middle tone for the above four words, you would probably be understood; Thais would understand the meaning from the context.

If you are also able to use the correct tone with the above words, you are well on the way to speak Thai fluently. Understanding is the key. Note also that sometimes Thai people minimize the tones in such a way that you can hardly distinguish them.

F. Take it further

Refer to the book:

Dhyan Manik: *Understanding the Thai Language and Grammar:*

- More about Thai consonant and vowel sounds can be found in Chapter 1, sections 1.1 and 1.2.
- There is a comprehensive list of different types of Thai foods, vegetables, fruits, drinks, spices etc. in Chapter 9.
- A list of spices can be found in Chapter 9, section 9.6.
- A more extensive list of colours can be found in Chapter 11, section 11.4.

Chapter 9

At the pharmacy and not being well

phŏm pen-wàt
ผม เป็น หวัด
I have a cold.

Highlights

ráan-khǎai-yaa	ร้าน ขาย ยา	pharmacy, drug store
mâi-sàbaai	ไม่ สบาย	to be not well
pùuat-hǔua	ปวด หัว	to have a headache
rôok	โรค	disease
yaa	ยา	medicine
mɔ̌ɔ	หมอ	doctor

A. Sentences

1. tʃǎn *mâi-sàbaai* nít-nɔ̀i ฉัน ไม่ สบาย นิด หน่อย
I *no-well* bit-little – *I am not feeling well.*

2. mii *rôok* lǎai yàang มี โรค หลาย อย่าง
have *disease* many kind
There are many kinds of diseases.

3. thúk-khon *mâi-sàbaai* baang-khráng
ทุก คน ไม่ สบาย บาง ครั้ง
every-person *no-well* some-time
Everybody is sick sometimes.

4. tʃǎn *pùuat-thɔ́ɔng* ฉัน ปวด ท้อง
I *pain-stomach* – *I have a stomach ache.*

5. tʃǎn *pùuat-hǔua* ฉัน ปวด หัว
I *ache-head* – *I have a headache.*

6. tʃǎn *pen-wàt* ฉัน เป็น หวัด
I *be-cold* – *I have a cold.*

(7) phûuak kháu *pen-máreng* พวก เขา เป็น มะเร็ง
group-he *be-cancer* – They have a cancer.

(8) phûuan tʃán pen *rôok-bau-wăan*
เพื่อน ฉัน เป็น โรค เบา หวาน
friend I be *disease-urine-sweet* – My friend has diabetes.

(9) lăai khon *tìt-tʃúua* หลาย คน ติด เชื้อ
many person *catch-virus*
Many people have an infection.

(10) bang khon *hŭua-tsai-waai* บาง คน หัว ใจ วาย
some person *head-heart-finish*
Some people have a heart attack.

(11) khun tông kin *yaa* คุณ ต้อง กิน ยา
you must eat *medicine* – You must take some medicine.

(12) *ráan-khăai-yaa* yùu thîi năi ร้าน ขาย ยา อยู่ ที่ ไหน
store-sell-medicine stay at where – Where is a drug store?

(13) tʃán tông-kaan *yaa-kêɛ-pùuat* ฉัน ต้อง การ ยา แก้ ปวด
I need-task *medicine-fix-pain* – I need some painkiller.

(14) *tʃái* yang-ngai ใช้ ยังไง
use how – How do I use this?

(15) àat-tsà tông pai hăa *mɔ̆ɔ* อาจ จะ ต้อง ไป หา หมอ
maybe-will must go search *doctor*
Perhaps, I must visit a doctor.

Common expressions
(kham thîi tʃái bòi-bòi คำ ที่ ใช้ บ่อยๆ)

duu-lɛɛ tuua-eeng ná ดู แล ตัว เอง นะ
see-look body-self ná – *Take care of yourself.*

> khɔ̆ɔ hâi hăai reu-reu ขอ ให้ หาย เร็วๆ
> ask give recover fast-fast – *Get well soon.*
>
> khít-thŭng mâak คิด ถึง มาก
> think-about very – *I miss you very much.*
>
> tsəə-kan ná khá / khráp เจอ กัน นะ คะ / ครับ
> meet-with ná khá / khráp – *Let us meet soon.*

B. Vocabulary

mâi-sàbaai	ไม่ สบาย	to be sick, not well
nít-nɔ̀i	นิด หน่อย	a little, a little bit
rôok	โรค	disease
mii	มี	to have, there is
lăai	หลาย	many, several
yàang	อย่าง	type, kind
thúk-khon	ทุก คน	everyone, everybody
baang-khráng	บาง ครั้ง	sometimes
baang	บาง	some
khráng	ครั้ง	time, occasion
pùuat-thɔ́ɔng	ปวด ท้อง	to have a stomach ache
pùuat-hŭua	ปวด หัว	to have a headache
pen-wàt	เป็น หวัด	to have a cold
wàt	หวัด	common cold
phûuak-kháu	พวก เขา	they
phûuak	พวก	group
kháu	เขา	she, he

Chapter 9

pen máreng	เป็น มะเร็ง	to have a cancer
pen	เป็น	to be
máreng	มะเร็ง	cancer
phûɯan tʃán	เพื่อน ฉัน	my friend
pen rôok bau-wăan	เป็น โรค เบา หวาน	to have diabetes
rôok	โรค	disease
bau	เบา	urine
wăan	หวาน	to be sweet
lăai khon	หลาย คน	many people
tìt-tʃúɯa	ติด เชื้อ	to be infected
tìt	ติด	to catch, to attach, to stick
tʃúɯa	เชื้อ	virus, bacteria
bang khon	บาง คน	some people
hŭua-tsai-waai	หัว ใจ วาย	heart attack
hŭua-tsai	หัว ใจ	heart
hŭua	หัว	head
tsai	ใจ	heart, mind, spirit
waai	วาย	to be finished
tôŋ-kaan	ต้อง การ	to need
ráan-khăai-yaa	ร้าน ขาย ยา	pharmacy, drug store
ráan	ร้าน	shop, store
khăai	ขาย	to sell
yaa	ยา	medicine
yaa-kɛ̂ɛ-pùuat	ยา แก้ ปวด	painkiller
kɛ̂ɛ-pùuat	แก้ ปวด	to fix pain
kɛ̂ɛ	แก้	to fix, to solve
pùuat	ปวด	pain
tʃái	ใช้	to use

yang-ngai	ยังไง	how?
tông	ต้อง	must
pai hăa	ไป หา	to visit
pai	ไป	to go
hăa	หา	to look for
mɔ̆ɔ	หมอ	a doctor
duu-lɛɛ	ดู แล	to take care
tuua-eeng	ตัว เอง	yourself
ná	นะ	polite particle
khɔ̆ɔ	ขอ	to ask
hâi	ให้	for, to give
hăai	หาย	to get well, to recover
reu-reu	เร็วๆ	fast
khít-thŭng	คิด ถึง	to miss, to long for
khít	คิด	to think, to consider
thŭng	ถึง	of, about
mâak	มาก	much
tsǝǝ-kan	เจอ กัน	to meet
tsǝǝ	เจอ	to meet
kan	กัน	to be with
ná-khráp	นะ ครับ	polite particles for men

C. How the language works

A) In English, we usually express body disorders with the verb *to have, to have a headache*, etc. The same in Thai is expressed with different verbs such as **pùuat** ปวด *to ache,* **tsèp** เจ็บ *to be hurt,* **tit** ติด *to catch,* **pen** เป็น *to be,* **waai** วาย *to be finished.*

Chapter 9

Examples:

1. **pùuat** ปวด *to ache* and **tsèp** เจ็บ *to be hurt.*

> **1.1** tʃán *pùuat* thɔ́ɔng ฉัน ปวด ท้อง
> I *ache* stomach – *I have a stomach ache.*

- Here the Thai language uses the verb **pùuat** ปวด *to ache.*

> **1.2** tʃán *pùuat* hŭua ฉัน ปวด หัว
> I *ache* head – *I have a headache.*

- Here the Thai language uses the verb **pùuat** ปวด *to ache.*

> **1.3** kháu *tsèp-tsai* mâak เขา เจ็บ ใจ มาก
> he *hurt-heart* very
> *He is very much hurt! (heart-broken)*

- Here the Thai language uses the verb **tsèp** เจ็บ *to be hurt.*

> **1.4** kháu *bàat-tsèp* เขา บาด เจ็บ
> he *cut-hurt* – *He was injured.*

- Here the Thai language uses the verb **tsèp** เจ็บ *to be hurt.*

2. **tit** ติด *to catch*

> **2.1** lăai khon *tìt* tʃʉ́ʉa หลาย คน ติด เชื้อ
> many person *catch* infection
> *Many people have an infection.*

- Here the Thai language uses the verb **tit** ติด *to catch.*

3. pen เป็น *to be*

> **3.1** tɕán *pen* wàt   ฉัน เป็น หวัด
> I *be* cold – *I have a cold.*

- Here the Thai language uses the verb **pen** เป็น *to be*.

> **3.2** phûuak-kháu *pen* máreng   พวก เขา เป็น มะเร็ง
> group-he *be* cancer – *They have a cancer.*

- Here the Thai language uses the verb **pen** เป็น *to be*.

> **3.3** phûɯan tɕán *pen* rôok-bau-wăan
> เพื่อน ฉัน เป็น โรค เบา หวาน
> friend I *be* disease-urine-sweet – *My friend has diabetes.*

- Here the Thai language uses the verb **pen** เป็น *to be*.

4. waai วาย *to be finished*

> **4.1** bang khon *hŭua-tsai-waai*   บาง คน หัว ใจ วาย
> some person *head-heart-finish*
> *Some people have a heart attack.*

- Here the Thai language uses the verb **waai** วาย *to be finished*.

B) In Thai, combining two or three words can create new meanings. **yaa** ยา *medicine* is a good example. Consider the following:

yaa	ยา	*medicine*
yaa-kɛ̂ɛ-pùuat	ยา แก้ ปวด	*pain killer*
yaa-kɛ̂ɛ-pùuat-hŭua	ยา แก้ ปวด หัว	*medicine for headache*
yaa-kɛ̂ɛ-pùuat-thɔ́ɔng	ยา แก้ ปวด ท้อง	*medicine for stomach ache*
yaa-kɛ̂ɛ-pùuat-fan	ยา แก้ ปวด ฟัน	*medicine for toothache*

yaa-sèep-tìt	ยา เสพ ติด	*drugs, narcotics*
yaa-máa	ยา ม้า	*amphetamine, yaba*
yaa-bâa	ยา บ้า	*amphetamine*
tìt-yaa	ติด ยา	*to be addicted to drugs*

- Normally, when two or more words are combined to create new meanings, we use hyphens in transliterations to emphasize the fact that these words are best understood as one word or a phrase.

D. New sounds

Consonants:

- **l** as in the Thai word **ling** ลิง *monkey*
  – English sound: **l**ike, **l**eft, be**ll**y (rating: good, but pay attention)
- **r** as in the Thai word **ruua** เรือ *boat*
  – English sound: **r**ed, te**rr**ible, **wr**ong
  (rating: OK, but pay attention)
- These two consonant sounds (**l** and **r**) are so called sonorant sounds in Thai. Often Thais replace **r**-sound with **l**. So, the **ruua** เรือ *boat* could also be pronounced as **luua** เรือ *boat*. You need to be aware of this. That is an informal way to speak.

Vowels:

- short **ʉ** as in the word **phʉ̂ng** เพิ่ง *just, a moment ago*
  – English sound: sh**ou**ld, c**ou**ld, w**ou**ld
  (rating: not very good, pay attention)
- long **ʉʉ** as in the word **tʃʉ̂ʉ** ชื่อ *name*
  – English sound: **new**, r**u**de, f**ew**
  (rating: not very good, pay attention)
- Vowels in Thai are always clearly pronounced either long or short.

E. Simple advice

The Thai writing system is not always that easy to comprehend. Here again, we have five similar sounding words which are written differently in the Thai script.

Examples:

yaa	ยา	*medicine*
yàa	อย่า	*do not*
yàa	หย่า	*divorce*
yâa	ย่า	*grandmother*
yâa	หญ้า	*grass*

If you go to any of the language schools in Thailand, you are most likely first taught the Thai script, writing system and tones. There is nothing wrong with that. The truth is that with such a method you cannot learn to speak Thai quickly. If you decide to go that way, the task is vast.

So, what can we do? We may estimate that you are understood about 70–80 % of the time if you manage to choose simple common words in the right context and pronounce them correctly. Hence, by using the middle tone only for the above words, Thais would understand the meaning from the context and your speaking would sound quite natural.

On the other hand, if you try to speak with correct tones at the beginning, your speaking may sound unnatural since you are not used to speak that way. Thai people may not understand you. The first tone, the middle tone, sometimes called the level tone or the common tone, lies between all the other four tones. So, the trick here would be to use the *middle tone* as in the first word **yaa** ยา medicine for all five words. Then, meaning would be understood from the context only.

Having said that, we must emphasize the fact that tones are a very important part of the Thai language, and they cannot be ignored. The point we are trying to make here is that in the beginning it is more important to choose the right words in the given context and pronounce them correctly. It takes longer and needs some considerable effort to master all five tones of the Thai language well and naturally.

Note also that **yàa** อย่า *do not* and **yàa** หย่า *divorce* are both pronounced with the same tone, *low tone*. However, they are written differently in the Thai script and have a completely different meaning. The same applies to **yâa** ย่า *grandmother* and **yâa** หญ้า *grass*. The tone is a *falling tone*. So, even if you would use the correct tone for these words while speaking, the meaning must be understood from the context anyway.

Hence, the context and the word choice are very important in Thai. There are many more examples like this. It is very important to learn to use simple correct words in the given situation. If you are able to do that, Thais would forgive you even though your tone is not perfect.

F. Take it further

Refer to the book:

Dhyan Manik: *Understanding the Thai Language and Grammar:*

- More about Thai consonant and vowel sounds can be found in Chapter 1, sections 1.1 and 1.2.
- Health words: More about health & diseases and personal items can be found in Chapter 10, sections:
- 10.1 Some common health vocabulary (**phέε** แพ้ to be allergic)
- 10.2 Not feeling well (**pùuat-hŭua** ปวด หัว to have a headache)
- 10.3 Some common diseases (**pen-rôok-bau-wăan** เป็น โรค เบา หวาน to have diabetes)
- 10.4 To heal illnesses (**ráan-khăai-yaa** ร้าน ขาย ยา pharmacy, drug store)
- 10.5 Personal items (**sàbùu** สบู่ soap)

Chapter 10

Using prepositions, nouns, adjectives and adverbs

mɛɛu nɔɔn bon tó
แมว นอน บน โต๊ะ
The cat lies on the table.

Highlights

Nouns

rót	รถ	car
rót-yon	รถ ยนต์	car
rót-théksîi	รถ แท็กซี่	taxi
hôŋ	ห้อง	room
tó	โต๊ะ	table

Prepositions

thîi	ที่	at, to
nai	ใน	in
bon	บน	on, on the top
tâi	ใต้	under
tsàak	จาก	from

Adjectives and adverbs

mài	ใหม่	to be new
sŭuai	สวย	to be beautiful, beautifully
bau-bau	เบาๆ	to be gentle, gently, softly
nàk	หนัก	to be heavy, heavily
reu	เร็ว	to be fast
dii	ดี	to be good, well

A. Sentences

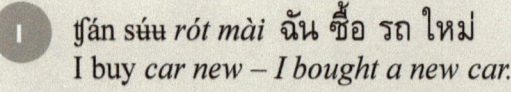 tʃán súu *rót mài* ฉัน ซื้อ รถ ใหม่
I buy *car new* – *I bought a new car.*

2 tʃán tʃɔ̂ɔp *phûu-tʃaai lɔ̀ɔ* ฉัน ชอบ ผู้ ชาย หล่อ
I like *person-male handsome* – *I like handsome men.*

3 tʃán yàak-dâai *măa tuua-lék* ฉัน อยาก ได้ หมา ตัว เล็ก
I want-get *dog body-small* – *I want to get a small dog.*

4 tʃán yàak nâng *rót-théksîi* ฉัน อยาก นั่ง รถ แท็กซี่
I want sit *car-taxi* – *I want to take a taxi.*

5 fɛɛn kháu yùu *thîi* paarîit แฟน เขา อยู่ ที่ ปารีส
girlfriend he stay *at* Paris – *His girlfriend stays in Paris.*

6 phûuan tʃán tham-ngaan *nai* hông
เพื่อน ฉัน ทำ งาน ใน ห้อง
friend I do-work *in* room – *My friend works in the room.*

7 mɛɛu nɔɔn *bon* tó แมว นอน บน โต๊ะ
cat sleep *on* table – *The cat lies on the table.*

8 dèk-dèk tʃɔ̂ɔp nâng *nai* rôm เด็กๆ ชอบ นั่ง ใน ร่ม
child-child like sit *in* umbrella
Children like to sit under the umbrella.

9 tʃán maa *tsàak* krungthêep ฉัน มา จาก กรุงเทพ
I come *from* Bangkok – *I come from Bangkok.*

10 phɔ̂ɔ-mɛ̂ɛ tʃán tham-ngaan *nàk* พ่อ แม่ ฉัน ทำงาน หนัก
father-mother I do-work *heavy* – *My parents work hard.*

11 kháu khàp *dii* เขา ขับ ดี
he drive *good* – *He drives well.*

12 kháu khàp rót *dâai-reu* เขา ขับ รถ ได้ เร็ว
he drive car *can-fast* – *He drives a car fast.*

13 Chanida dəən *dâai-sŭuai* ชนิดา เดิน ได้ สวย
Chanida walk *can-beautiful* – *Chanida walks beautifully.*

14 Peter khui *sànùk* ปีเตอร์ คุย สนุก
Peter chat *fun* – *Peter is funny!*

15 *ráwang nɔ̀i* ระวัง หน่อย
be *careful little* – *Be careful!*

16 *bau-bau* khâ เบาๆ ค่ะ
gentle-gentle khâ – *Do it gently!*

Common expressions
(kham thîi ʧái bɔ̀i-bɔ̀i คำ ที่ ใช้ ป่อยๆ)

khun maa *tsàak* pràthêet arai คุณ มา จาก ประเทศ อะไร
you come *from* country what – *What country are you from?*

bâan khun yùu *thîi-năi* บ้าน คุณ อยู่ ที่ ไหน
home you stay *place-where* – *Where is your home?*

khun mii *lûuk* mái คุณ มี ลูก ไหม
you have *child* "question" – *Do you have any children?*

khun lên *kiilaa* arai คุณ เล่น กีฬา อะไร
you play *sport* what – *Do you play any sport?*

B. Vocabulary

ʧán	ฉัน	I
súu	ซื้อ	to buy
rót	รถ	car
mài	ใหม่	to be new
ʧɔ̂ɔp	ชอบ	to like

khon	คน	person, people
lɔ̀ɔ	หล่อ	to be handsome
yàak-dâai	อยาก ได้	to want to get
yàak	อยาก	to want
dâai	ได้	to get
măa	หมา	dog
tuua	ตัว	to be body
lék	เล็ก	to be small
nâng	นั่ง	to sit
rót-théksîi	รถ แท็กซี่	taxi
rót	รถ	car
kháu	เขา	she/he
yùu	อยู่	to stay, to live
thîi	ที่	at, to
paarîit	ปารีส	Paris
phɨ̂ɨan tʃán	เพื่อน ฉัน	my friend
phɨ̂ɨan	เพื่อน	friend
tʃán	ฉัน	I
tham-ngaan	ทำ งาน	to work
nai	ใน	in
hɔ̂ng	ห้อง	room
mɛɛu	แมว	cat
nɔɔn	นอน	to sleep
bon	บน	on, on the top
tó	โต๊ะ	table
dèk-dèk	เด็กๆ	children
tʃɔ̂ɔp	ชอบ	to like
nâng	นั่ง	to sit

rôm	ร่ม	umbrella, shade
maa	มา	to come
tsàak	จาก	from
krungthêep	กรุงเทพ	Bangkok
phɔ̂ɔ-mɛ̂ɛ	พ่อ แม่	parents
phɔ̂ɔ	พ่อ	father
mɛ̂ɛ	แม่	mother
tham-ngaan	ทำ งาน	to work
nàk	หนัก	hard
khàp	ขับ	to drive
dii	ดี	to be good, well
dâai-reu	ได้ เร็ว	fast
dəən	เดิน	to walk
dâai-sŭuai	ได้ สวย	beautifully
dâai	ได้	can, to be able to
sŭuai	สวย	to be beautiful, beautifully
sànùk	สนุก	to be fun, funny
khui	คุย	to chat, to speak
ráwang	ระวัง	be careful, watch out!
nɔ̀i	หน่อย	a little
bau-bau	เบาๆ	gently, softly
pràthêet	ประเทศ	country
arai	อะไร	what?
bâan khun	บ้าน คุณ	your home
yùu	อยู่	to be, to stay, to live
thîi-năi	ที่ ไหน	where?
mii	มี	to have

lûuk	ลูก	child, children
mái	ไหม	basic question word
lên	เล่น	to play
kiilaa	กีฬา	sport

C. How the language works

A) Prepositions in Thai are usually placed before nouns as in English.

Examples:

 phûuan ʧán tham-ngaan *nai hɔ̂ng*
เพื่อน ฉัน ทำ งาน ใน ห้อง
friend I do-work *in room – My friend works in the room.*

Here the Thai preposition **nai** ใน *in* is used in the same way as the English preposition *in*.

B) In Thai, there are some multifunctional words which are used in several different grammatical functions and meanings in the sentence. **thîi** ที่ is one of them.

1. **thîi** ที่ as a preposition *at, to*

    thîi bâan   ที่ บ้าน   *at home*

2. **thîi** ที่ as a relative pronoun, *that, which, who*

thîi-sǎam	ที่ สาม	*third*
thîi-lǔua	ที่ เหลือ	*remainder, excess, leftover*
thîi-nîi	ที่ นี่	*here*
thîi-sùt	ที่ สุด	*most*
thîi-nǎi	ที่ ไหน	*where?*
thîi-rák	ที่ รัก	*sweetheart*

3. **thîi** ที่ *place*, before verbs, can create new nouns

   thîi-nɔɔn ที่ นอน *place to sleep*
   is translated into English as a *bed*.

   thîi-sài-náam ที่ ใส่ น้ำ *place to put water*
   is translated into English as a *water tank*.

   thîi-plɔ̀ɔt-bùrìi ที่ ปลอด บุหรี่ *place to be free of smoke*
   is translated into English as a *non-smoking area*.

   thîi-phák ที่ พัก *place to stay*
   is translated into English as a *residence*, a *home*.

   thîi-nâng ที่ นั่ง *place to sit*
   is translated into English as a *seat*, a *sitting place*.

   thîi-yùu ที่ อยู่ *place to live*
   is translated into English as an *address*.

3.1 Other usages

   plìian-thîi เปลี่ยน ที่ *to change place*
   is translated into English as *to move* or *to change the place*.

   baang-thîi บาง ที่ *some place*
   is translated into English as *somewhere*.

Note that there is another word **thii** ที *time, occasion*, which is pronounced in the similar way; it is pronounced with the middle tone, while **thîi** ที่ is pronounced with falling tone.

thii	ที	*time, occasion*
baang-thii	บาง ที	*sometimes, perhaps*

C) Often adjectives and adverbs in Thai are understood from the context.

Examples:

> ① kháu *dii* เขา ดี
> he *good* – *He is good.*

- Here **dii** ดี *good* is an adjectiv. In this sentence the adjective **dii** ดี *good* also plays the role of the verb *to be* in English.

> ② kháu khǐian *dii* เขา เขียน ดี
> he write *good* – *He writes well.*

- Here **dii** ดี *good* is an adverb. When an adjective follows a verb, it is translated into English as an adverb, here *well*.

> ③ kháu khǐian *dâai dii* เขา เขียน ได้ ดี
> he write *can good* – *He writes well.*

- Here we have placed **dâai** ได้ *can*, before the adjective **dii** ดี *good*, and the translation into English is the same as in the sentence 2. However, the colour of the sentence is slightly different and more expressive in Thai.
- **dâai** ได้ can be placed before an adjective in order to express that the action is being done that way. In English, we express the same with adverbs.

> ④ kháu khǐian *dii dâai* เขา เขียน ดี ได้
> he write *good can* – *He can write well.*

- We can also place **dâai** ได้ after an adjective, normally at the end of the sentence. The meaning changes compared to the sentence 3.
- Here the meaning is *he can write well* or *he is allowed to write well*.

D) dèk-dèk เด็กๆ *children*

- We already know that Thai nouns are often doubled in order to show plurals. Many times plurals are understood from the context, however.

E) nâng นั่ง *to sit*

> ʧán yàak nâng *rót-théksîi* ฉัน อยาก นั่ง รถ แท็กซี่
> I want sit *car-taxi – I want to take a taxi.*

- **nâng** นั่ง *to sit* is often used when taking a car or a motorcycle. **nâng rót** นั่ง รถ means *taking a car (sitting in a car as a passenger)*.

- Often, Thais like to include **rót** รถ *car* before words like **théksîi** แท็กซี่ *taxi* to emphasize the fact that the car is a vehicle.

- **rót** รถ *vehicle* in Thai can be used with many other words to form different meanings.

Examples:

rót-fai	รถ ไฟ	*train* (literally: vehicle electricity)
rót-mee	รถ เมล์	*bus* (literally: vehicle mail)
rót-tûu	รถ ตู้	*van* (literally: vehicle box)
rót-máa	รถ ม้า	*horse carriage* (literally: vehicle horse)
rót-khèɛng	รถ แข่ง	*car racing* (literally: vehicle race)
rót-tìt	รถ ติด	*traffic jam* (literally: vehicle stuck)
mau-rót	เมา รถ	*to be carsick* (literally: drunk vehicle)

So, **rót** รถ *car, vehicle* in Thai has much wider meaning than the English word *car*. It can also refer to *bicycles, trolleys* etc.

F) lên เล่น *to play* can be used in several different ways.

Chapter 10

Examples:

lên-kiilaa	เล่น กีฬา	*to sport: to play tennis, volleyball, football, etc.*
phûut-lên	พูด เล่น	*to joke*
lɔ́ɔ-lên	ล้อ เล่น	*to tease, to joke*
tʃûɯ-lên	ชื่อ เล่น	*nickname*
dəən-lên	เดิน เล่น	*to take a walk*
lên-náam	เล่น น้ำ	*to swim, to play in the water*

- There is another word for swimming **wâai-náam** ว่าย น้ำ *to swim*.
- **lên-náam** เล่น น้ำ *to swim* sounds like swimming is more fun.

G) ráwang ระวัง *to be careful, to watch out*

- When we place the *verb* first in the sentence, the statement can commonly be understood as a command.

Examples:

ráwang nɔ̀i	ระวัง หน่อย	*be careful!*
khàp dii-dii	ขับ ดีๆ	*drive properly*
dəən reu-reu	เดิน เร็วๆ	*walk fast*
yùt dĭau-níi	หยุด เดี๋ยว นี้	*stop now*

D. New sounds

Consonants:

- **ng** as in the Thai word **ng**uu งู *snake*
  – English sound: ri**ng**ing, havi**ng**, thi**ng**
  (rating: OK, but pay attention).

- **h** as in the Thai word nók-**h**ûuk นก ฮูก *owl*
  – English sound: **h**e, **h**ave, **h**elp (rating: good)

- In English, **ng**-sound does not appear at the beginning of the word, but in Thai it is common. You need some practise to get this sound right at the beginning of the word.

Vowels:

We have now introduced all pure vowel sounds in Thai. There are nine pure short vowel sounds in Thai. When we consider that every short vowel sound has its long counterpart, then we actually have 18 pure vowel sounds in Thai. As we have already learned, one letter in the transliteration denotes a short vowel sound and two letters denote a long vowel sound. They are:

à อะ – aa อา, ì อิ – ii อี, ù อุ – uu อู, è เอะ – ee เอ, ə̀ เออะ – əə เออ, ɛ̀ แอะ – ɛɛ แอ, **ʉ̀ อึ – ʉʉ อื**อ, ò โอะ – oo โอ, ɔ̀ เอาะ – ɔɔ ออ

We have marked those vowel sounds with **bold** where you, as an English speaker, may require some extra practise. With these 18 pure and clear vowel sounds we can produce a number of vowel combinations which will be introduced in the following chapters.

E. Simple advice

Learning Thai script is an art. It is good to be aware of the fact that learning the Thai script does not help you to understand the Thai sounds any better. Sounds are sounds, and it does not matter how they are written. You need to learn every sound first, one by one. The same also applies to English. The only difference is that the Thai writing system is far more complex. Once you know all the sounds, then you can learn how to write sounds in Thai if you wish to do so.

Note that if you do the opposite and try to learn Thai sounds from the Thai script, your task will be far more complex and difficult compared to learning all pure sounds first. You may get confused and give up. There are many more alphabet symbols than actual sounds in the Thai language.

For example:

Let's suppose that you would like to know how the following Thai symbols are pronounced:

ถ, ฐ, ท, ธ, ฑ, ฒ

You might spend a lot of time working out the exact pronunciation of each symbol. However, if you already know that the correct sound for all these Thai symbols is **th** as in the English word **t**ime, then you only need to memorize that all these consonants represent this sound (aspirated **th**-sound).

Actually, things are somewhat more complicated than that. You should also learn which consonant groups each of the above six consonants belong to (there are three groups, low, middle and high). For the beginner that would be too much. Learning all that would take energy from learning to speak Thai fluently.

So, learn all the sounds first and then subsequently the Thai script if you want to. It is not necessary to know the Thai script in order to speak Thai fluently. To explain the Thai writing system goes beyond the scope of this book. We just point out those difficulties you might encounter on the way.

F. Take it further

Refer to the book:

Dhyan Manik: *Understanding the Thai Language and Grammar:*

- More about Thai consonant and vowel sounds can be found in Chapter 1, sections 1.1 and 1.2.
- A comprehensive presentation of adjectives, adverbs and prepositions can be found in the following Chapters: 11 adjectives, 12 adverbs and 15 prepositions.

Chapter 11

Using adverbs of frequency – "how often" -words

ʧǎn tsà yùu thîi nîi tàlɔ̀ɔt-pai
ฉัน จะ อยู่ ที่ นี่ ตลอด ไป
I will stay here forever.

Highlights

sàmɔ̌ə	เสมอ	*always*
baang-khráng	บาง ครั้ง	*sometimes*
thammádaa	ธรรมดา	*usually*
thúk-wan	ทุก วัน	*everyday*
pòkkàtì	ปกติ	*normally*
bɔ̀ɔi-bɔ̀ɔi	บ่อยๆ	*often*

A. Sentences

1 *pòkkàtì* thîi mɯɯang-thai rɔ́ɔn mâak
ปกติ ที่ เมือง ไทย ร้อน มาก
normally at state-thai hot very
Normally, it is very hot in Thailand.

2 kháu moo-hǒo *bɔ̀ɔi-bɔ̀ɔi* เขา โมโห บ่อยๆ
he angry *often-often* – He is often angry.

3 phûuak-kháu tsà yùu dûuai kan *sàmɔ̌ə*
พวก เขา จะ อยู่ ด้วย กัน เสมอ
group-he will stay with together *always*
They will always stay together.

4 *baang-khráng* sànùk *baang-khráng* nâa-bɯ̀ɯa
บาง ครั้ง สนุก บาง ครั้ง น่า เบื่อ
some-time fun *some-time* nâa-boring
Sometimes it is fun, sometimes boring!

5 *thammádaa* kháu kin kaafɛɛ ธรรมดา เขา กิน กาแฟ
usually he drink coffee – Usually, he drinks coffee.

6 ʧán kin nám-sôm *thúk-wan* ฉัน กิน น้ำ ส้ม ทุก วัน
I drink water-orange *every-day*
I drink orange juice every day.

7 kháu maa thîi nîi *pràtsam* เขา มา ที่ นี่ ประจำ
he come place-this *regularly* – *He comes here regularly.*

8 khun pai thîau *bɔ̀i* mái คุณ ไป เที่ยว บ่อย ไหม
you go travel *often* "question" – *Do you travel a lot?*

9 ʧán pai thîau *aathít-lá sɔ̌ɔng khráng*
ฉัน ไป เที่ยว อาทิตย์ ละ สอง ครั้ง
I go tour *week-lá two time* – *I go out twice a week.*

10 ʧán *mâi-khəəi* pai ʧiiang-raai ฉัน ไม่ เคย ไป เชียงราย
I *no-once* go Chiang Rai
I have never been to Chiang Rai.

11 ʧán *mâi-khɔ̂i* ʧɔ̂ɔp kháu ฉัน ไม่ ค่อย ชอบ เขา
I *no-really* like he – *I don't really like him.*

12 ʧán tsà yùu thîi nîi *tàlɔ̀ɔt-pai* ฉัน จะ อยู่ ที่ นี่ ตลอด ไป
I will stay place-this *always-go* – *I will stay here forever.*

13 kháu bɔ̀n *tàlɔ̀ɔt-weelaa* เขา บ่น ตลอด เวลา
he complain *always-time*
He is complaining all the time.

Common expressions
(kham thîi ʧái bɔ̀i-bɔ̀i คำ ที่ ใช้ บ่อยๆ)

kamlang pháyaayaam yùu กำลัง พยายาม อยู่
kamlang try be – *I am trying!*

> thii-lá-lék thii-lá-nɔ́ɔi ที ละ เล็ก ที ละ น้อย
> time-lá-small time-lá-little – *Little by little!*
>
> ngaan sèt lɛ́ɛu งาน เสร็จ แล้ว
> work finish already – *Job is done!*
>
> rúu sɯ̀k bau-tsai รู้ สึก เบา ใจ
> know-awareness relieved-heart – *I feel relieved.*

B. Vocabulary

pòkkàtì	ปกติ	normally
thîi	ที่	at
rɔ́ɔn	ร้อน	to be hot
mɯɯang-thai	เมือง ไทย	Thailand
mâak	มาก	very, much, a lot
kháu	เขา	he
moo-hŏo	โมโห	to be angry
bɔ̀i-bɔ̀i	บ่อยๆ	often
phûuak-kháu	พวก เขา	they
yùu	อยู่	to stay, to live
dûuai	ด้วย	with
kan	กัน	together
sàmɔ̆ə	เสมอ	always
baang-khráng	บาง ครั้ง	sometimes
sànùk	สนุก	to be fun
bɯ̀ɯa	เบื่อ	to be boring
thammádaa	ธรรมดา	usually
kin	กิน	to eat, (to drink)

tʃán	ฉัน	I
nám-sôm	น้ำ ส้ม	orange juice
thúk-wan	ทุก วัน	every day
thúk	ทุก	every
wan	วัน	day
maa	มา	to come
thîi-nîi	ที่ นี่	here
pràtsam	ประจำ	regularly
khun	คุณ	you
pai	ไป	to go
thîau	เที่ยว	to travel, to go out
rɯ̌ɯ-mái	หรือ ไม่	or not?
aathít-lá	อาทิตย์ ละ	weekly
sɔ̌ɔng	สอง	two
khráng	ครั้ง	time
khəəi	เคย	once, used to
mâi-khɔ̂i	ไม่ ค่อย	not really
mâi	ไม่	no
khɔ̂i	ค่อย	quietly, gradually, hardly
tʃɔ̂ɔp	ชอบ	to like
mâi-khəəi	ไม่ เคย	never
tsà	จะ	will
tàlɔ̀ɔt-pai	ตลอด ไป	forever
tàlɔ̀ɔt	ตลอด	always
bòn	บ่น	to complain
tàlɔ̀ɔt-weelaa	ตลอด เวลา	always, all the time
weelaa	เวลา	time
kamlang	กำลัง	action in progress

pháyaayaam	พยายาม	to try
yùu	อยู่	action exists
thii-lá-lék thii-lá-nɔ́ɔi	ที ละ เล็ก ที ละ น้อย	little by little
ngaan	งาน	work
sèt	เสร็จ	to finish
lɛ́ɛu	แล้ว	already
rúu-sùk	รู้ สึก	to feel
bau-tsai	เบา ใจ	to be relieved, lightened
bau	เบา	to lighten, to slow down
tsai	ใจ	heart, mind, spirit

C. How the language works

In this chapter, we learn how to use "how often" -words (*time words of frequency*) correctly, sometimes also called *adverbs of frequency*. The only difficulty is that we need to know when to place them at the beginning of the sentence and when at the end of the sentence.

There are some rules to be observed.

A) Time words of frequency at the *end* of the sentence only.

These time words of frequency are placed at the end of the sentence only and can never be placed at the beginning of the sentence.

Examples:

sàmɔ̌ɔ	เสมอ	*always*
pràtsam	ประจำ	*regularly*
bɔ̀i-bɔ̀i	บ่อยๆ	*often*
tàlɔ̀ɔt-weelaa	ตลอด เวลา	*all the time*
tàlɔ̀ɔt-pai	ตลอด ไป	*forever*
mǔuan-khəəi	เหมือน เคย	*as usual*

Chapter 11

> **1** tʃán tsà yùu thîi nîi *tàlɔ̀ɔt-pai* ฉัน จะ อยู่ ที่ นี่ ตลอด ไป
> I will stay place-this *always-go* – *I will stay here forever.*

- Here **tàlɔ̀ɔt-pai** ตลอด ไป *forever* is placed at the end of the sentence. It cannot be placed at the beginning of the sentence.

> **2** tʃán pai tʃiiang-raai *pràtsam* ฉัน ไป เชียงราย ประจำ
> I go Chiang Rai *regular* – *I go to Chiang Rai regularly.*

- Here **pràtsam** ประจำ *regularly* is placed at the end of the sentence. It cannot be placed at the beginning of the sentence.

B) **tàlɔ̀ɔt** ตลอด *during, entire, always, all*

tàlɔ̀ɔt ตลอด is also a multifunctional word in Thai. It can create new meanings when placed before either nouns or verbs.

Examples:

tàlɔ̀ɔt-weelaa	ตลอด เวลา	*all the time*
tàlɔ̀ɔt-wan	ตลอด วัน	*all day long*
tàlɔ̀ɔt-khɯɯn	ตลอด คืน	*all night long*
tàlɔ̀ɔt-pii	ตลอด ปี	*all year round*
tàlɔ̀ɔt-pai	ตลอด ไป	*forever*
tàlɔ̀ɔt-maa	ตลอด มา	*all along, consistently*
tàlɔ̀ɔt tʃiiwít	ตลอด ชีวิต	*throughout the life*

C) Time words at the *beginning* of the sentence only.

Examples:

thammádaa	ธรรมดา	*normally*
pòkkàtì	ปกติ	*usually, normally*

> **I** *pòkkàtì* thîi mɯɯang-thai rɔ́ɔn mâak
> ปกติ ที่ เมือง ไทย ร้อน มาก
> *normally at state-thai hot very*
> Normally, it is very hot in Thailand.

- These words cannot be placed at the end of the sentence alone.

> **I.1** thîi mɯɯang-thai rɔ́ɔn mâak *pen-pòkkàtì*
> ที่ เมือง ไทย ร้อน มาก เป็น ปกติ
> *at state-thai hot very be-normally*
> Normally, it is very hot in Thailand.

However, if you do place **pòkkàtì** ปกติ *usually, normally* or **thammádaa** ธรรมดา *normally*, at the end of the sentence, then you must use the verb **pen** เป็น *to be* in front of the adverb as in this sentence.

c) Time words of frequency at the *beginning* or at the *end* of the sentence.

Depending on the emphasis, we may place some words either at the beginning or at the end of the sentence.

Examples:

| **thúk-wan** | ทุก วัน | *every day* |
| **baang-khráng** | บาง ครั้ง | *sometimes* |

> **I** tʃǎn kin nám-sôm *thúk-wan* ฉัน กิน น้ำ ส้ม ทุก วัน
> I eat water-orange *every-day*
> I drink orange juice every day.

- Here **thúk-wan** *every day* is placed at the end of the sentence. The emphasis is on drinking.
- Note also that in Thai we can use the word **kin** กิน *to eat* for drinking. It is an informal expression.

2 *thúk-wan* ɟǎn kin nám-sôm ทุก วัน ฉัน กิน น้ำ ส้ม
every-day I eat water-orange
Every day I drink orange juice.

- Here **thúk-wan** *every day* is placed at the beginning of the sentence. The emphasis is on "how often".

E) **thúk** ทุก *every, each* is a handy word. It can be placed before many nouns.

Examples:

thúk-wan	ทุก วัน	*every day*
thúk-khon	ทุก คน	*everybody*
thúk-khráng	ทุก ครั้ง	*every time*
thúk-sìng	ทุก สิ่ง	*every thing*
thúk-yàang	ทุก อย่าง	*each, all, all kind*
thúk-duuan	ทุก เดือน	*every month*
thúk-pii	ทุก ปี	*every year*
thúk-khuun	ทุก คืน	*every night*
thúk-thîi	ทุก ที่	*everywhere*

F) The particle **lá** ละ can be used to show how many times an action takes place in a certain time period.

lá ละ is placed after the time periods (days, nights, weeks, months, etc.) and before the number of times to emphasize the fact how many times the action takes place during a certain time period.

Examples:

aathít-lá sɔ̌ɔng khráng	อาทิตย์ ละ สอง ครั้ง	*twice a week*
pii-lá sìi khráng	ปี ละ สี่ ครั้ง	*four times a year*
duuan-lá sǎam khráng	เดือน ละ สาม ครั้ง	*three times a month*

khuun-lá nùng khráng คืน ละ หนึ่ง ครั้ง *once a night*
thii-lá lék thii-lá nɔ́ɔi ที ละ เล็ก ที ละ น้อย *little by little*

> **1** tʃán pai thîau *aathít-lá sɔ̌ɔng khráng*
> ฉัน ไป เที่ยว อาทิตย์ ละ สอง ครั้ง
> I go tour *week-lá two time – I go out twice a week.*

- This construction is normally placed at the end of the sentence.

G) **khəəi** เคย *once, used to* and **khɔ̂i** ค่อย *quietly, gradually, hardly.*

> **1** tʃán pai tʃiiang-raai *mǔuan-khəəi*
> ฉัน ไป เชียงราย เหมือน เคย
> I go Chiang Rai *as-used to*
> *I have been to Chiang Rai as usual.*

- **khəəi** เคย can be used in two different ways. Here **khəəi** เคย is used as a *time word of frequency,* and is placed at the end of the sentence; the meaning is **mǔuan-khəəi** เหมือน เคย *as usual.*

> **2** tʃán *mâi-khəəi* pai tʃiiang-raai ฉัน ไม่ เคย ไป เชียงราย
> I *no-once* go Chiang Rai
> *I have never been to Chiang Rai.*

- In this sentence, **khəəi** เคย is placed before the main verb.
- Here we have used **mâi-khəəi** ไม่ เคย *never* as a helping verb before the main verb **pai** ไป *to go*. See more about how to use **khəəi** เคย as a past time tense marker in Chapter 15.

> **3** tʃán *mâi-khɔ̂i* tʃɔ̂ɔp kháu ฉัน ไม่ ค่อย ชอบ เขา
> I *no-really* like he – *I don't really like him.*

- **khɔ̂i** ค่อย *quietly, gradually, hardly* may sound similar to **khəəi** เคย *once, used to* but the meaning is totally different. **khɔ̂i** ค่อย *quietly, gradually, hardly* is not normally used in past time sentences.

D. New sounds

We have now introduced all the Thai consonant and vowel sounds. There are altogether twenty consonant sounds and eighteen pure vowel sounds.

1. All 20 *Thai consonant sounds:*
   p/ph, m/n, b/d, **t**/th, s/f, **ts**/ʧ, k/kh, y/w, **l**/**r**, **ng**/h

2. All 18 *Thai pure vowel sounds:*
   à อะ – aa อา, ì อิ – ii อี, ù อุ – uu อู, è เอะ – ee เอ, ə̀ เออะ – əə เออ, ɛ̀ แอะ – ɛɛ แอ, **ʉ** อึ – **ʉʉ** อือ, ò โอะ – oo โอ, ɔ̀ เอาะ – ɔɔ ออ

For English speakers, we have marked those sounds with **bold** which need some attention.

E. Simple advice

Royal Thai is the only official transliteration system in use in Thailand. It is mainly used for names and road signs in Thailand. However, it has several shortcomings in describing Thai sounds accurately. For instance, it does not differentiate between short and long vowels. It usually omits the tone marks altogether. It is, therefore, not often used in language schools or in Thai learning books. The symbols and letters we have chosen to use in this book describe Thai sounds more accurately than many other systems.

You just must get used to the fact that the same sound may be transliterated in many ways in different books. If you study the Thai sounds first as they are spelled in this book, then you will be able to read other transliteration systems easier. We must admit, however, that it is not very easy for the beginner to understand all the different transliteration methods, not to mention understanding the Thai script. Do not try to guess how the unfamiliar sounds are pronounced. Your guess will most likely be wrong. Spend enough time at the beginning to get all sounds correct. After that nobody can fool you.

In Thai, all 18 pure vowel sounds are written with a unique symbol. As you know in English there are only five vowel symbols (i, a, u, e, o). With these five vowel symbols one should be able to produce 20–22 different vowel sounds including diphthongs. That means that one vowel symbol represents several different sounds depending on the word. To be truthful, nobody really knows how many vowel sounds there are in English since in different English dialects the vowel sounds are produced somewhat differently. Therefore, it does not make much sense to transliterate Thai vowel sounds the way English uses vowel symbols. It would be confusing. Nevertheless, some transliteration systems try to do so; then, it is quite difficult to know what the actual Thai sound is.

In this book, we have adapted a phonetic way to describe sounds. That means that we use only one symbol to describe one particular sound. That way it will be easier for you to identify the Thai sounds. The Thai sounds are not that difficult to learn. Consonants and vowels are pronounced clearly and consistently in Thai.

F. Take it further

Refer to the book:

Dhyan Manik: *Understanding the Thai Language and Grammar:*

- More about Thai consonant and vowel sounds can be found in Chapter 1, sections 1.1 and 1.2.
- An extensive list of Thai adverbs can be found in Chapter 12.
- More about "how often" -words (adverbs of frequency) can be found in Chapter 12, section 12.3.

Adverbs are a large group of different types of words. Sometimes, adverbs in Thai are used in the similar way as adjectives, and it is not always easy to distinguish adverbs from adjectives.

Chapter 12

Comparisons: *more, less, most, same, equal, as*

kháu sǔung-kwàa ʧǎn
เขา สูง กว่า ฉัน
She is taller than I.

Chapter 12

Highlights

kwàa	กว่า	*more*
nɔ́ɔi-kwàa	น้อย กว่า	*less than*
mâak-kwàa	มาก กว่า	*more than*
mǔuan	เหมือน	*as*
thâu-kàp	เท่า กับ	*equal to*
thîi-sùt	ที่ สุด	*most*

A. Sentences

1. kháu kin lâu *mâak-kwàa* tʃán
   เขา กิน เหล้า มาก กว่า ฉัน
   he eat alcohol *much-more* I
   He drinks more alcohol than I do.

2. tʃán tham-ngaan *nɔ́ɔi-kwàa* kháu
   ฉัน ทำ งาน น้อย กว่า เขา
   I do-work *little-less* he – *I work less than he does.*

3. kháu *sǔung-kwàa* tʃán เขา สูง กว่า ฉัน
   he *tall-more* I – *He is taller than I.*

4. pràthêet-thai *yài-kwàa* pràthêet-laau
   ประเทศ ไทย ใหญ่ กว่า ประเทศ ลาว
   country-Thai *big-more* country-Lao
   Thailand is bigger than Laos.

5. bâan tʃán yùu *klai-kwàa* bâan khun
   บ้าน ฉัน อยู่ ไกล กว่า บ้าน คุณ
   home I *far-more* home you
   My home is further than yours.

6 an-níi sŭuai *mǔuan* an-nán อัน นี้ สวย เหมือน อัน นั้น
piece-this *as* piece-that – *This is as beautiful as that one.*

7 kháu *mǔuan* phɔ̂ɔ เขา เหมือน พ่อ
he *as* father – *He is like his father.*

8 kháu sŭung *thâu-kàp* mɛ̂ɛ เขา สูง เท่า กับ แม่
she tall *equal-with* mother – *She is as tall as her mother.*

9 rót-fai reu *thâu-kàp* rót-bát รถ ไฟ เร็ว เท่า กับ รถ บัส
car-fire fast *equal-with* car-bus
The train is as fast as the bus.

10 khrai wîng dâai *reu-thîi-sùt* ใคร วิ่ง ได้ เร็ว ที่ สุด
who run can *fast-that-most* – *Who can run fastest?*

11 thîi-níi *thùuk-thîi-sùt* ที่ นี่ ถูก ที่ สุด
place-this *cheap-that-most* – *This place is the cheapest.*

12 rau mii ŋən *mâak-thîi-sùt* เรา มี เงิน มาก ที่ สุด
we have money *much-that-most*
We have the most money.

13 sàthăanii rót-fai yùu *klâi-thîi-sùt*
สถานี รถ ไฟ อยู่ ใกล้ ที่ สุด
station car-fire stay *close-that-most*
The train station is closest.

Common expressions
(kham thîi ʧái bɔ̀i-bɔ̀i คำ ที่ ใช้ บ่อยๆ)

sànăam kiilaa hèŋ-ʧâat yùu thîi-năi
สนาม กีฬา แห่ง ชาติ อยู่ ที่ ไหน
field sport place-nation stay place where
Where is the National Sport Stadium?

> kàrúnaa khàp ʧáa-ʧáa กรุณา ขับ ช้าๆ
> please drive slow-slow – *Please, drive slowly!*
>
> rót-tìt mâak รถ ติด มาก
> car-close very – *There is a traffic jam.*
>
> tsɔ̀ɔt thîi-nîi khâ / khráp จอด ที่ นี่ ค่ะ / ครับ
> stop place-this khâ / khráp – *Please, stop here!*

B. Vocabulary

kin	กิน	to eat, to drink
lâu	เหล้า	alcoholic drinks (whisky, vodka, etc.)
mâak-kwàa	มาก กว่า	to be more than
nɔ́ɔi-kwàa	น้อย กว่า	to be less than
sǔung-kwàa	สูง กว่า	to be taller than
yài-kwàa	ใหญ่ กว่า	to be bigger than
pràthêet-laau	ประเทศ ลาว	Laos
kwaa	กว่า	more
mǔuan	เหมือน	as
thâu-kàp	เท่า กับ	to be equal to
thîi-sùt	ที่ สุด	to be most
bâan	บ้าน	home, house
yùu	อยู่	to live, to stay
klai-kwàa	ไกล กว่า	to be further than
an-níi	อัน นี้	this one
sǔuai	สวย	to be beautiful
mǔuan	เหมือน	as

Chapter 12

an-nán	อัน นั้น	that one
kháu	เขา	she, he
phɔ̂ɔ	พ่อ	father
sǔung	สูง	to be tall
thâu-kàp	เท่า กับ	to be equal, equally
mɛ̂ɛ	แม่	mother
rót-fai	รถ ไฟ	train
rót-bát	รถ บัส	bus
rót	รถ	car
fai	ไฟ	fire
bát	บัส	bus
khrai	ใคร	who?
wîng	วิ่ง	to run
reu-thîi-sùt	เร็ว ที่ สุด	to be fastest
reu	เร็ว	to be fast
thîi-sùt	ที่ สุด	most, maximum
thîi	ที่	that
sùt	สุด	peak, most, greatest
thîi-nîi	ที่ นี่	here, this place
thùuk-thîi-sùt	ถูก ที่ สุด	to be cheapest
thùuk	ถูก	to be cheap
rau	เรา	we
mii	มี	have
ngən	เงิน	money
mâak-thîi-sùt	มาก ที่ สุด	to be most
sàthǎanii	สถานี	station
klâi-thîi-sùt	ใกล้ ที่ สุด	to be closest

klâi	ใกล้	to be close, near
sànăam	สนาม	stadium
kiilaa	กีฬา	sport
hèng	แห่ง	place
tʃâat	ชาติ	nation
kàrúnaa	กรุณา	please!
khàp	ขับ	to drive
tʃáa-tʃáa	ช้าๆ	slowly
rót-tìt	รถ ติด	traffic jam
tsɔ̀ɔt	จอด	to stop
thîi-nîi	ที่ นี่	here

C. How the language works

 The word **kwàa** กว่า *more* is mainly used with adjectives and adverbs in order to compare two different entities. **kwàa** กว่า *more* is not usually used alone.

Examples:

> kháu *kèng-kwàa* tʃán เขา เก่ง กว่า ฉัน
> he *skilful-more* I – *He is more skilful than I am.*

- Here we compare **kháu** เขา *he* with **tʃán** ฉัน *I*. **kèng** เก่ง is an adjective *to be skilful*.
- **kèng-kwàa** เก่ง กว่า *more skilful than* is placed before the object, **tʃán** ฉัน *I*.
- In English, we need to add the word *than*. Actually here in Thai, we get by with four words. In English, we need to use seven words.

> **2** tɕán kin lâu *nɔ́ɔi-kwàa* kháu ฉัน กิน เหล้า น้อย กว่า เขา
> I eat alcohol *little-less* he
> *I drink less alcohol than he does.*

- Here we compare **tɕán** ฉัน *I* with **kháu** เขา *he*.
- **nɔ́ɔi-kwàa** น้อย กว่า *to be less* is placed before the object, **kháu** เขา *he*.
- Note that in colloquial Thai, the verb **kin** กิน *to eat* is commonly used instead of the verb **dùum** ดื่ม *to drink*. The meaning is the same.

B) Another word for *more* is **mâak-khûn** มาก ขึ้น. **khûn** ขึ้น means *to rise, to increase, to enter.*

> **1** thúk-wan tɕán tham-ngaan *mâak-khûn*
> ทุก วัน ฉัน ทำ งาน มาก ขึ้น
> every-day I do-work *much-increase*
> *Everyday, I work more and more.*

- Here we must use **mâak-khûn** มาก ขึ้น since there is no one or nothing else to be compared with.

> **2** thúk-wan tɕán tham-ngaan *mâak-kwàa*
> ทุก วัน ฉัน ทำ งาน มาก กว่า
> every-day I do-work *much-more*
> *Everyday, I work more and more.*

- This sentence is not correct.
- We cannot use **mâak-kwàa** มาก กว่า *much more than* here since there is not anything to be compared with.

3 More examples of the word **khûn** ขึ้น *to rise, to increase, to enter*

dii-khûn	ดี ขึ้น	*to get better*
kə̀ət-khûn	เกิด ขึ้น	*to happen, to occur*
phə̂əm-khûn	เพิ่ม ขึ้น	*to increase, more*
khûn-rót	ขึ้น รถ	*to enter a car or a bus*

C) **mǔuan** เหมือน *as, like* and different usages

mǔuan เหมือน *as, like* is very common word in Thai. However, it is used somewhat differently according to the context.

Examples:

> **1** khun *mǔuan* kháu   คุณ เหมือน เขา
> you *as* he – *You are like him.*

> **2** kháu *mǔuan* phɔ̂ɔ   เขา เหมือน พ่อ
> he *as* father – *He is like his father.*

- In the sentences 1 and 2 **mǔuan** เหมือน *as, like* is used to connect words.

> **3** kháu sǔuai *mǔuan-dəəm*   เขา สวย เหมือน เดิม
> she beautiful *as-before* – *She is beautiful as always.*

- In this sentence **mǔuan** เหมือน *as* is again used differently.
- **mǔuan-dəəm** เหมือน เดิม *as before* is translated here into English as *as always*.

> **4** tʃán mâi rúu *mǔuan-kan*   ฉัน ไม่ รู้ เหมือน กัน
> I no know *as-together* – *I don't know either.*

- This sentence is not very easy to translate into English.
- **mǔuan** เหมือน *as, like* is used to express literally the idea *I also don't know*.
- It is better translated as *I don't know either*. In Thai, this kind of structure is quite commonly used.

D) **thâu-kàp** เท่า กับ *equal to* is used to connect words and phrases.

Examples:

> **1** kháu sǔung *thâu-kàp* mêɛ เขา สูง เท่า กับ แม่
> she tall *equal-with* mother – *She is as tall as her mother.*

- **thâu-kàp** เท่า กับ *equal to* is placed before the object, here **mêɛ** แม่ *mother*.

> **2** rót-fai reu *thâu-kàp* rót-bát รถ ไฟ เร็ว เท่า กับ รถ บัส
> car-fire fast *equal-with* car-bus
> *The train is as fast as the bus.*

- **thâu-kàp** เท่า กับ *equal to* is placed before the object, here **rót-bát** รถ บัส *bus*.

E) **thîi-sùt** ที่ สุด is used to express superlatives such as *most, greatest, maximum* etc.

Examples:

> **1** khun *yîiam-thîi-sùt* คุณ เยี่ยม ที่ สุด
> you *excellent-that-most* – *You are the greatest.*

- **thîi-sùt** ที่ สุด *to be most* comes at the end of the sentence.
- The adjective **yîiam** เยี่ยม *excellent, superb* is placed before **thîi-sùt** ที่ สุด.

> **2** kháu *sămkhan-thîi-sùt* เขา สำคัญ ที่ สุด
> she *important-that-most*
> She is the most important person.

- **thîi-sùt** ที่ สุด *to be most* comes at the end of the sentence.
- The adjective **sămkhan** สำคัญ *important* is placed before **thîi-sùt** ที่ สุด.

> **3** phŏm tʃɔ̂ɔp khun *mâak-thîi-sùt* ผม ชอบ คุณ มาก ที่ สุด
> I like you *much-that-most* – *I like you the most.*

- **thîi-sùt** ที่ สุด *to be most* comes at the end of the sentence.
- The adverb **mâak** มาก *much* is placed before **thîi-sùt** ที่ สุด.

4 More ways to use **thîi-sùt** ที่ สุด

dii-thîi-sùt	ดี ที่ สุด	*the best*
nai-thîi-sùt	ใน ที่ สุด	*at last, finally*
yài-thîi-sùt	ใหญ่ ที่ สุด	*the biggest*
nɔ́ɔi-thîi-sùt	น้อย ที่ สุด	*the smallest*
yɛ̂ɛ-thîi-sùt	แย่ ที่ สุด	*the worst*
sŭuai-thîi-sùt	สวย ที่ สุด	*the most beautiful*

D. New sounds

Now we are ready to introduce the Thai end sounds. Basically, the end sounds in Thai can be divided into two main groups, *open endings* (sometimes also called *live endings*) and *closed endings* (sometimes also called *dead endings*). The end sounds are important since they play a major role as far as the Thai tonal system is concerned. The pronunciation of end sounds can cause some problems for Western or English speakers. This is particularly the case with *closed (dead) endings*.

In this chapter we shall review *sonorant consonant end sounds*. They constitute the *open end sound;* that means that the sound is not stopped by the lips, by the tongue or in the glottis. These sounds are easy since they are pronounced in the similar way in English.

End sounds for sonorant consonants:

n น = **n**

r ร = **n**

l ล = **n**

m ม = **m**

ng ง = **ng**

So, we have only three end sounds for these five sonorant consonants. All the sonorant consonants in Thai constitute an *open ending* when at the end of a word or syllable.

Examples:

rɔ́ɔn	ร้อน	*hot*
bin	บิล	*bill**
kaan	การ	*prefix, task**
sŏm	สม	*to be suitable*
lɔɔng	ลอง	*to try*

* Note that the initial consonants **r** and **l** are pronounced as **n** at the end of a word or syllable. So, the borrowed English word bi**ll** is pronounced in Thai as bi**n**. Because of this pronunciation change, it is not easy to detect when Thais are using borrowed English words, and nowadays, there are a lot of borrowed words commonly used.

E. Simple advice

End sounds are very important in the Thai language. You are advised to make some effort in the beginning to get them right; otherwise, there is a chance that Thai people will not understand you easily. In English, the consonants are normally pronounced the same whether they are at the beginning or at the end of the word. Normally, you should not have any difficulty to produce the open Thai end sounds since they are pronounced naturally in the same way in Thai as well as in English. However, the closed consonant end sounds, which we shall review in Chapter 16, are produced differently in Thai and can cause some problems as far as the pronunciation is concerned.

Initial consonant sounds have already been dealt with in Chapters 1–8. In Thai, there are only 20 different initial consonant sounds, but there are 44 consonant symbols in Thai to represent these 20 sounds.

If you decide to learn the Thai script and writing system, then go for it and be prepared for an interesting and relatively long journey. Note also that knowing the Thai writing system does not help you to pronounce Thai sounds any better or to speak Thai more fluently. However, you will be able to read Thai text and perhaps also write in the Thai script.

In order to gain overall understanding about the Thai language, we need to point out the complexity of the Thai writing system and then try to make it easy for you to learn to speak Thai.

F. Take it further

Refer to the book:

Dhyan Manik: *Understanding the Thai Language and Grammar:*

- More about open end sounds can be found in Chapter 1, section 1.3.1.
- Names of stations, airports etc. can be found in Chapter 7, section 7.2.5.
- Names of countries of the world can be found in Chapter 7, section 7.3.
- An extensive list of Thai adjectives can be found in Chapter 11 and comparison of adjectives in section 11.5.
- An extensive list of Thai adverbs can be found in Chapter 12 and comparison of adverbs in section 12.11.

Chapter 13

Using hâi ให้ and dâai ได้ – to give and to get

yàak tham-hâi khun rúu-sùk sàbaai
อยาก ทำ ให้ คุณ รู้ สึก สบาย
I want to make you feel good.

Chapter 13

Highlights

hâi	ให้	to give, to let, to make
hâi ngən	ให้ เงิน	to give money
hâi pai	ให้ ไป	to let someone go
tham-hâi	ทำ ให้	to make someone do something, to cause something to happen
dâai	ได้	to get, can, to have a permission to
dâai ngən	ได้ เงิน	to get money
pai dâai	ไป ได้	can, to be able to go
tham-dâai	ทำ ได้	can be done

A. Sentences

hâi ให้

1. khrai *hâi* ngən khun khá ใคร ให้ เงิน คุณ คะ
   who *give* money you khá – *Who gave you money?*

2. káu *hâi* เขา ให้
   he *give* – *He gave me money.*

3. phɔ̂ɔ-mɛ̂ɛ *hâi* kháu pai thîau พ่อ แม่ ให้ เขา ไป เที่ยว
   father-mother *let* he go out – *His parents let him go out.*

4. tʃǎn *hâi* khun *pai* ฉัน ให้ คุณ ไป
   I *let* you go – *I let you go.*

(5) *hâi* ɡǎn ɡûuai ná ให้ ฉัน ช่วย นะ
let I help ná – *Let me help you!*

(6) kháu *tham-hâi* ɡǎn pai เขา ทำ ให้ ฉัน ไป
he *do-make* I go – *He made me go.*

(7) yàak *tham-hâi* khun rúu-sùk sàbaai
อยาก ทำ ให้ คุณ รู้ สึก สบาย
want *do-make* you know-awareness happy
I want to make you feel good.

(8) tham-tua *hâi-dii* nɔ̀i ทำ ตัว ให้ ดี หน่อย
do-body *make-good* little – *Try to behave well.*

(9) khrûɯang-níi *hâi* khun เครื่อง นี้ ให้ คุณ
machine-this *give* you – *This machine is for you.*

dâai ได้

(10) khrai *dâai* ngən khá ใคร ได้ เงิน คะ
who *get* money khá – *Who has received the money?*

(11) mâi mii khrai ไม่ มี ใคร
no have who – *Nobody!*

(12) *yàak-dâai* khrûɯang-nán อยาก ได้ เครื่อง นั้น
want-get machine-that
I would like to get (to have) that machine.

(13) ɡǎn *yàak-dâai* nǎngsɯ̌ɯ sǎam lêm khâ
ฉัน อยาก ได้ หนังสือ สาม เล่ม ค่ะ
I *want-get* book three copy khâ
I would like to get (to have) three books.

(14) ɡǎn khít wâa *pen-pai-dâai* ฉัน คิด ว่า เป็น ไป ได้
I think that *be-go-can* – *I think it is possible.*

15 ngaan-níi *tham-dâai* งาน นี้ ทำ ได้
work-this *do-can* – This work can be done.

16 tʃán pai *mâi-dâai* ฉัน ไป ไม่ ได้
I go *no-can* – I cannot go.

17 piitɜ̂ə *mâi-dâai* pai ปีเตอร์ ไม่ ได้ ไป
Peter *no-can* go – Peter did not have a chance to go.

18 tʃán *dâai* súɯ sûa-yɯ̂ɯt lɛ́ɛu ฉัน ได้ ซื้อ เสื้อ ยืด แล้ว
I *get* buy shirt-stretch
I already had an opportunity to buy a T-shirt.

19 kháu tham-tua *dâai-dii* เขา ทำ ตัว ได้ ดี
he do-body *can-good* – He behaves well.

Common expressions
(kham thîi tʃái bɔ̀i-bɔ̀i คำ ที่ ใช้ บ่อยๆ)

phûut thai *dâai* nít-nɔ̀i พูด ไทย ได้ นิด หน่อย
speak thai *can* small-little – I speak Thai a little.

khun kháu-tsai mái คุณ เข้า ใจ ไหม
you enter-heart "question" – Do you understand?

khun phûut angkrìt mái คุณ พูด อังกฤษ ไหม
you speak English "question" – Do you speak English?

phûut *dâai* tɛ̀ɛ mâi kèng พูด ได้ แต่ ไม่ เก่ง
speak *can* but no skilful – Yes, I can speak but not well.

B. Vocabulary

khrai	ใคร	who?
hâi	ให้	to give

ngən	เงิน	money
phɔ̂ɔ-mɛ̂ɛ	พ่อ แม่	parents
hâi	ให้	to let
pai thîau	ไป เที่ยว	to go out
hâi	ให้	to let / to offer help
tʃûuai	ช่วย	to help
nɔ̀i	หน่อย	a little
tham-hâi	ทำ ให้	to make (causative)
khrŵuang-níi	เครื่อง นี้	this machine
hâi	ให้	to give/for
yàak-dâai	อยาก ได้	to want to get, would like to have
pen-pai-dâai	เป็น ไป ได้	to be possible, can be done
năngsŵŵ	หนังสือ	book
săam	สาม	three
lêm	เล่ม	copy (classifier)
mâi-dâai	ไม่ ได้	did not, did not have a chance
mâi-dâai	ไม่ ได้	cannot
tham-tua	ทำ ตัว	to behave
dâai-dii	ได้ ดี	well
dâai	ได้	to get + a verb (to have an opportunity or a chance)
sŵŵ	ซื้อ	to buy
sûa-yûŵt	เสื้อ ยืด	T-shirt
lɛ́ɛu	แล้ว	already
ngaan-níi	งาน นี้	this job
tham-dâai	ทำ ได้	can be done
phûut	พูด	to speak
thai	ไทย	Thai

dâai	ได้	can, to be able to
nít-nɔ̀i	นิด หน่อย	a little
khun	คุณ	you
kháu-tsai	เข้า ใจ	to understand
kháu	เข้า	to enter
tsai	ใจ	heart, mind
mái	ไหม	basic question word
angkrìt	อังกฤษ	English
tɛ̀ɛ	แต่	but
mâi	ไม่	no
kèng	เก่ง	to be skilled, talented, efficient

C. How the language works

To give and *to get* are basic needs in life. They go together and need to be in balance. Thai people express these meanings by **hâi** ให้ *to give* and **dâai** ได้ *to get*.

Moreover, **hâi** ให้ *to give* and **dâai** ได้ *to get* are used in several different ways in Thai. Note that the translation into English will be different depending on where these two verbs stand in the sentence and also what other verbs are used with them. We shall explain here the most important ways to use **hâi** ให้ and **dâai** ได้ in the sentence. If this is too much for you now, then just learn a few expressions first.

In many cases, **hâi** ให้ and **dâai** ได้ are used grammatically in a similar way but the meaning is different.

The most simple way to use the verb **hâi** ให้ is to use it as a main verb *to give something to someone.* **hâi** ให้ also has another meaning, namely *to let,* when used as a helping word in the sentence.

Chapter 13

dâai ได้ *to get* something is used as a main verb in the similar way as the English words *to get, to receive* or *to obtain*. **dâai** ได้ also has other meanings, namely *can, to be able to, to be permitted to,* when used as a helping verb at the end of the sentence.

In many sentences, **hâi** ให้ has some causative connotation; hence, it may be understood as a *command*. On the other hand, **dâai** ได้ is often understood as *can*; something is *possible*. It is not a command. See if you can get the difference in meaning from the following examples.

A) Both **hâi** ให้ and **dâai** ได้ can be placed before nouns. The meaning is *to give* and *to get* something.

> **1** phǒm tsà *hâi ngən* khun   ผม จะ ให้ เงิน คุณ
> I will *give money* you – *I will give you money.*

- In this sentence, **hâi** ให้ *to give* is used as a main verb. It is placed before the object **ngən** เงิน *money*.
- What is given usually comes first in Thai, and to whom the object is given comes after.
- We could also translate this sentence into English as *I will give money to you.* That would be the same word order as in Thai.

> **2** phǒm kamlang-tsà *dâai ngən* tsàak ee-thii-em
> ผม กำลัง จะ ได้ เงิน จาก เอทีเอ็ม
> I kamlang-will *get money* from ATM
> *I am just about going to get money from the ATM.*

- In this sentence, **dâai** ได้ *to get* is used as a main verb. It is placed before the object **ngən** เงิน *money*.
- Note **kamlang-tsà** กำลัง จะ is the future time *tense marker* (near future, *just about*) which we will study in more detail in Chapter 15.

> **3** khrûɯang-níi *hâi* khun เครื่อง นี้ ให้ คุณ
> machine-this *give* you – *This machine is for you.*

- **hâi** ให้ *to give* is a verb in Thai, but sometimes it is difficult to translate it into English.
- In this structure, we need to use the preposition *for* in order to make the English meaning clear.

B) Both **hâi** ให้ and **dâai** can be placed before adjectives; the meaning is *to do something that way*.

> **1** khĭian *hâi sŭuai* เขียน ให้ สวย
> write *give beautiful* – *Write beautifully!*

- This is quite a strong command.
- In this sentence, **hâi** ให้ *to give* is a helping verb. It is placed before the adjective **sŭuai** สวย *beautiful*.
- **hâi** ให้ *to give* can be dropped but the emphasis of the sentence changes slightly. It is less demanding. However, the translation into English remains the same.

> **2** kháu khĭian *dâai sŭuai* เขา เขียน ได้ สวย
> he write *can beautiful* – *He writes beautifully.*

- This is not a command. It only tells that he writes that way.
- Actually in this structure, it would be better to understand **dâai** ได้ as *can* instead of *to get*.
- In this sentence, **dâai** ได้ *can* is a helping verb. It is placed before the adjective **sŭuai** สวย *beautiful*.
- The meaning is clearly different compared to the sentence 1.
- **dâai** ได้ *can* may be dropped, but the colour of the sentence changes slightly. However, the translation into English remains the same.

Chapter 13

c) Both **hâi** ให้ and **dâai** can be used as helping verbs in the sense *to let, to allow, to give permission*.

> **1** phǒm *hâi* khun *pai* ผม ให้ คุณ ไป
> I will *let* you *go* – *I let you go!*

- **hâi** ให้ is used here as a causative verb (to allow someone else to do something).
- It is best translated into English here as *to let, to allow, to give permission to someone to do something*; *you can go because I let you go*. It is up to me.
- **hâi** ให้ *to let* is placed before the object, here **khun** คุณ *you*. What is allowed comes after, here **pai** ไป *to go*.
- In a different context, this sentence can mean *I make you go* or *I have you go*.

> **2** *hâi* tʃǎn tʃûuai ná ให้ ฉัน ช่วย นะ
> *let* I help ná – *Let me help you!*

- This is a friendly imperative structure to offer help. In this structure, **hâi** ให้ *to give* is best translated into English as *to let, to allow, to give permission*.
- Here **hâi** ให้ *to let* is used somewhat differently. It is placed at the beginning of the sentence and before the speaker **tʃǎn** ฉัน *I*.
- It is used as a causative verb allowing someone *to do something*. What is allowed comes after, here **tʃûuai** ช่วย *to help*.

> **3** khun pai *dâai* คุณ ไป ได้
> you go *can* – *You can go!*

- Here, **dâai** ได้ is best translated into English as *can, to be allowed to* or *to be permitted to*.

- **dâai** ได้ has *no causative* connotation, *you can go whatever the reason. It is up to you.*
- **dâai** ได้ *can* is used in the sense that someone has *permission* to do something. It is usually placed at the end of the sentence and after the subject and the main verb, here **khun** คุณ *you* and **pai** ไป *to go.*

> **4**   kháu kèng – kháu tham *dâai* เขา เก่ง – เขา ทำ ได้
> he skilful – he do *can* – *He is smart. He can do it.*

- In this structure, **dâai** ได้ is best translated into English as *can.*
- Here **dâai** ได้ *can* is used grammatically in the same way as in the sentence 3, but the meaning is now *can, to be able to.*

D) Both **hâi** ให้ and **dâai** can be used together with the verb **tham** ทำ *to make* but the meaning is clearly different.

> **1**   kháu *tham-hâi* tʃán maa เขา ทำ ให้ ฉัน มา
> he *do-make* I come – *He made me come.*

- Here **hâi** ให้ is used together with another verb **tham** ทำ *to do*. In this structure, **hâi** ให้ is best translated into English as *to make.*
- This structure has a strong causative meaning making someone do something.
- **tham-hâi** ทำ ให้ is placed before the object, here **tʃán** ฉัน *I*. What is done comes after, here **maa** มา *to come.*
- In this structure, **tham-hâi** ทำ ให้ is best translated into English as *to make, to have.*
- This sentence could also be translated into English as *He had me come.*

Chapter 13

> **2** kháu *tham-hâi* ʧǎn rúu-sùk yɛ̂ɛ เขา ทำ ให้ ฉัน รู้ สึก แย่
> he *do-make* I know-awareness bad (terrible)
> *He made me feel bad.*

- **tham-hâi** ทำ ให้ *to make* can also be used in connection with feelings which may be good or bad in the same way as in English.

> **3** ngaan-níi *tham-dâai* งาน นี้ ทำ ได้
> work-this *do-can* – *This job can be done.*

- Here **dâai** ได้ is used together with another verb **tham** ทำ *to make*.
- This structure has no causative meaning making someone do something as in the sentence 2 with **hâi** ให้.
- **tham-dâai** ทำ ได้ is placed after the subject, here **ngaan-níi** งาน นี้ *this job, this work.*
- **tham-dâai** ทำ ได้ is best translated into English here as *can be done.*
- It is possible to do the job in all circumstances.

E) Both **hâi** ให้ and **dâai** can be used in combination with other verbs in order to have special meanings.

Examples:

> **1** ʧǎn mâi *yɔɔm-hâi* khun ʧáná ฉัน ไม่ ยอม ให้ คุณ ชนะ
> I no *allow-give* you win – *I will not let you win.*

- Here **yɔɔm-hâi** ยอม ให้ can be translated into English as *to let, to allow.*
- **hâi** ให้ reinforces the main verb and also changes the meaning. **yɔɔm** ยอม alone means *to give up, to surrender.*

2 kháu *sàng-hâi* phŏm pai tham-ngaan
เขา สั่ง ให้ ผม ไป ทำ งาน
he *order-give* I go do-work
He ordered me to go to work.

- The meaning of **sàng** สั่ง is *to order, to command*.
- Here **sàng-hâi** สั่ง ให้ can be translated into English as *to order someone to do something*.
- **hâi** ให้ reinforces the meaning of the main verb and makes the statement into a stronger command.

3 ʧán *dâai-yin* wâa man *phɔɔ-duu-dâai*
ฉัน ได้ ยิน ว่า มัน พอ ดู ได้
I *get-hear* that it *enough-see-can*
I have heard that it was OK.

- **dâai-yin** ได้ ยิน means *to have heard*. **dâai** ได้ *to get* and **yin** ยิน *to hear* cannot usually be separated.
- **phɔɔ-duu-dâai** พอ ดู ได้ is an idiomatic expression that means *not bad, fairly good, OK*.

4 ʧán *tsam-dâai* ฉัน จำ ได้
I *remember-can* – *I remember.*

- **tsam** จำ *to remember* is normally used together with **dâai** ได้ *can*. **tsam-dâai** จำ ได้ is *to remember*.

F) Both **hâi** ให้ and **dâai** can be used in many different idiomatic expressions.

Examples:

> ① *hâi-pen-pai* ให้ เป็น ไป
> let-be-go – Let it be!

- This is a command! The object is dropped here since it is understood from the context.

> ② *pen-pai-dâai* เป็น ไป ได้
> be-go-can – It is possible!

This is not a command. The subject, **man** มัน *it,* is dropped here. It is understood from the context.

G) Both **hâi** ให้ and **dâai** can be used when asking (for) something, making a request and being polite.

> ① phŏm *khɔ̌ɔ-hâi* khun tʃûuai nɔ̀i khráp
> ผม ขอ ให้ คุณ ช่วย หน่อย
> I *ask-give* you help little khráp
> *Could you help me a little?*

- This is also a kind of command since we use the verb **hâi** ให้.
- However, the request is made softer by several words: **khɔ̌ɔ** ขอ *to ask,* **nɔ̀i** หน่อย *a little* and **khráp** ครับ. The request sounds now like asking for help in a polite way.
- This sentence is grammatically correct, but may sound a bit too complicated. The next sentence 2 is perhaps more normal in speaking.

> ② tʃûuai tʃǎn nɔ̀i *dâai-mái* khá ช่วย ฉัน หน่อย ได้ ไหม คะ
> help I little *can-question* khá
> *Could you help me a little?*

- This is also a kind of command since the verb **tʃûuai** ช่วย *to help* is placed at the beginning of the sentence.
- The request is made softer by **nɔ̀i** หน่อย *a little,* **dâai-mái** ได้ไหม *could you* and **khá** คะ at the end of the statement.
- The request sounds like asking for help in a polite way. The subject is often dropped in commands like this.

H) In Thai, the request is usually softened by polite ending particles.

The most common polite ending particles are:

nɔ̀i	หน่อย	*a little*
dûuai	ด้วย	*also*
dâai-mái	ได้ไหม	*can you?*
khâ	ค่ะ	*polite particle for women*
khráp	ครับ	*polite particle for men*
ná	นะ	*OK?*

D. New sounds

Any *long pure vowel sound* in Thai constitutes an *open end sound*. There are nine pure long vowel sounds in Thai. These long vowel sounds are new in a sense that they are treated here as end sounds. It makes sense to study initial sounds separately from end sounds since end sounds are directly related to the tones of the Thai language.

They are:

aa, ii, uu, ee, ɛɛ, oo, ɔɔ, əə, ʉʉ (long vowels = open ending)

You may like to review some sentences and see where these long vowel sounds form an end sound at the end of a word or syllable. They are pronounced as *open end sounds* (sometimes called live endings) in Thai. Good news is that the English long vowel sounds are pronounced in the same way as the Thai long vowel sounds at the end of the word.

However, there are not that many in English. English examples would be: see, tea, flee. In Thai, long vowel end sounds are very common.

Examples:

taa	ตา	*eye*
muu	มือ	*hand*
mŭu	หมู	*pork*
sĭi	สี	*colour*
thîi	ที่	*at, to, that*

E. Simple advice

You need to learn a new and more consistent way of using letters and sounds similar to that which we use in this book. The English language does not give you much help in this regard. For example, the English language is not at all consistent as far as vowels are pronounced; the same vowel letter may denote many different sounds depending on the word it appears in. For example, the letter **a** in the English word s**a**d is pronounced as ɛɛ. However, the same letter is pronounced in the English word m**a**ke as **ei**, in the word **a**bout as ə, in the word t**au**ght as ɔɔ, and in the word l**au**gh as **aa** and so on. Thai vowels are spelled clearly either short or long. On the other hand, many Thai consonants are pronounced differently at the beginning of a word or syllable compared to how they are pronounced at the end of a word. The change in the pronunciation follows a clear and consistent rule, however.

Build up your confidence gradually and start by using words which everyone uses daily. They are generally easily understood even if you do not pronounce the word exactly right. Learn to choose simple correct words to express yourself in the relevant situation. That is the Thai way.

F. Take it further

Refer to the book:

Dhyan Manik: *Understanding the Thai Language and Grammar:*

- More about open end sounds can be found in Chapter 1, section 1.3.1.

Refer to the books:

1. Dhyan Manik: *Learning Thai with **hâi** ให้*
   (ISBN 978-952-6651-15-6)
2. Dhyan Manik: *Learning Thai with **dâai** ได้ – Book I*
   (ISBN 978-952-6651-20-0)
3. Dhyan Manik: *Learning Thai Tenses with **dâai** ได้ – Book II*
   (ISBN 978-952-6651-20-0)

- In order to learn to speak Thai fluently, you need to know how to use **hâi** ให้ and **dâai** ได้ in a sentence. Depending on the context, these two words have several different meanings.
- When you are ready, you may wish to review these three books which explain thoroughly how Thais use **hâi** ให้ and **dâai** ได้ in daily conversation in many different ways.

Chapter 14

Using lɛ́ɛu แล้ว and kɔ̂ɔ ก็

sɔ̌ɔng rɔ́ɔi kɔ̂ɔ-lɛ́ɛu-kan
สอง ร้อย ก็ แล้ว กัน
Two hundred. Agreed!

Chapter 14

Highlights

lέεu	แล้ว	*already*
lέεu-tὲε	แล้ว แต่	*depends on... up to...*
sèt-lέεu	เสร็จ แล้ว	*already finished*
kɔ̂ɔ	ก็	*also, likewise, then, so, therefore*
lέεu-kɔ̂ɔ	แล้ว ก็	*and, and then*

A. Sentences

lέεu แล้ว *already*

1. khɔ̀ɔp khun – *phɔɔ lέεu* khâ   ขอบ คุณ – พอ แล้ว ค่ะ
   thank you – *enough already* khâ
   Thank you! That's enough.

2. kin *lέεu* khâ   กิน แล้ว ค่ะ
   eat *already* khâ – **I have already eaten.**

3. tʃán tsà pai *lέεu*   ฉัน จะ ไป แล้ว
   I will go *already* – **I will go now.**

4. *lέεu-tὲε* khun   แล้ว แต่ คุณ
   already-but khun – **It is up to you.**

5. kháu tham man *ìik-lέεu*   เขา ทำ มัน อีก แล้ว
   he do it *more-already* – **He did it again.**

6. tʃán tham man *sèt-lέεu*   ฉัน ทำ มัน เสร็จ แล้ว
   I do it *finish-already* – **I have already finished it.**

Chapter 14

7. *aathít thîi-lɛ́ɛu tʃán pai hăa phɔ̂ɔ-mɛ̂ɛ*
อาทิตย์ ที่ แล้ว ฉัน ไป หา พ่อ แม่
week that-already I go search father-mother
Last week, I visited my parents.

lɛ́ɛu แล้ว and **kɔ̂ɔ** ก็ *and, and then, likewise, also*

8. *khrai tsà pai* ใคร จะ ไป
who will go – *Who is going?*

9. *tʃán lɛ́ɛu-kɔ̂ɔ phûɯan tʃán* ฉัน แล้ว ก็ เพื่อน ฉัน
I *then-also* friend I – *I and my friend.*

10. *khun yàak tham arai* คุณ อยาก ทำ อะไร
you want do what – *What do you want to do?*

11. *arai-kɔ̂ɔ-dâai* อะไร ก็ ได้
what-also-can – *Whatever you like. / Anything is fine.*

12. *rót-khan níi tʃái-lɛ́ɛu mái* รถ คัน นี้ ใช้ แล้ว ไหม
car-vehicle this *use-already* "question"
Are these cars used?

13. *rót-khan nán thîi tʃái-lɛ́ɛu* – *rakhaa thâu-rai*
รถ คัน นั้น ที่ ใช้ แล้ว – ราคา เท่า ไร
car-vehicle that that *use-already* – price equal-what
What is the price of that used car?

14. *kɔ̂ɔ* – *an-nán raakhaa kâau mɯ̀ɯn bàat thâu-nán*
ก็ – อัน นั้น ราคา เก้า หมื่น บาท เท่า นั้น
also – piece-that cost nine ten-thousand baht equal-that
Well, the price is only ninety thousand baht.

15 tsèt mùun ookhee sămràp rót mɯɯ-sɔ̌ɔng mái
เจ็ด หมื่น โอเค สำหรับ รถ มือ สอง ไหม
seven ten-thousand okay for hand-two "question"
Is seventy thousand baht okay for a used car?

16 ookhee pɛ̀ɛt mùun *kɔ̂ɔ-lɛ́ɛu-kan*
โอเค แปด หมื่น ก็ แล้ว กัน
OK eight-ten *also-already-with*
OK, eighty thousand baht is fine.

17 rót sǐi-dɛɛng trong nóon *kɔ̂ɔ-dii*
รถ สี แดง ตรง โน้น ก็ ดี
car colour-red at-there *also-good*
The red car over there is also good.

18 raakhaa thâu-kan ราคา เท่า กัน
price equal-together – *The price is the same.*

Common expressions
(kham thîi ʧái bɔ̀i-bɔ̀i คำ ที่ ใช้ บ่อยๆ)

sèt rɯ́-yang เสร็จ รึ ยัง
finish or-not – *Have you finished?*

sèt *lɛ́ɛu* เสร็จ แล้ว
finish *already* – *Yes, I have finished.*

phrɔ́ɔm *lɛ́ɛu* พร้อม แล้ว
ready *already* – *I am ready.*

yang mâi sèt ยัง ไม่ เสร็จ
yet no finish-already – *No, I have not yet finished.*

B. Vocabulary

khɔ̀ɔp khun	ขอบ คุณ	thank you
phɔɔ lέɛu	พอ แล้ว	already enough
khâ	ค่ะ	polite particle for women
phɔɔ	พอ	to be enough
lέɛu	แล้ว	already
kin	กิน	to eat
arai	อะไร	what?
lέɛu-tὲɛ	แล้ว แต่	up to..., depends on...
man	มัน	it
ìik-lέɛu	อีก แล้ว	again
ìik	อีก	again, more
tsà	จะ	will
sèt-lέɛu	เสร็จ แล้ว	to be finished
sèt	เสร็จ	to finish, to complete
aathít thîi-lέɛu	อาทิตย์ ที่ แล้ว	last week
pai hăa	ไป หา	to go to search
phɔ̂ɔ-mε̂ɛ	พ่อ แม่	parents
khrai	ใคร	who?
lέɛu-kɔ̂ɔ	แล้ว ก็	and, and then
yàak	อยาก	to want
tham	ทำ	to do
arai-kɔ̂ɔ-dâai	อะไร ก็ ได้	anything is fine, whatever
rót	รถ	car
khan	คัน	vehicle (classifier)
níi	นี้	this
nán	นั้น	that

rakhaa	ราคา	price
tʃái-lɛ́ɛu	ใช้ แล้ว	to be used, second-hand
tʃái	ใช้	to use
mɯɯ-sɔ̌ɔng	มือ สอง	to be second-hand, used
mɯɯ	มือ	hand
sɔ̌ɔng	สอง	two
kâau mɯ̀ɯn	เก้า หมื่น	ninety thousand
kâau	เก้า	nine
mɯ̀ɯn	หมื่น	ten thousand
bàat	บาท	Thai baht
thâu-nán	เท่า นั้น	only
thâu	เท่า	to be equal to
tsèt mɯ̀ɯn	เจ็ด หมื่น	seventy thousand
sǎmràp	สำหรับ	for
pèɛt mɯ̀ɯn	แปด หมื่น	eighty thousand
ookhee	โอเค	OK
kɔ̂ɔ-lɛ́ɛu-kan	ก็ แล้ว กัน	OK, fine, agreed
sǐi-dɛɛng	สี แดง	to be red
trong nóon	ตรง โน้น	over there
kɔ̂ɔ-dii	ก็ ดี	also good
thâu-kan	เท่า กัน	to be same, equal
kan	กัน	together, with
sèt rɯ́-yang	เสร็จ รึ ยัง	to be finished or not
phrɔ́ɔm lɛ́ɛu	พร้อม แล้ว	to be ready now
phrɔ́ɔm	พร้อม	to be ready
yang	ยัง	yet, still, not, not yet
yang mâi sèt	ยัง ไม่ เสร็จ	not yet finished
mâi	ไม่	no

C. How the language works

Depending on the context, **lɛ́ɛu** แล้ว may have several meanings such as *already, a certain state has been reached, a new situation exists, a state or circumstance has changed, then, after that etc.*

 lɛ́ɛu แล้ว and adjectives

Place **lɛ́ɛu** แล้ว *already* after an adjective to express the fact that a certain state *has been reached, obtained* or *attained*. The meaning is similar to the phrase *it is already the case*. **lɛ́ɛu** แล้ว at the end of the sentences indicates a *change of circumstances*. A new situation exists.

Sometimes, we can translate **lɛ́ɛu** แล้ว into English as *already* and sometimes as *now*. The meaning is very similar.

Examples:

> phɔɔ *lɛ́ɛu* พอ แล้ว
> enough *already* – It is already enough. / It is enough now.

- **lɛ́ɛu** แล้ว *already* can be used with adjectives to express the fact that there has been a change in the circumstances; a certain condition has been reached.
- Before, it was not enough. Now, it is enough.

> **2** dii *lɛ́ɛu* ดี แล้ว
> good *already-only* – It already is good. / It is good now.

- **lɛ́ɛu** แล้ว *already* can be used with adjectives to express the fact that a certain condition has been reached or obtained.
- Before, it was not good. Now, it is good.

thùuk *lέεu* ถูก แล้ว
correct *already* – *It is already correct. / It is correct now.*

- **lέεu** แล้ว *already* can be used with adjectives to express the fact that a certain condition has been reached or obtained.
- Before, it was not correct. Now, it is correct.
- In all of the above examples (1–3) the adjective also plays the role of the verb. The focus is on the *present time, now*.

B) **lέεu** แล้ว after verbs

lέεu แล้ว *already* can also be used with verbs to express the fact that a certain condition or an action has been reached or obtained. However, here grammatical function can be different compared to when used with adjectives as in the sentences 1–3.

Much depends on the type of verb we use and the context. Often, **lέεu** แล้ว denotes the present tense or an *ongoing action*. Sometimes, in another context, **lέεu** แล้ว expresses a *past tense*, a *completed action*.

Examples:

a) Present time

kháu-tsai *lέεu* เข้า ใจ แล้ว
enter-heart *already*
I understand already. / I understand now.

- **kháu-tsai** เข้า ใจ *to understand* is a state verb that describes a certain *state* or *condition similar to adjectives*. After state verbs and adjectives **lέεu** แล้ว tends to reflect the present tense.
- This sentence reflects the *simple present tense*, an *ongoing state*. Now, I understand. Before, I did not understand.

> **2** fǒn-tòk *lɛ́ɛu* ฝน ตก แล้ว
> rain-fall *already* – *It is already raining.*

- With some verbs that describe action which you can see with your own eyes, **lɛ́ɛu** แล้ว tends to reflect the present tense. **fǒn-tòk** ฝน ตก *to rain* is such a verb.
- This sentence reflects the *present continuous tense*, an *ongoing action.* Now, it is raining. Before, it was not raining.

> **3** kháu tham-ngaan *lɛ́ɛu* เขา ทำ งาน แล้ว
> he do-work *already* – *He is already working.*

- With some longer term action verbs, **lɛ́ɛu** แล้ว tends to reflect the present tense. **tham-ngaan** ทำ งาน is such a verb.
- This sentence reflects the *present continuous tense*, an *ongoing action.* Now, he is working. Before, he was not working.

b) **Completed action**

> **1** sòng *lɛ́ɛu* ส่ง แล้ว
> send *already* – *I have already sent it.*

- Depending on the context and the type of verb we use, the tense can be different.
- After short time action verbs, **lɛ́ɛu** แล้ว normally reflects the past tense. **sòng** ส่ง *to send* is such a short time action verb.
- This sentence reflects the past tense, an *action completed*.

> **2** kháu maa *lɛ́ɛu* เขา มา แล้ว
> he come *already* – *He has already arrived.*

Chapter 14

- Depending on the context and the type of verb we use, the tense can be different.
- After short time action verbs, **lɛ́ɛu** แล้ว normally reflects the past tense. **maa** มา *to come* is such a short time action verb.
- This sentence reflects the past tense, an *action completed*.

> **3** kin *lɛ́ɛu* กิน แล้ว
> eat *already – I have already eaten.*

- Depending on the context and the type of verb we use, the tense can be different.
- After short time action verbs, **lɛ́ɛu** แล้ว normally reflects the past tense. **kin** กิน *to eat* is such a *short time action verb*.
- This sentence reflects the past tense, an *action completed*.

C) **thîi-lɛ́ɛu** ที่ แล้ว and **ìik-lɛ́ɛu** อีก แล้ว

thîi-lɛ́ɛu ที่ แล้ว *ago* and **ìik-lɛ́ɛu** อีก แล้ว *again* are handy expressions that Thai people use frequently.

Examples:

> **1** khául pai sǎam-sìp naathii *thîi-lɛ́ɛu*
> เขา ไป สาม สิบ นาที ที่ แล้ว
> he go three-ten minute *that-already*
> *He left thirty minutes ago.*

- **thîi-lɛ́ɛu** ที่ แล้ว *ago* is often placed after the time (minutes, hours, days, months etc.).
- For different emphasis, it can be placed either at the end or at the beginning of the sentence.
- Here we have placed **thîi-lɛ́ɛu** ที่ แล้ว *ago* at the end of the sentence to emphasize the fact that he *has left*.
- This sentence reflects the past tense, an *action completed*.

Chapter 14

> **2** dɯɯan *thîi-lɛ́ɛu* ʧán yáai maa thîi nîi
> เดือน ที่ แล้ว ฉัน ย้าย มา ที่ นี่
> month *that-already* I move come place-this
> *I moved here a month ago.*

- Here we have placed **thîi-lɛ́ɛu** ที่ แล้ว *ago* at the beginning of the sentence to emphasize the fact that the action happened a *month ago*.
- For different emphasis, it can be placed either at the end or at the beginning of the sentence.
- This sentence reflects the past tense, an *action completed*.

> **3** kháu maa *ìik-lɛ́ɛu* เขา มา อีก แล้ว
> he come *more-already* – *He came again.*

- **ìik-lɛ́ɛu** อีก แล้ว *again* comes normally at the end of the sentence.
- This sentence reflects the past tense, an *action completed*.

> **4** mâi yàak pai *ìik-lɛ́ɛu* ไม่ อยาก ไป อีก แล้ว
> no want go *more-already*
> *I don't want to go there anymore.*

- In the negative sentence **ìik-lɛ́ɛu** อีก แล้ว is translated into English as *not anymore*.
- This sentence reflects the *present* or *future tense*; an *action is not desired*.

D) lɛ́ɛu-tɛ̀ɛ แล้ว แต่ and **lɛ́ɛu-kɔ̂ɔ** แล้ว ก็

lɛ́ɛu-tɛ̀ɛ แล้ว แต่ *it depends on..., it is up to...* and **lɛ́ɛu-kɔ̂ɔ** แล้ว ก็ *and, and then* are used frequently by Thais every day.

> **1** *lɛ́ɛu-tɛ̀ɛ* khun แล้ว แต่ คุณ
> *already-but* you – *It is up to you.*

- **lɛ́ɛu-tɛ̀ɛ khun** แล้ว แต่ คุณ *it depends on you, it is up to you.*
- **lɛ́ɛu-tɛ̀ɛ** แล้ว แต่ *it depends on* is normally placed before the object, here **khun** คุณ *you*.
- Thai people use this expression frequently.

> **2** *lɛ́ɛu-tɛ̀ɛ* kháu แล้ว แต่ เขา
> *already-but* he – *It is up to him.*

- **lɛ́ɛu-tɛ̀ɛ kháu** แล้ว แต่ เขา *it depends on him, it is up to him.*
- **lɛ́ɛu-tɛ̀ɛ** แล้ว แต่ *it depends on* is normally placed before the object, here **kháu** เขา *him*.

> **3** tʃán *lɛ́ɛu-kɔ̂ɔ* phŵan tʃán tsà pai thîau
> ฉัน แล้ว ก็ เพื่อน ฉัน จะ ไป เที่ยว
> I *then-also* friend I will go out
> *I and my friend will go out.*

- **lɛ́ɛu-kɔ̂ɔ** แล้ว ก็ *and, and then* is a nice way to connect words, phrases and sentences.
- Here **lɛ́ɛu-kɔ̂ɔ** แล้ว ก็ connects **tʃán** ฉัน *I* and **phŵan** เพื่อน *friend*. The meaning is *and*.

> **4** tʃán *lɛ́* phŵan tʃán tsà pai thîau
> ฉัน และ เพื่อน ฉัน จะ ไป เที่ยว
> I *and* friend I will go out – *I and my friend will go out.*

- **lɛ́** และ *and*, is another way to connect words, phrases and sentences.
- **lɛ́** และ *and* is perhaps slightly more official than **lɛ́ɛu-kɔ̂ɔ** แล้ว ก็ *and* which is often used in speaking.

> **5** ␣chán kàp phûuan chán tsà pai thîau
> ฉัน กับ เพื่อน ฉัน จะ ไป เที่ยว
> I *with* friend I will go out – *I and my friend will go out.*

- **kàp** กับ *with* is another way to connect words. Usually, Thais like to connect nouns or pronouns this way.
- In this sentence, we could use **lɛ́ɛu-kɔ̂ɔ** แล้ว ก็ or **lɛ́** และ, and the meaning would be the same *and*. However, the colour of the sentence would be slightly different in Thai.

E) kɔ̂ɔ ก็

kɔ̂ɔ ก็ *well, also, then, so, therefore* is a very mysterious word in Thai. Thais use it every day in many different ways, but nobody can tell you the exact meaning. We give here a few different ways how it is used.

Examples:

> **1** *kɔ̂ɔ* – mâi thùuk ləəi ก็ – ไม่ ถูก เลย
> *also* – no correct at-all – *Well! It is not correct at all.*

- **kɔ̂ɔ** ก็ can be used at the beginning of the statement as an introduction. It gives the speaker some more time to think about the reply.
- It is used in a similar way as the English word *well* at the beginning of the sentence.

> **2** *arai-kɔ̂ɔ-dâai* อะไร ก็ ได้
> *what-also-can* – *Anything is fine! / Whatever you like!*

- **arai-kɔ̂ɔ-dâai** อะไร ก็ ได้ *whatever* is an idiomatic expression. It can be used as a complete reply to a question.
- It is used in a similar way as **lɛ́ɛu-tɛ̀ɛ khun** แล้ว แต่ คุณ *it depends on you, it is up to you.*

> **3** sɔ̌ɔng rɔ́ɔi *kɔ̂ɔ-lɛ́ɛu-kan* สอง ร้อย ก็ แล้ว กัน
> two hundred *also-then-together* – Two hundred. Agreed!

- **kɔ̂ɔ-lɛ́ɛu-kan** ก็ แล้ว กัน *agreed* is an idiomatic expression, which can be used to indicate an agreement after negotiations. However, you must repeat what you have agreed upon, here **sɔ̌ɔng rɔ́ɔi** สอง ร้อย *two hundred*.

> **4** an-níi *kɔ̂ɔ-dii* อัน นี้ ก็ ดี
> piece-this *also-good* – This one is quite good.

- **kɔ̂ɔ** ก็ can be placed before an adjective to make a comparison with something else.
- Here **kɔ̂ɔ-dii** ก็ ดี is used to tell that *this one is not so bad* compared to something else. In fact, it is quite good.

F) **mùun** หมื่น *10,000* and **tʃái-lɛ́ɛu** ใช้ แล้ว *used, second hand*

Example:

> **1** **mùun** หมื่น *ten thousand*

- **mùun** หมื่น *ten thousand* is a very handy expression when counting big numbers. Similarly, in English we can say sixteen thousand (16,000).
- In Thai, we would express 16,000 as **nùng mùun hòk phan** หนึ่ง หมื่น หก พัน (literally: one ten-thousand and six thousand).
- In speaking, Thais would often use the short form and say **mùun hòk** (literally: ten-thousand six = 16,000)

2 In Thai, we have two expressions for the English word *second-hand*

Examples:

> **2.1** **tʃái-lɛ́ɛu** ใช้ แล้ว *used, second-hand*

- is commonly used since **tʃái** ใช้ means *to use* and **lɛ́ɛu** แล้ว means *already* (literally: used already).

> **2.2** **mɯɯ-sɔ̌ɔng** มือ สอง *second-hand, used* (literally: hand-two)

- This expression may have been borrowed from English.

3 **mɯɯ** มือ *hand* can be used with several other words to form new meanings. Here are some commonly used.

Examples:

- **khrûuang-mɯɯ** เครื่อง มือ *tools*
- **mɯɯ-thɯ̌ɯ** มือ ถือ *mobile phone*
- **fǐi-mɯɯ** ฝี มือ *skill, craftsmanship*
- **khwǎa-mɯɯ** ขวา มือ *right side*
- **sáai-mɯɯ** ซ้าย มือ *left side*
- **laai-mɯɯ** ลาย มือ *handwriting*

G) **yang** ยัง *still, not*

yang ยัง *still, not, not yet, or not* can have several meanings depending on the situation and other words it is used with. Words like this are best learned by using the language in the context.

Examples:

> **1** kin *lɛ́ɛu-rɯ̌ɯ-yang* กิน แล้ว หรือ ยัง
> eat *already-or-yet* – Have you already eaten or not?

- Here **yang** ยัง is used in a question. This is a typical question in Thai. Thai people often like to know whether you have eaten.
- In fact, it is often only used as a nice way to start a conversation.

> **2** *yang* ยัง
> yet (not) – Not yet!

- Usually in Thai, a reply to a question includes a part of the question.
- In reply, **yang** ยัง alone is enough; it means *no, not yet*.

> **3** kin *lɛ́ɛu* กิน แล้ว
> eat *already* – Yes, I have eaten already.

- In Thai, normally a reply to a question includes a part of the question. Here **lɛ́ɛu** แล้ว means *yes, already*.

> **4** *tɛ̀ɛ-kɔ̂ɔ-yang* hǐu yùu แต่ ก็ ยัง หิว อยู่
> but-also-yet hungry be – But I am still hungry.

- Here **yang** ยัง means *still*. The person gives more information about her/his eating.
- **tɛ̀ɛ-(kɔ̂ɔ)-yang hǐu yùu** แต่ (ก็) ยัง หิว อยู่ *I am still hungry.*
- We may drop the word **kɔ̂ɔ** ก็, and the translation into English remains the same. However, the Thai sentence would lose some colour and flow.

D. New sounds

Special vowels and short vowel combinations also constitute an open end sound in Thai.

Even though we don't teach the Thai writing system in this book, we follow the Thai sound structure. There are three special vowel sounds in

Thai, sometimes called consonant-like vowels. That is perhaps because **am** อำ has a vowel and also a consonant in one sound.

a) Special vowels: **am** อำ, **au** เอา, **ai** ใอ, ไอ

Examples:

kh**am**	คำ	*word*
m**au**	เมา	*to be drunk*
s**ài**	ใส่	*to put on, to wear*
m**âi**	ไม่	*no*

- Any special vowel constitutes an *open end sound*.

b) Short vowel combinations: **iu** อิว, **ui** อุย, **eu** เอ็ว, **ai** อัย

Examples:

h**ĭu**	หิว	*to be hungry*
khui	คุย	*to chat*
reu	เร็ว	*to be fast*
sàm**ăi**	สมัย	*time era*

- Any short vowel combination constitutes an *open end sound*.
- Just to point out that the sound **ai** is written in three different ways in Thai script, **ai** อัย, **ai** ใอ and **ai** ไอ. This has nothing to do with the pronunciation of the sound. It has to do with the writing and the meaning of the word.

E. Simple advice

Be also aware that the Thai language contains a large number of words which are not used by ordinary Thais in everyday conversation. The common problem with many language books is that they teach you words that are not commonly used by Thais. In order to be understood easily, you should learn to use the most common words. If you use an unfamiliar word, however correct it may be, you are not likely to be immediately understood. That is the reason why you cannot simply learn words from a dictionary. You need to know how and when to use a certain word contextually. This is absolutely essential in Thai.

Original Thai words are used by Thais every day. They constitute a core of the Thai language. As we have already learned, there are also a number of borrowed words which are also used by Thais every day. Good examples are the names of days and months. In this book, we concentrate on original Thai words and those borrowed words which are commonly used by Thais.

F. Take it further

Refer to the book:

Dhyan Manik: *Understanding the Thai Language and Grammar:*

- More about open end sounds can be found in Chapter 1, section 1.3.1.
- Further analyses about different types of verbs together with **léɛu** แล้ว *already* can be found in Chapter 13.

Refer to the books:

1. Dhyan Manik: *Learning Thai and Thai Tenses with **léɛu** แล้ว* (ISBN 978-952-6651-44-6), coming in 2020
2. Dhyan Manik: *Learning Thai with **kɔ̂ɔ** ก็* (ISBN 978-952-6651-45-3), coming in 2021

- When you are ready, you may wish to review these two books which explain thoroughly how to use **léɛu** แล้ว and **kɔ̂ɔ** ก็ in daily conversation in many different ways as Thai people do.
- The exact publishing dates can be checked on the following page www.thaibooks.net
- More information can also be found in the following two books:

3. David Smyth: *Thai – An Essential Grammar*
4. James Higbie & Snea Thinsan: *Thai Reference Grammar*

Chapter 15

Expressing Thai tenses

tʃán rian năngsɯ̌ɯ yùu
ฉัน เรียน หนังสือ อยู่
I am studying!

Highlights

Time words (present, past and future)

tɔɔn-níi	ตอน นี้	*now*
phrûng-níi	พรุ่ง นี้	*tomorrow*
mûɯa-waan	เมื่อ วาน	*yesterday*
pii thîi-lɛ́ɛu	ปี ที่ แล้ว	*last year*

Tense markers (present, past and future)

kamlang	กำลัง	*action in progress (now, present)*
khəəi	เคย	*happened at least once in the past, used to (past)*
phûŋ	เพิ่ง	*just, a moment ago (recent past)*
tsà	จะ	*will (future)*
kamlang-tsà	กำลัง จะ	*just about going to (near future)*

Time indicators (present, past and future)

lɛ́ɛu	แล้ว	*already, a new situation exists (present, past and future)*
yùu	อยู่	*state or condition exists (present, now)*

A. Sentences

1 **Present tense**

1.1 rɔ́ɔn mâak ร้อน มาก
hot very – *It is very hot.*

1.2 wan-níi rót-tìt *lɛ́ɛu* วัน นี้ รถ ติด แล้ว
today car-stuck *already* – *Today, there is a traffic jam.*

1.3 *tɔɔn-níi* năao mâak ตอน นี้ หนาว มาก
at-this cold very – *It is very cold now.*

1.4 kháu *kamlang* tham-ngaan เขา กำลัง ทำ งาน
he *kamlang* do-work – *He is working.*

1.5 tʃán kin kaafɛɛ *yùu* ฉัน กิน กาแฟ อยู่
I drink coffee *be* – *I am drinking coffee.*

1.6 kháu too *lɛ́ɛu* khâ เขา โต แล้ว ค่ะ
he big *already* khâ – *He is already grown up.*

1.7 tʃán mâi yàak kin *ìik-lɛ́ɛu* ฉัน ไม่ อยาก กิน อีก แล้ว
I no want eat *more-already*
I don't want to eat any more.

2 **Past tense**

2.1 *mûɯa-waan* tʃán pai thîiau kàp fɛɛn
เมื่อ วาน ฉัน ไป เที่ยว กับ แฟน
yesterday I go trip with boyfriend
Yesterday, I went out with my boyfriend.

2.2 *pii thîi-lɛ́ɛu* fŏn-tòk mâak ปี ที่ แล้ว ฝน ตก มาก
year that-already rain-fall much – *It rained a lot last year.*

2.3 kin *lɛ́ɛu* rɯ̌ɯ-yang กิน แล้ว หรือ ยัง
eat *already* or-not – *Have you already eaten?*

2.4 kin *lɛ́ɛu* khâ กิน แล้ว ค่ะ
eat *already* khâ – *Yes, I have already eaten.*

2.5 kháu pai *lɛ́ɛu* เขา ไป แล้ว
he go *already* – *He has gone already.*

2.6 tʃǎn *khəəi* riian phaasǎa-tsiin ฉัน เคย เรียน ภาษา จีน
I *once* study language-China – *I have studied Chinese.*

2.7 kháu *phɯ̂ng* tham เขา เพิ่ง ทำ
he *just* do – *He has just done it.*

3 Future tense

3.1 tʃǎn *tsà* yùu thîi-nîi naan-naan ฉัน จะ อยู่ ที่ นี่ นานๆ
I *will* stay long-long – *I will stay here for a long time.*

3.2 *pii-nâa* kháu *tsà* riian phaasǎa-angkrìt
ปี หน้า เขา จะ เรียน ภาษา อังกฤษ
next-year he *will* study language-England
Next year, he will study English.

3.3 *phrûng-níi* tʃǎn *tsà* pai hǎa phɔ̂ɔ-mɛ̂ɛ
พรุ่ง นี้ ฉัน จะ ไป หา พ่อ แม่
tomorrow I will go search father-mother
Tomorrow, I will visit my parents.

3.4 tʃǎn *kamlang-tsà* pai nɔɔn lɛ́ɛu
ฉัน กำลัง จะ ไป นอน แล้ว
I *kamlang-will* go sleep already
I am just about going to sleep already.

Chapter 15

Common expressions
(kham thîi ɟ́ái bɔ̀i-bɔ̀i คำ ที่ ใช้ บ่อยๆ)

tsà pai thîi-nǎi kɔ̂ɔ-dâai จะ ไป ที่ ไหน ก็ ได้
will go place-where also-can – *I can go anywhere.*

tsà pai yùu lɛ́ɛu จะ ไป อยู่ แล้ว
will go be-already – *I am just going there anyway.*

tsà pai yang-ngai kɔ̂ɔ-dii จะ ไป ยังไง ก็ ดี
will go how also-good – *I will go anyhow.*

tsà pai yang-ngai kɔ̂ɔ-taam จะ ไป ยังไง ก็ ตาม
will go how also-follow – *I will go whatever happens.*

B. Vocabulary

tɔɔn-níi	ตอน นี้	now
rɔ́ɔn	ร้อน	to be hot
too	โต	to be big, grown up
lɛ́ɛu	แล้ว	already, state or condition reached
rót-tìt	รถ ติด	traffic jam
tìt	ติด	to be jammed, stuck
yàak	อยาก	to want
ìik-lɛ́ɛu	อีก แล้ว	again, anymore
kamlang	กำลัง	action in progress (now)
tham-ngaan	ทำ งาน	to work
yùu	อยู่	state or condition exists (now)
lɛ́ɛu rǔɯ-yang	แล้ว หรือ ยัง	already or not?
kin lɛ́ɛu	กิน แล้ว	yes, I have already eaten

mûua-waan	เมื่อ วาน	yesterday
pai thîiau	ไป เที่ยว	to go out
kàp	กับ	with, together
fɛɛn	แฟน	boyfriend, girlfriend, lover
pii thîi-lɛ́ɛu	ปี ที่ แล้ว	a year ago
fǒn-tòk	ฝน ตก	to rain
fǒn	ฝน	rain
tòk	ตก	to fall, to drop down
mâak	มาก	much
khəəi	เคย	happened at least once before, used to
phaasǎa-tsiin	ภาษา จีน	Chinese
phûng	เพิ่ง	just, a moment ago
pii-nâa	ปี หน้า	next year
tsà	จะ	will
riian	เรียน	to study
phrûng-níi	พรุ่ง นี้	tomorrow
pai hǎa	ไป หา	to visit
pai	ไป	to go
hǎa	หา	to look for
phɔ̂ɔ-mɛ̂ɛ	พ่อ แม่	parents
yùu	อยู่	to stay, to live
kamlang-tsà	กำลัง จะ	just about (near future)
naan-naan	นานๆ	a long time
tsà pai	จะ ไป	will go
thîi-nǎi	ที่ ไหน	where?
kɔ̂ɔ-dâai	ก็ ได้	possible
yùu-lɛ́ɛu	อยู่ แล้ว	anyway
yang-ngai	ยังไง	how

kɔ̂ɔ-dii	ก็ ดี	to be quite good
kɔ̂ɔ-taam	ก็ ตาม	whatever

C. How the language works

You may have wondered how to express Thai tenses. Well, in grammatical terms, the Thai language does not have any tenses. The main verb is always in its basic form. In English, we normally speak about *tenses* since the main verb is conjugated to denote a specific tense. However, the English term "tense" is also a handy way to talk about the present, past and future activities in Thai.

Thai tenses are only expressed differently compared to English. Yet, in both languages, we talk about actions which happened in the past, are happening now or will happen in the future. The English tense system is far more complex, however. The Thai way is straight forward and quite intuitive. Generally, we can say that the correct tense in Thai is often understood from the context only, and there is not any need for additional indicators. However, time words, time indicators or tense makers are often used to make the tense clear when it is not understood from the context.

When the action is happening at the time of speaking, Thai people like to use the tense marker **kamlang** กำลัง *action in progress* or the time indicator **yùu** อยู่ *state* or *condition exists.*

The past is normally understood from the context and time words such as **mûua-kɔ̀ɔn** เมื่อ ก่อน *before.*

There are also two past tense markers:

khəəi	เคย	*happened at least once before, used to* (past)
phûng	เพิ่ง	*just, a moment ago* (past)

Normally, Thai people prefer to use the *future tense marker* **tsà** จะ *will* whenever the action refers to the future. This is perhaps because the future in Thai is very much hypothetical. They like to underline the fact that the action *may* happen or *should* happen in the future. One can not be so sure about it. The future tense in Thai is made in the similar way as the *simple future tense* is made in English with the helping verb *will*.

Let us walk through the Thai way of expressing the present, past and future; we hope that we can make it clear for you. We have the following words to play with.

Examples:

1. Time words (present, past and future)

tɔɔn-níi	ตอน นี้	*now*
phrûng-níi	พรุ่ง นี้	*tomorrow*
mûɯa-waan	เมื่อ วาน	*yesterday*
pii thîi-lɛ́ɛu	ปี ที่ แล้ว	*last year*

2. Tense markers (present, past and future)

kamlang	กำลัง	*action in progress* (now, present)
khəəi	เคย	*happened at least once before, used to* (before, past)
phûng	เพิ่ง	*just, a moment ago* (before, just, past)
tsà	จะ	*will* (future)
kamlang-tsà	กำลัง จะ	*just about going to* (near future)

3. Time indicators (present, past and future)

lɛ́ɛu แล้ว *already, state* or *condition reached* (present, past, future – circumstances have changed, a new state or condition has emerged)*

yùu อยู่ *state* or *condition exists* **(present, now)**

* You may also wish to review the previous Chapter 14 and see how **lɛ́ɛu** แล้ว already can effect tenses.

Chapter 15

1 Present tense

> **1.1** rɔ́ɔn mâak ร้อน มาก
> hot very – *It is very hot.*

- Here we use only two simple words; the tense is understood from the context.
- Note also that the adjective **rɔ́ɔn** ร้อน *hot* in Thai also plays the role of a verb.
- In English, we can express the same with the *simple present tense* (It is...).

> **1.2** tɔɔn-níi năao mâak ตอน นี้ หนาว มาก
> at-this cold very – *It is very cold now.*

- We may add the *time word* **tɔɔn-níi** ตอน นี้ *now* at the beginning of the sentence to emphasize the present time.
- The English tense is the *simple present tense* (It is...).

> **1.3** kháu too *lɛ́ɛu* khâ เขา โต แล้ว ค่ะ
> he big *already* khâ – *He is already big.*

- **lɛ́ɛu** แล้ว is very special word since it can be used with all tenses, *present, past* and *future*. Much depends on the context and the main verb.
- After an adjective (state verb), **lɛ́ɛu** แล้ว usually indicates the *present time*.
- The English tense is the *simple present tense* (He is...).
- Note that we have also reviewed the time indicator **lɛ́ɛu** แล้ว *already* in Chapter 14.

> **1.4** kháu *kamlang* tham-ngaan เขา กำลัง ทำ งาน
> he *kamlang* do-work – *He is working.*

- When **kamlang** กำลัง *action in progress* is placed before the main verb, the sentence reflects the *present continuous tense* (verb + -ing, *working*) in English.
- The action happens normally at the time of speaking.

> **1.5** tʃán kin kaafɛɛ *yùu* ฉัน กิน กาแฟ อยู่
> I drink coffee *be* – *I am drinking coffee.*

- We can express the same idea with the time indicator **yùu** อยู่ *action exists* instead of **kamlang** กำลัง *action in progress*.
- **yùu** อยู่ *action exists* is placed after the main verb and at the end of the sentence. **yùu** อยู่ is a more familiar term compared to **kamlang** กำลัง *action in progress*. Therefore, it is more often used in speaking.
- This sentence reflects the *present continuous tense* (verb + -ing, *drinking*) in English.

> **1.6** tʃán *kamlang* kin kaafɛɛ *yùu* ฉัน กำลัง กิน กาแฟ อยู่
> I *kamlang* drink coffee *be* – *I am drinking coffee.*

- It is not uncommon that both **kamlang** กำลัง *action in progress* and **yùu** อยู่ *action exists* are used in the same sentence.
- Note that the *tense marker* **kamlang** กำลัง is always placed before the main verb, and the time indicator **yùu** อยู่ is placed at the end of the sentence.
- The English tense is the same in the sentences 4–6, the *present continuous tense* (verb + -ing). In Thai, the emphasis of the expression is slightly different, however.

1.7 phŏm *yùu* thîi krungthêep   ผม อยู่ ที่ กรุงเทพ
I *live* at Bangkok – *I live* in Bangkok.

- **yùu** อยู่ can also be used as a main verb meaning *to live* or *to stay*. On the other hand, **kamlang** กำลัง *action in progress* cannot be used alone as a main verb.
- Here, the tense is understood from the context; we conclude that if the action does not refer to past or future, it must refer to now.
- The English tense is the *present simple tense* (I live...).

2 Past tense

2.1 kin *lɛ́ɛu-rɯ̌ɯ-yang*   กิน แล้ว หรือ ยัง
eat *already-or-not* – *Have you already eaten?*

2.2 kin *lɛ́ɛu* khâ   กิน แล้ว ค่ะ
eat *already* khâ – *Yes, I have already eaten.*

- In these two sentences, the *past tense* is understood from the context and from the time indicator **lɛ́ɛu** แล้ว *already*.
- If we drop **lɛ́ɛu** แล้ว, the sentence would not make sense.
- Note the simple Thai structure; in English, we need to conjugate two verbs, *have* and *eaten*.
- The English tense is the *present perfect tense* (I have eaten...).

2.3 kháu pai *lɛ́ɛu*   เขา ไป แล้ว
he go *already* – *He has already gone.*

- Here the *past tense* is understood from the context and from the time indicator **lɛ́ɛu** แล้ว.
- If we drop **lɛ́ɛu** แล้ว, the sentence would not make sense.

- Note the simple Thai structure. In English, we need to conjugate two verbs, *has* and *gone*.
- In English, tense is the *present perfect tense* (He has gone...) which is normally used when the exact time of the action is not given.
- In Thai, we rather talk about the *past* only.

> **2.4** *mûɨa-waan* tʃán pai thîiau kàp fɛɛn
> เมื่อ วาน ฉัน ไป เที่ยว กับ แฟน
> *yesterday* I go trip with boyfriend
> *Yesterday, I went out with my boyfriend.*

- Here the *past tense* is understood from the context and from the past time word **mûɨa-waan** เมื่อ วาน *yesterday*.
- If we drop **mûɨa-waan** เมื่อ วาน, the Thai tense would not be clear; then, depending on the context, this sentence could also refer to the present or future time.
- The English tense here is the *past simple tense* (I went...) which is usually used when the exact time is given.

> **2.5** *pii thîi-lɛ́ɛu* fǒn-tòk mâak ปี ที่ แล้ว ฝน ตก มาก
> *year that-already* rain-fall much – *It rained a lot last year.*

- Here the *past tense* is understood from the context and from the time word **pii thîi-lɛ́ɛu** ปี ที่ แล้ว a *year ago*.
- If we drop **pii thîi-lɛ́ɛu** ปี ที่ แล้ว, the Thai tense would not be clear; then, depending on the context, it could also refer to the present or future time.
- The English tense here is the *past simple tense* (It rained...) which is usually used when the exact time is given.

> **2.6** tʃán *khəəi* riian phaasǎa-tsiin ฉัน เคย เรียน ภาษา จีน
> I *once* study language-China – *I have studied Chinese.*

Chapter 15

- Here the *past tense* is understood from the context and from the *tense marker* **khəəi** เคย *once, used to*.
- If we drop **khəəi** เคย *once, used to*, the Thai tense would not be clear; then, depending on the context, this sentence could also refer to the present or future time.
- The English tense here is the *present perfect tense* (I have studied...) which is usually used when the exact time is not given.

> **2.7** kháu *phûng* tham sèt เขา เพิ่ง ทำ เสร็จ
> he *just* do finish – *He has just done it.*

- Here the *past tense* is understood from the context and from the *tense marker* **phûng** เพิ่ง *just, a moment ago*.
- If we drop **phûng** เพิ่ง *just, a moment ago*, the Thai sentence would not make sense.
- The English tense here is the *present perfect tense* (He has just done...).

3 Future tense

The future tense in Thai is very simple. It is normally made with the future tense marker **tsà** จะ *will*. **tsà** จะ *will* is used in the same way as the English helping word *will*. In both languages, the helping verb will is placed before the main verb to tell that the action refers to the anticipated future event.

> **3.1** *pii-nâa* phŏm *tsà* riian phaasăa-thai
> ปี หน้า ผม จะ เรียน ภาษา ไทย
> next-year I *will* study language-Thai
> *Next year, I will study Thai.*

- Here the *future tense* is understood from the *future time word* **pii-nâa** ปี หน้า *next year* and from the *tense marker* **tsà** จะ *will*.

- We could drop the *tense marker* **tsà** จะ *will*, and the sentence would be grammatically correct.
- However, as we have already pointed out, Thai people normally like to use **tsà** จะ *will* in most of the sentences that refer to the future.
- Note also that the Thai future tense is formed grammatically in the similar way as it is formed in English. Both languages use the helping verb **tsà** จะ *will*.
- The English tense is the *future simple tense* (I will...).

> **3.2** *phrûng-níi* tʃán *tsà* pai hăa phɔ̂ɔ-mɛ̂ɛ
> พรุ่ง นี้ ฉัน จะ ไป หา พ่อ แม่
> *tomorrow* I *will* go search father-mother
> *Tomorrow, I am going to visit my parents.*

- Here the *future tense* is understood from the context and from the *future time word* **phrûng-níi** พรุ่ง นี้ *tomorrow* and from the *tense marker* **tsà** จะ *will*.
- We could drop the *tense marker* **tsà** จะ *will*, and the sentence would be grammatically correct.
- However, as we have already pointed out, Thai people normally like to use **tsà** จะ *will* in most of the sentences which refer to the future.
- Here we have used *going to* in English to express the *simple future*.

> **3.3** tʃán *tsà* yùu thîi-níi naan-naan ฉัน จะ อยู่ ที่ นี่ นานๆ
> I *will* stay place-this long-long
> *I will stay here for a long time.*

- Here the *future tense* is understood from the *tense marker* **tsà** จะ *will* only.
- The English tense is the *future simple tense* (I will...).

Chapter 15

> **3.4** rót-fai *tsà* ɔ̀ɔk pɛ̀ɛt moong tʃáu
> รถ ไฟ จะ ออก แปด โมง เช้า
> car-fire *will* leave eight hour morning
> *The train leaves at eight in the morning.*

- In this sentence, the *future tense* is understood from the *tense marker* **tsà** จะ *will* only.
- Here we have used the English *present simple tense* (The train leaves...) to express the *future*.

> **3.5** tʃán *kamlang-tsà* pai noon *lɛ́ɛu*
> ฉัน กำลัง จะ ไป นอน แล้ว
> I *kamlang-will* go sleep *already*
> *I am just about going to go to sleep already.*

- In this sentence, the *future tense* is understood from the *tense marker* **kamlang-tsà** กำลัง จะ *just about going to*.
- Here we have used the English verb form *just about going to* to express the *future*.

4. More examples about tenses

> **4.1** Basic sentence
> tʃán pai thiiau kàp phʉ̂ʉan ฉัน ไป เที่ยว กับ เพื่อน
> I go trip with friend – *I went out with my friend.*

- This Thai sentence does not have any time word nor has it any tense marker.
- Hence, depending on the context, it could refer to the *present, past* or *future time*. When the tense is understood, there is no need for any additional indicators in Thai.

So, depending on the context, the translation into English could be:

- I *am going* out with my boyfriend.
- I *went* out with my boyfriend.
- I *will* go out with my boyfriend.

We can make the Thai tense clear by adding more words as follows:

 yùu อยู่ *state* or *condition exists*

tʃán pai thîiau kàp phʉ̂ʉan *yùu*
ฉัน ไป เที่ยว กับ เพื่อน อยู่
I go trip with friend *be – I am going out with my friend.*

- If you would like to express the fact that the action is taking place at the *time of speaking*, then just place the *time indicator* **yùu** อยู่ *state* or *condition exists* at the end of a statement or sentence.
- The English tense is the *present continuous tense* (I am going...).

 kamlang กำลัง *action in progress*

tʃán *kamlang* pai thîiau kàp phʉ̂ʉan
ฉัน กำลัง ไป เที่ยว กับ เพื่อน
I *kamlang* go trip with friend
I am going out with my friend.

- The present can also be expressed by the *tense marker* **kamlang** กำลัง *action in progress* which is placed before the main verb.
- **kamlang** กำลัง is somewhat more formal style compared to **yùu** อยู่ which is often used in speaking.
- The English tense is the *present continuous tense* (I am going...).

mûua-waan เมื่อ วาน *yesterday*

mûua-waan tʃán pai thîiau kàp phûuan
เมื่อ วาน ฉัน ไป เที่ยว กับ เพื่อน
yesterday I go trip with friend
Yesterday, I went out with my friend.

- The simplest way to express the past tense in Thai is to use the past *time word* such as **mûua-waan** เมื่อ วาน *yesterday*. Now, we have made it clear that the action took place *yesterday*.
- The English tense is the *past simple tense* (I went...).

 lɛ́ɛu แล้ว *already*

tʃán pai thîiau kàp phûuan *lɛ́ɛu*
ฉัน ไป เที่ยว กับ เพื่อน แล้ว
I go trip with friend *already*
I have been out with my friend already.

- Here the emphasis is on *already, it is already the case*. We can assume that the action has happened *recently*.
- With some verbs such as *coming, going, eating, sending,* etc., the *time indicator* **lɛ́ɛu** แล้ว *already* at the end of the sentence denotes a past tense.
- The English tense is the *present perfect tense* (I have been).

 khɔ́ɔi เคย *happened at least once before*

tʃán *khɔ́ɔi* pai thîiau kàp phûuan
ฉัน เคย ไป เที่ยว กับ เพื่อน
I *once* go trip with friend
I have been out with my friend.

- **khɔ́ɔi** เคย *happened at least once before, used to*

- Here the emphasis is on the fact that the action happened at *least once* in the past; the *past tense* is understood from the context and from the *tense marker* **khəəi** เคย *once, used to*.
- There is not any exact time given. The emphasis here is on the fact that the action has already taken place in the past.
- However, the English sentence *I have been out with my friend* implies that the action has taken place recently, while the Thai sentence tells nothing about when the action has taken place.
- The English tense is the *present perfect tense* (I have been...).

 tsà จะ *will*

tʃán *tsà* pai thîiau kàp phûuan
ฉัน จะ ไป เที่ยว กับ เพื่อน
I *will* go trip with friend
I will be going out with my friend.

- Future is very easy in Thai. Here the *future tense* is understood from the *tense marker* **tsà** จะ *will*.
- The *tense marker* **tsà** จะ *will* is often used in all types of future actions.
- The English tense used here is the *future continuous tense* (I will be going...)

 aathít-nâa อาทิตย์ หน้า *next week*

aathít-nâa tʃán *tsà* pai thîiau kàp phûuan
อาทิตย์ หน้า ฉัน จะ ไป เที่ยว กับ เพื่อน
week-next I *will* go trip with friend
Next week, I am going to go out with my friend.

- Here the *future tense* is understood from the *time word* **aathít-nâa** อาทิตย์ หน้า *next week* and from the *tense marker* **tsà** จะ *will*.

- The future *tense marker* **tsà** จะ *will* is often used in all types of future actions.
- The English tense is the future with *going to*.

D. New Sounds

Long diphthongs and vowels combinations

a) Long diphthongs: **iia** เอีย, **ʉʉa** เอือ, **uua** อัว
   All long diphthongs constitute an *open-end sound*.

Examples:

sĭia	เสีย	to waste
lʉ̆ʉa	เหลือ	to be excessive
hŭua	หัว	head

In Thai, these sounds are called diphthongs. For our purposes, they can also be called vowel combinations. However, we shall follow the Thai way to classify sounds in this book.

b) Long vowel combinations: **eeu** เอว, **əəi** เอย, **ooi** โอย, **ɛɛu** แอว, **aai** อาย, **aau** อาว, **ɔɔi** ออย, **iiau** เอียว, **ʉʉai** เอือย, **uuai** อวย. These vowel combinations are special in the sense that they all end with either **i** or **u**.

All long vowel combinations constitute an *open-end sound*.

Examples:

leeu	เลว	to be bad
nəəi	เนย	butter
dooi	โดย	by, by means of
mɛɛu	แมว	cat
bàai	บ่าย	afternoon
yaau	ยาว	to be long

sɔɔi	ซอย	*side street*
diiau	เดียว	*alone*
nùuai	เหนื่อย	*to be tired*
dûuai	ด้วย	*by, with, also*

In Thai, we have many more vowel combinations than the English language has. All these vowel combinations are made from the pure simple vowel sounds.

We don't try to give here any English examples of these sounds since the Standard English vowel combinations are far less numerous.

We have now introduced all open-end sounds in Thai. In the following chapters, we shall talk about *closed end sounds* (dead endings).

E. Simple advice

As you may already have noticed, expressing the Thai time factor is quite simple compared to English. In Thai, several different English tenses merge into one Thai tense. For example, the future in English can be expressed by the *present simple tense, future simple tense,* the *future with going to,* etc. In Thai, anticipated future actions are normally expressed by the *future tense marker* **tsà** จะ *will.* You may think of it as if you would be expressing all the anticipated future actions in English with helping verb *will.* That is the Thai way.

When you hear Thai people speaking English, they may sometimes say: *yesterday, I go swimming* or *tomorrow I go to school.* There is not any difficulty to understand what is meant even though it is considered to be broken English. Often, Thais like to make things simple and speak English in the Thai way. The thinking goes: "What is the point to learn all those irregular verbs and complicated English tenses when you are understood anyway?"

So, as you already know, in Thai everything is in basic form; we just add words or understand the correct tense from the context. In English, we also need to use the correct tense forms when referring to different time phases.

When you are speaking Thai, things become much easier if you can think as Thai people do. It does not help you at all to bring the idea of the complicated English tense system into the Thai language. Thai people think about time as completed actions (past), actions that are happening now (present) and anticipated actions which may or may not happen in the future (wishes, hopes, possibilities etc.).

F. Take it further

Refer to the book:

Dhyan Manik: *Understanding the Thai Language and Grammar:*

- More about open end sounds can be found in Chapter 1, section 1.3.1.
- More about Thai tenses can be found in the following Chapters:
- Chapter 12: Adverbs – Adverbs of time, section 12.2
- Chapter 13: Commonly used verbs and **lɛ́ɛu** แล้ว *already*
- Chapter 17: The summary of the Thai tenses

Refer to the books:

1. Dhyan Manik: *Learning Thai Tenses with* **dâai** ได้ *– Book II* (ISBN 978-952-6651-20-0)
2. Dhyan Manik: *Learning Thai and Thai Tenses with* **lɛ́ɛu** แล้ว (ISBN 978-952-6651-44-6), coming out late 2020
3. David Smyth: *Thai – An Essential Grammar*
4. James Higbie & Snea Thinsan: *Thai Reference Grammar*
- When you are ready, you may wish to learn more about Thai tenses from these four books.

More information about Thai learning books can be found at www.thaibooks.net

Chapter 16

Thai tenses – duration of time / point of time

tɔɔn-níi tsɔɔn pen nák-sùksăa maa-dâai sìp dʉʉan lɛ́ɛu
ตอน นี้ จอห์น เป็น นัก ศึกษา มา ได้ สิบ เดือน แล้ว
Now, John has been a student for ten months already.

Chapter 16

Highlights

lέεu	แล้ว	*already*
maa	มา	*come*
dâai	ได้	*get*
pai	ไป	*go*
maa-dâai	มา ได้	*come and get*
tâng-tὲε	ตั้ง แต่	*since, from*
thîi-lέεu	ที่ แล้ว	*ago*
tsà	จะ	*will*
phai-nai	ภาย ใน	*within*

A. Sentences

1. Focusing on the ongoing actions – "up to now"

1.1 maa มา *come* and **lέεu** แล้ว *already*

tʃán rian năngsɯ̌ɯ *maa* tsèt dɯɯan *lέεu*
ฉัน เรียน หนังสือ มา เจ็ด เดือน แล้ว
I study book *come* seven month *already*
I have already been studying for seven months.

1.2 dâai ได้ *get* and **lέεu** แล้ว *already*

tʃán duu năng *dâai* săam tʃûua-moong *lέεu*
ฉัน ดู หนัง ได้ สาม ชั่ว โมง แล้ว
I see-movie *get* three during-hour *already*
I have already been watching a movie for three hours.

1.3 **maa-dâai** มา ได้ *come and get* and **lέεu** แล้ว *already*

tɔɔn-níi tsɔɔn pen nák-sùksăa *maa-dâai* sìp dʉʉan lέεu
ตอน นี้ จอห์น เป็น นัก ศึกษา มา ได้ สิบ เดือน แล้ว
at-this John be person-study *come-get* ten month
Now, John has been a student for ten months already.

1.4 **lέεu** แล้ว *already*

kháu yùu thîi-nîi naan *lέεu* เขา อยู่ ที่ นี่ นาน แล้ว
he stay place-this long *already*
He has already stayed here for a long time.

1.5 **tâng-tὲε** ตั้ง แต่ *since*

kháu khàp rót-théksîi *tâng-tὲε* pii *thîi-lέεu*
เขา ขับ รถ แท็กซี่ ตั้ง แต่ ปี ที่ แล้ว
he drive car-taxi long *set-since* year *that-already*
He has been driving a taxi since last year.

2 Focusing on the completed actions – past

2.1 **maa** มา *come*

tʃán tham-ngaan thîi mʉʉang-thai *maa* sǎam dʉʉan
ฉัน ทำ งาน ที่ เมือง ไทย มา สาม เดือน
I do-work state-Thai *come* three month
I have worked in Thailand for three months.

2.2 **dâai** ได้ *get*

tʃán duu năng *dâai* sǎam tʃûua-moong
ฉัน ดู หนัง ได้ สาม ชั่ว โมง
I see-movie *get* three during-hour
I have watched a movie for three hours.

2.3 **maa-dâai** มา ได้ *come and get*

piitɔ̂ɔ *khəəi* pen nák-kiilaa *maa-dâai* nùng pii
ปีเตอร์ เคย เป็น นัก กีฬา มา ได้ หนึ่ง ปี
Peter *once* be sportsman *come-get* one year
Peter used to be a sportsman for one year.

2.4 **pai** ไป *go*

tʃáu-níi tʃán tham-ngaan *pai* sǎam tʃûua-moong
เช้า นี้ ฉัน ทำ งาน ไป สาม ชั่ว โมง
morning-this I do-work *go* three during-hour
I worked for three hours this morning.

2.5 **mûua-kɔ̀ɔn** เมื่อ ก่อน *previously*

mûua-kɔ̀ɔn tʃán pen nák-sàdɛɛng hòk pii
เมื่อ ก่อน ฉัน เป็น นัก แสดง หก ปี
when-before I be actor six year
Previously, I was an actor for six years.

2.6 **thîi-lɛ́ɛu** ที่ แล้ว *ago*

tʃán kin-khâao sǎam sìp naa-thii *thîi-lɛ́ɛu*
ฉัน กิน ข้าว สาม สิบ นา ที ที่ แล้ว
I eat-rice three-ten minute *that-already*
I have eaten thirty minutes ago.

3 Focusing on the anticipated future actions

3.1 **tsà** จะ *will* and **dâai** ได้ *get*

pii-nâa tʃán *tsà* pai thîiau *dâai* tsèt wan
ปี หน้า ฉัน จะ ไป เที่ยว ได้ เจ็ด วัน
year-next I *will* go trip *get* seven day
Next year, I will go for a holiday for seven days.

3.2 **tsà** จะ *will* and **ìik** อีก *more*

tʃán *tsà* tham-ngaan *ìik* sìi pii ฉัน จะ ทำ งาน อีก สี่ ปี
I *will* do-work *more* four year
I will work for four more years.

3.3 **tsà** จะ *will* and **lɛ́ɛu** แล้ว *already*

ìik sɔ̌ɔng aathít tʃán tsà pai *lɛ́ɛu*
อีก สอง อาทิตย์ ฉัน จะ ไป แล้ว
more two week I will go *already*
In two weeks, I will already be gone.

3.4 **tsà** จะ *will* and **phai-nai** ภาย ใน *within*

tʃán tsà tham hâi sèt *phai-nai* hâa naathii
ฉัน จะ ทำ ให้ เสร็จ ภาย ใน ห้า นาที
I will do make finish – *part-in* five minute
I will finish it within five minutes.

Common expressions
(kham thîi tʃái bɔ̀i-bɔ̀i คำ ที่ ใช้ บ่อยๆ)

phaasǎa-thai yâak mái ภาษา ไทย ยาก ไหม
language-Thai difficult "question" – *Is Thai difficult?*

mâi mǔuan phaasǎa-angkrìt ไม่ เหมือน ภาษา อังกฤษ
no as language-English – *Not the same as English.*

phaasǎa-thai sànùk ภาษา ไทย สนุก
language-Thai fun – *Thai language is fun.*

hěn-dûuai mái เห็น ด้วย ไหม
see-with "question" – *Do you agree?*

B. Vocabulary

rian năngsɯ̌ɯ	เรียน หนังสือ	to study, to go to school
rian	เรียน	to study
năngsɯ̌ɯ	หนังสือ	book
maa tsèt dɯɯan lɛ́ɛu	มา เจ็ด เดือน แล้ว	for seven months
maa	มา	to come
lɛ́ɛu	แล้ว	already
tham-ngaan	ทำ งาน	to work
tham	ทำ	to do
ngaan	งาน	work
maa săam pii lɛ́ɛu	มา สาม ปี แล้ว	for three years
duu	ดู	to see, to watch
tʃûua-moong	ชั่ว โมง	hour
tʃûua	ชั่ว	during
moong	โมง	hour, o'clock
rót-théksîi	รถ แท็กซี่	taxi
tâng-tɛ̀ɛ	ตั้ง แต่	since
tâng	ตั้ง	up to, to set
tɛ̀ɛ	แต่	from, since, but
pii-thîi-lɛ́ɛu	ปี ที่ แล้ว	last year
naan-lɛ́ɛu	นาน แล้ว	long time ago
mɯɯang-thai	เมือง ไทย	Thailand
mɯɯang	เมือง	state, city
khəəi	เคย	once, used to be
pen	เป็น	to be
nák-kiilaa	นัก กีฬา	sportsman
mûɯa-kɔ̀ɔn	เมื่อ ก่อน	before, earlier

Chapter 16

nák-sàdɛɛng	นัก แสดง	actor
tʃáu-níi	เช้า นี้	this morning
pai	ไป	to go
tʃûua-moong	ชั่ว โมง	hour, hours
pii-nâa	ปี หน้า	next year
pai-thîiau	ไป เที่ยว	to go out, to take a holiday
tsèt wan	เจ็ด วัน	seven days
ìik sɔ̌ɔng aathít	อีก สอง อาทิตย์	in two weeks
tsà pai lɛ́ɛu	จะ ไป แล้ว	will be gone
tsà tham	จะ ทำ	will do
hâi sèt	ให้ เสร็จ	to finish
phai-nai	ภาย ใน	in, within
hâa naathii	ห้า นาที	five minutes
tɔɔn-níi	ตอน นี้	now
nák-sùksăa	นัก ศึกษา	student
maa	มา	to come
sìp dɯɯan	สิบ เดือน	ten months
ìik sìi pii	อีก สี่ ปี	four more years
phaasăa-thai	ภาษา ไทย	Thai language
yâak	ยาก	difficult
mái	ไหม	basic question word
mâi	ไม่	no
mɯ̌ɯan	เหมือน	as, like
phaasăa-angkrìt	ภาษา อังกฤษ	English
sànùk	สนุก	fun
hěn-dûuai	เห็น ด้วย	to agree
hěn	เห็น	to see
dûuai	ด้วย	also, with, as well

C. How the language works

With the sentences referring to the duration of time, the time indicator **lέεu** แล้ว *already* at the end of the statement is used for more flow and emphasis; it tells that the action has already been going on *up to now, so far* (for so long).

There are several verbs which can be placed before the duration of time.

For different emphasis, we may use either **dâai** ได้, **maa** มา, **maa-dâai** มา ได้ or **pai** ไป before the duration of time.

In English, we usually express this structure with the *present perfect continuous tense* (I have been living...) or with the *present perfect tense* (I have lived...) and the preposition *for* before the duration of time.

However, the English tense does not tell anything about the nuances we can express with **dâai** ได้, **maa** มา, **maa-dâai** มา ได้ or **pai** ไป when placed before the duration of time.

Examples:

 Focusing on the ongoing actions – "up to now"

When the time indicator **lέεu** แล้ว is placed at the end of the sentence and after the duration of time, it expresses the continuation of the action: *so far, up to now, already.*

> tɕʰán rian nǎngsɯ̌ɯ tsèt dɯɯan *lέεu*
> ฉัน เรียน หนังสือ เจ็ด เดือน แล้ว
> I study book seven month *already*
> *I have already been studying for seven months.*

- The simplest way to express the ongoing action is to place **lέεu** แล้ว *already* after the duration of time at the end of the sentence.

- In this sentence, we have dropped the helping verbs (**dâai** ได้ or **maa** มา) before the duration of time.

- **lɛ́ɛu แล้ว** *already* at the end of the statement is enough to denote the fact that the action is an ongoing action; the feeling is *"up to now, so far"*.
- The English tense is the *present perfect continuous tense* (I have been...)

> **2** tʃǎn rian nǎngsɯ̌ɯ *maa* tsèt dɯɯan *lɛ́ɛu*
> ฉัน เรียน หนังสือ มา เจ็ด เดือน แล้ว
> I study book *come* seven month *already*
> *I have already been studying for seven months.*

- We may add the helping verb **maa** มา *to come* before the duration of time. **maa** มา *to come* is translated into English as *for*; the feeling is *"having time"*.
- **lɛ́ɛu แล้ว** *already* at the end of the statement tells that the action is an ongoing action; the feeling is *"up to now, so far"*.
- The English tense is the *present perfect continuous tense* (I have been...)

> **3** tʃǎn rian nǎngsɯ̌ɯ *dâai* naan *lɛ́ɛu*
> ฉัน เรียน หนังสือ ได้ นาน แล้ว
> I study book *get* long *already*
> *I have already been studying for a long time.*

- We may add the helping verb **dâai** ได้ *to get* before the duration of time. **dâai** ได้ *to get* is translated into English as *for*; the feeling is *"getting time"*.
- **lɛ́ɛu แล้ว** *already* at the end of the statement tells that the action is an ongoing action; the feeling is *"up to now, so far"*.
- The English tense is the *present perfect continuous tense* (I have been...)

> **4** tʃán rian nǎngsɯ̌ɯ *maa-dâai* naan *lɛ́ɛu*
> ฉัน เรียน หนังสือ มา ได้ นาน แล้ว
> I study book *come-get* long *already*
> *I have already been studying for a long time.*

- We may add the helping verb **maa-dâai** ได้ *to come-to get* before the duration of time. **maa-dâai** ได้ *to come-to get* is translated into English as *for*; the feeling is *"having and getting time"*.
- **lɛ́ɛu** แล้ว *already* at the end of the statement tells that the action is an ongoing action; the feeling is *"up to now, so far"*.
- The English tense is the *present perfect continuous tense* (I have been...)

> **5** tʃán rian nǎngsɯ̌ɯ *pai* naan *lɛ́ɛu*
> ฉัน เรียน หนังสือ ไป นาน แล้ว
> I study book *go* long *already*
> *I have already been studying for a long time.*

- We may add the helping verb **pai** ได้ *to go* before the duration of time. **pai** ได้ *to go* is translated into English as *for*; the feeling is *"losing time"*.
- **lɛ́ɛu** แล้ว *already* at the end of the statement tells that the action is an ongoing action; the feeling is *"up to now, so far"*.
- The English tense is the *present perfect continuous tense* (I have been...)

> **6** tʃán rian nǎngsɯ̌ɯ *tâng-tɛ̀ɛ* pii thîi-lɛ́ɛu
> ฉัน เรียน หนังสือ ตั้ง แต่ ปี ที่ แล้ว
> I study book *set-from* year that-already
> *I have already been studying since last year.*

Chapter 16

- This is also an ongoing action. **tâng-tɛ̀ɛ** ตั้ง แต่ *since* is placed before the *point of time;* it is used in the similar way as the English word *since* is used.
- The English tense is the *present perfect continuous tense* (I have been...)

B) Focusing on completed actions – past

> **1** tʃán rian năngsŭɯ tsèt dɯɯan
> ฉัน เรียน หนังสือ เจ็ด เดือน
> I study book seven month
> *I have studied for seven months.*

- Here we have dropped all time words and tense markers. Depending on the context, the sentence can be understood as past tense.
- The action has been completed sometimes in the past.
- The English tense is the *present perfect tense* (I have…)

> **2** *mɯ̂ɯa-kɔ̀ɔn* tʃán rian năngsɯ̌ɯ *maa* tsèt dɯɯan
> เมื่อ ก่อน ฉัน เรียน หนังสือ มา เจ็ด เดือน
> *when-before* I study book *come* seven month
> *Previously, I have studied for seven months.*

> **3** *mɯ̂ɯa-kɔ̀ɔn* tʃán rian năngsɯ̌ɯ *dâai* tsèt dɯɯan
> เมื่อ ก่อน ฉัน เรียน หนังสือ ได้ เจ็ด เดือน
> *when-before* I study book *get* seven month
> Previously, I have studied *for* seven months.

- In the sentences 2 and 3, we have placed the time word **mɯ̂ɯa-kɔ̀ɔn** *before* เมื่อ ก่อน at the beginning of the sentence to emphasize the fact that the action has taken place before now.
- For different emphasis, we may add **dâai** ได้ *to get* or **maa** มา before the duration of time.

- The translation into English remains the same in both sentences 2 and 3.
- The English tense is the *present perfect tense* (I have…)

> **4** tʃán *khəəi* rian nǎngsǔɯ *dâai* tsèt dɯɯan
> ฉัน เคย เรียน หนังสือ ได้ เจ็ด เดือน
> I *once* study book *get* seven month
> *I have studied for seven months.*

- **khəəi** เคย *once, used to* is a tense marker and needs to be placed before the action verb. See more about how to use tense markers in the previous Chapter 15.
- With **khəəi** เคย the sentence always refers to the past.
- The English tense is the *present perfect tense* (I have…)

> **5** tʃán rian nǎngsǔɯ tsèt dɯɯan *thîi-lɛ́ɛu*
> ฉัน เรียน หนังสือ เจ็ด เดือน ที่ แล้ว
> I study book seven month *that-already*
> *I studied seven months ago.*

- When **thîi-lɛ́ɛu** ที่ แล้ว *ago* is placed after the time phase, the meaning changes from *for seven months* to *seven months ago*.
- The English tense is the *past simple tense* (I studied…)

C) Focusing on anticipated actions – future

> **1** tʃán *tsà* rian nǎngsǔɯ tsèt dɯɯan
> ฉัน จะ เรียน หนังสือ เจ็ด เดือน
> I *will* study book seven month
> *I will study for seven months.*

- In this sentence we have used the future tense marker **tsà** จะ *will* to express the future.

Chapter 16

- The English tense is the *future simple tense* (I will…)

> **2** tʃán *tsà* rian năngsɯ̌ɯ *dâai* tsèt dɯɯan
> ฉัน จะ เรียน หนังสือ ได้ เจ็ด เดือน
> I *will* study book *get* seven month
> *I will study for seven months.*

- In this sentence we have used the future tense marker **tsà** จะ *will* to express the future.
- For different emphasis, we may add **dâai** ได้ *to get* before the duration of time; the translation into English remains the same as the previous sentence 1.
- **dâai** ได้ can be used with ongoing, completed or future actions.
- The English tense is the *future simple tense* (I will…)

> **2.1** tʃán *tsà* rian năngsɯ̌ɯ *maa* tsèt dɯɯan
> ฉัน จะ เรียน หนังสือ ได้ เจ็ด เดือน
> I *will* study book *come* seven month
> *I will study for seven months.*

- This sentence is not correct.
- **maa** มา *to come* is not used before the duration of time with anticipated future actions.
- **maa** มา *to come* is commonly only used before the duration of time with actions that have started *in the past and are ongoing* or *completed in the past*.
- So, this sentence would be grammatically wrong.

> **3** *pii-nâa* tʃán *tsà* rian năngsɯ̌ɯ (*dâai*) tsèt dɯɯan
> ปี หน้า ฉัน จะ เรียน หนังสือ (ได้) เจ็ด เดือน
> year-next I *will* study book (*get*) seven month
> *Next year, I will study for seven months.*

- We may add the future time word **pii-nâa** ปีหน้า *next year* at the beginning of the sentence to give the actual time when the action will take place.
- **dâai** ได้ *to get* may be dropped here; the translation into English would be the same.
- Colour of the sentence in Thai is different, however.
- The English tense is the *future simple tense* (I will…)

D. New sounds

Basically, we can divide the Thai end sounds in two broad categories, *open sounds* and *closed sounds*. Previously, we introduced the open consonant and vowel end sounds.

In this chapter, we shall study the closed consonant end sounds in more detail since they play an important role as far as the tonal structure of the Thai language is concerned. Closed end sounds at the end of the word or syllable are made by so called stop consonants. The sound is suddenly stopped in the mouth either by the lips or tongue, or is stopped in the glottis.

There are only three stop consonant end sounds which constitute a closed end sound in Thai. They are **p, t** and **k**.

Note that in transliterations you will only meet **p, t** or **k** as the end sound. So, unless you already know or want to know the Thai script, it is enough to understand how to pronounce these sounds. Stop end sounds are also sometimes called *dead endings*. They are not released but suddenly stopped in the mouth. They are kind of buried in the mouth. The stop end sound **k** is a special sound since you need to stop the sound deep in the glottis, often also called a *glottal stop*.

The good news is that even if you pronounce these unaspirated end sounds (**p, t** and **k**) aspirated as in English (**ph, th** and **kh**), you will be understood. For instance, if you say lûu**kh** *child* (aspirated **kh**) instead of lûu**k** ลูก *child* (unaspirated **k**), you will be most likely understood – but with a slight smile from your Thai listener who may be thinking that you are making a simple thing unnecessarily complicated.

E. Simple advice

In casual speech, we can omit **dâai** ได้, **maa** มา, **pai** ไป or **maa-dâai** มา ได้ before the duration of time, and the sentence would be correct. The translation into English would still be the same. Then, it is a simple statement telling *for how long*. It is your personal choice whether you like to emphasize nuances with **dâai** ได้, **maa** มา, **maa-dâai** มา ได้, **pai** ไป or leave them out. We take them up here since you will meet these verbs on many occasions and also in Thai learning books; the difference is not always clearly explained.

If you would like to express actions which have started in the past and are not yet completed, then just place the time indicator **lέεu** แล้ว *already* after the duration of time at the end of the sentence. Then, the meaning is that the action has already been going on *up to now, so far* for so long.

While looking at signs in Thailand, you may see that the word **sàwàt-dii** สวัสดี *welcome* is often written as **sawasdii** สวัสดี. In a way, it is correct because in the Thai script, this closed end sound is written with the consonant **s**. The third consonant in the Thai script is the consonant **s** ส. However, since in transliterations we write Thai sounds with western letters, then **t** would be more correct since it is the actual spoken sound in Thai.

F. Take it further

Refer to the book:

Dhyan Manik: *Understanding the Thai Language and Grammar:*

- More about closed end sounds can be found in Chapter 1, section 1.3.2.
- More about the glottal stop can be found in Chapter 1, section 1.3.3.
- More information about the duration of time and the point of time can be found in Chapter 17, section 17.8.

Refer to the books:

1. Dhyan Manik: *Learning Thai Tenses with **dâai** ได้ – Book II* (ISBN 978-952-6651-20-0)
2. Dhyan Manik: *Learning Thai and Thai Tenses with **lɛ́ɛu** แล้ว* (ISBN 978-952-6651-44-6), coming out late 2020
3. David Smyth: *Thai – An Essential Grammar*
4. Higbie & Thinsan: *Thai Reference Grammar – The Structure of Spoken Thai*

- When you are ready, you may wish to learn more about Thai tenses and how to express the duration of time from these four books.

Chapter 17

Expression of time: clock time, days, months, years...

bàai-moong khrûng sàdùuak mái
บ่าย โมง ครึ่ง สะดวก ไหม
Is 1.30 p.m. convenient for you?

Highlights

Clock time

tɔɔn-tʃáu	ตอน เช้า	in the morning, early morning (7–9 a.m.)
tɔɔn-bàai	ตอน บ่าย	in the afternoon (1–3 p.m.)
tɔɔn-yen	ตอน เย็น	in the late afternoon (3–6 p.m.)
tɔɔn-khâm	ตอน ค่ำ	at sunset, in the evening (6–11 p.m.)
tɔɔn-klaang-khɯɯn	ตอน กลาง คืน	at night time
tɔɔn-thîiang-khɯɯn	ตอน เที่ยง คืน	at midnight (12 a.m.)
tɔɔn-klaang-wan	ตอน กลาง วัน	at day time
tɔɔn-thîiang-wan	ตอน เที่ยง วัน	at noon (12 p.m.)

Days, weeks, months etc.

wan-tsan	วันจันทร์	Monday
aathít-nâa	อาทิตย์ หน้า	next week
pii-thîi-lɛ́ɛu	ปี ที่ แล้ว	last year
mók-kàraa-khom	มกราคม	January
wan thîi sǎam-sìp-èt	วัน ที่ สาม สิบ เอ็ด	the 31st

A. Sentences

 tsəə-kan *mûua-rai* khá   เจอ กัน เมื่อ ไร คะ
meet-with *when* khá – When shall we meet?

2 *tɔɔn-yen* ookhee mái ตอน เย็น โอเค ไหม
at-cool OK "question" – *Is the late afternoon OK?*

3 *kìi-moong* khá กี่ โมง คะ
how-many hour khá – *What time?*

4 *sìi moong yen* dii mái สี่ โมง เย็น ดี ไหม
four hour cool good "question"
Is four o'clock in the afternoon fine?

5 *sìi moong khrûng* dii-kwàa สี่ โมง ครึ่ง ดี กว่า
four hour half good-more – *Half past four is even better.*

6 lɛ́ɛu – tsəə-kan *sìi moong khrûng*
แล้ว – เจอ กัน สี่ โมง ครึ่ง
then – meet-with *four hour half*
Let us meet half past four then.

Going out

7 khun yàak pai thîau phrûng-níi *tɔɔn-bàai* mái
คุณ อยาก ไป เที่ยว พรุ่ง นี้ ตอน บ่าย ไหม
you want go out tomorrow *afternoon* "question"
Do you want to go out tomorrow afternoon?

8 *lɛ́ɛu-tɛ̀ɛ khun* แล้ว แต่ คุณ
then-just you – *It is up to you!*

9 *bàai-moong* sàdùuak mái บ่าย โมง สะดวก ไหม
afternoon-hour convenient "question"
Is 1 p.m. convenient for you?

10 khɔ̌ɔ-thôot ná – *mâi sàdùuak* khâ – *tʃán yûng*
ขอโทษ นะ – ไม่ สะดวก ค่ะ – ฉัน ยุ่ง
ask-pardon ná – *no convenient* khâ – *I busy*
Sorry, it is not convenient. I am busy.

11 *kìi-moong dii – tɔɔn-khâm dii mái*
กี่ โมง ดี – ตอน ค่ำ ดี ไหม
how-many hour good – *at evening good* "question"
What time is fine? Is the evening time OK?

12 *kìi-moong kɔ̂ɔ-dâai* กี่ โมง ก็ ได้
how-many hour also can – Any time is fine!

13 *săam thûm khun àat-tsà wâang*
สาม ทุ่ม คุณ อาจ จะ ว่าง
3 p.m. you perhaps-will free
Perhaps, you are free at 9 p.m.

14 mâi wâang khâ – tʃán mii nát *léeu*
ไม่ ว่าง ค่ะ – ฉัน มี นัด แล้ว
no free khâ – I have appointment *already*
I am not free. I already have an appointment.

15 tsəə-kan aathít-nâa wan-angkhaan *thîiang-wan*
เจอ กัน อาทิตย์ หน้า วัน อังคาร เที่ยง วัน
meet-with week-next day-Tuesday *at noon*
Let's meet next Tuesday at noon then.

16 ookhee khâ – tʃán tsà thoo-hăa khun phrûng-níi *bàai săam moong*
โอเค ค่ะ – ฉัน จะ โทร หา คุณ พรุ่ง นี้ บ่าย สาม โมง
OK I will phone-search you tomorrow *afternoon three hour*
Ok, I'll call you tomorrow 3 p.m.

Travelling

17 *dɯɯan sɔ̌ɔng* pii-nâa tʃán tsà pai tʃiiang-mài
เดือน สอง ปี หน้า ฉัน จะ ไป เชียงใหม่
month two year-next I will go Chiang Mai
In February, next year, I will go to Chiang Mai.

18 tsà pai *yang ngai* จะ ไป ยังไง
will go *like-how* – *How are you going to go?*

19 tsà *nâng khrŵang-bin* จะ นั่ง เครื่อง บิน
will *sit machine-fly* – *I am going to fly.*

20 tsà ɔ̀ɔk *kìi-moong* khá จะ ออก กี่ โมง คะ
will leave *what-hour* khá – *What time will you leave?*

21 khrŵang-bin tʃán tsà ɔ̀ɔk *sìp moong tʃáu*
เครื่อง บิน ฉัน จะ ออก สิบ โมง เช้า
machine-fly I will leave *10 hour morning*
My plane leaves at 10 a.m.

22 tsà klàp maa *mŵa-rai* khá จะ กลับ มา เมื่อ ไร คะ
will return come *when* khá – *When will you be returning?*

23 wan thîi sǎam-sìp-èt mókkàraa-khom kɔ̀ɔn *thîiang-khuun*
วัน ที่ สาม สิบ เอ็ด มกรา คม ก่อน เที่ยง คืน
day at three-ten-one January before *midnight*
Thirty-first of January before midnight.

24 tʃán mii *tǔua-pai-klàp* lɛ́ɛu ฉัน มี ตั๋ว ไป กลับ แล้ว
I have *ticket-go-return* already – *I already have a return ticket.*

Common expressions
(kham thîi tʃái bɔ̀i-bɔ̀i คำ ที่ ใช้ บ่อยๆ)

arai-kɔ̂ɔ-dâai อะไร ก็ ได้
what also can – *Anything is OK.*

tham taam sàbaai ทำ ตาม สบาย
do as happy – *Do as you wish.*

> tham taam tsai ʧɔ̂ɔp ทำ ตาม ใจ ชอบ
> do as heart like – *Do as you like.*
>
> sàbaai-sàbaai สบายๆ
> happy-happy – *To feel at ease.*

B. Vocabulary

tsəə	เจอ	to meet
kan	กัน	together, with
mûɯa-rai	เมื่อ ไร	when?
tɔɔn-yen	ตอน เย็น	late afternoon, (3–6 p.m.)
tɔɔn	ตอน	at
yen	เย็น	to be cool
mái	ไหม	basic question word
kìi-moong	กี่ โมง	what time
kìi	กี่	how much, how many?
moong	โมง	hour
sìi moong yen	สี่ โมง เย็น	4 p.m.
sìi moong khrɯ̂ng	สี่ โมง ครึ่ง	half past four
khûn	ขึ้น	to rise, to progress
lɛ́ɛu	แล้ว	then, already
yàak	อยาก	to want
pai thîau	ไป เที่ยว	to go out
tɔɔn-bàai	ตอน บ่าย	in the afternoon
bàai	บ่าย	afternoon
lɛ́ɛu-tɛ̀ɛ khun	แล้ว แต่ คุณ	it is up to you
lɛ́ɛu-tɛ̀ɛ	แล้ว แต่	up to, depends on

Chapter 17

bàai-moong	บ่าย โมง	in the afternoon
sàdùuak	สะดวก	convenient, comfortable
khɔ̌ɔ-thôot	ขอโทษ	sorry, excuse me
yûng	ยุ่ง	to be busy
tɔɔn-khâm	ตอน ค่ำ	at sunset, evening
arai-kɔ̂ɔ-dâai	อะไร ก็ ได้	whatever, anything is fine
àat-tsà	อาจ จะ	perhaps, maybe
sǎam thûm	สาม ทุ่ม	9 p.m.
wâang	ว่าง	to be free
mii nát	มี นัด	to have a date, an appointment
tsəə-kan	เจอ กัน	to meet
aathít-nâa	อาทิตย์ หน้า	next week
wan-angkhaan	วัน อังคาร	Tuesday
thîiang-wan	เที่ยง วัน	at noon
thoo-hǎa	โทร หา	to call
bàai sǎam moong	บ่าย สาม โมง	3 p.m.
dɯɯan sɔ̌ɔng	เดือน สอง	February
pii-nâa	ปี หน้า	next year
tsà pai	จะ ไป	will go
yang-ngai	ยังไง	how
tsà bin	จะ บิน	going to fly
khrûɯang-bin	เครื่อง บิน	airplane
khrûɯang	เครื่อง	machine
tsà ɔ̀ɔk	จะ ออก	will leave
kìi-moong	กี่ โมง	when, at what time?
khrûɯang-bin tʃán	เครื่อง บิน ฉัน	my plane
sìp moong tʃáu	สิบ โมง เช้า	10 a.m.

tsà klàp	จะ กลับ	will return
mûa-rai	เมื่อไร	when?
wan thîi săam-sìp-èt	วัน ที่ สาม สิบ เอ็ด	31st of...
mókkàraa-khom	มกรา คม	January
thîiang khɯɯn	เที่ยง คืน	at midnight
tŭua-pai-klàp	ตั๋ว ไป กลับ	return ticket
tŭua	ตั๋ว	ticket
pai	ไป	to go
klàp	กลับ	to return
arai-kɔ̂ɔ-dâai	อะไร ก็ ได้	whatever, anything is fine
tham	ทำ	to do
taam	ตาม	to follow, as
sàbaai	สบาย	to be happy, to be well
tsai	ใจ	heart
tʃɔ̂ɔp	ชอบ	to like

C. How the language works

To express the clock time in Thai is somewhat complicated. There are two different ways to tell the time. However, we discuss here the most common way which is normally used by Thais everyday while speaking.

The Thai clock time is divided into 4 sections, each containing 6 hours. The difficulty arises from the fact that the clock time in the morning, afternoon, evening and at night is expressed differently.

We have the following words to play with:

moong	โมง	*hour* (used in the morning and afternoon)
tʃáu	เช้า	*morning* (6 a.m.–12 a.m.)

bàai	บ่าย	*early afternoon* (1 p.m.–4 p.m.)
yen	เย็น	*late afternoon* (4 p.m.–7 p.m.)
thûm	ทุ่ม	*evening time* (7 p.m.–12 a.m.)
thîiang wan	เที่ยง วัน	*midday, noon* (12 p.m.)
thîiang khɯɯn	เที่ยง คืน	*midnight* (12 a.m.)
tii	ตี	*night time* (1 a.m.–5 a.m.)

In order to make the complicated Thai way to tell the clock time a little easier, we shall first divide the 24 hours into two parts: *when the sun is up (bright)* and *when the sun is down (dark)*. Bright and dark periods can be divided into two parts as follows:

A) When the sun is up, we use **moong** โมง *hour* in the morning and in the afternoon. It is bright.

1. Morning

moong โมง *hour* + **tʃáu** เช้า *morning* (bright)

6 a.m.	= hòk **moong tʃáu**	หก โมง เช้า
7 a.m.	= tsèt **moong tʃáu**	เจ็ด โมง เช้า
8 a.m.	= pɛ̀ɛt **moong tʃáu**	แปด โมง เช้า
9 a.m.	= kâau **moong tʃáu**	เก้า โมง เช้า
10 a.m	= sìp **moong tʃáu**	สิบ โมง เช้า
11 a.m.	= sìp èt **moong tʃáu**	สิบ เอ็ด โมง เช้า
12 p.m.	= **thîiang wan**	เที่ยง วัน 12 p.m. (noon, midday)

2. Afternoon

bàai บ่าย *early afternoon* + **moong** โมง *hour* (bright)

1 p.m.	= **bàai** (nɯ̀ng) **moong**	บ่าย (หนึ่ง) โมง
2 p.m.	= **bàai** sɔ̌ɔng **moong**	บ่าย สอง โมง
3 p.m.	= **bàai** sǎam **moong**	บ่าย สาม โมง
4 p.m.	= **bàai** sìi **moong**	บ่าย สี่ โมง

moong โมง *hour* + **yen** เย็น *cool, late afternoon*

4 p.m.	= sìi **moong yen**	สี่ โมง เย็น
5 p.m.	= hâa **moong yen**	ห้า โมง เย็น
6 p.m.	= hòk **moong yen**	หก โมง เย็น

At 1 p.m., the number 1 **nùng** หนึ่ง is usually dropped. After 4 p.m., Thais normally drop **bàai** บ่าย and start to talk about **yen** เย็น *cool* time.

B) When the *sun is down*, we use **thûm** ทุ่ม *evening time* and **tii** ตี *night time*. It is dark, and the sun has set.

In the old days when there were no clocks, the watchman would hit the drum at each hour to tell the time. **thûm** ทุ่ม *drum* (evening time) and **tii** ตี *hit* (night time) are still used today to tell the time.

3. Evening

thûm ทุ่ม *drum time* (dark)

7 p.m.	= nùng **thûm**	หนึ่ง ทุ่ม
8 p.m.	= sɔ̌ɔng **thûm**	สอง ทุ่ม
9 p.m.	= sǎam **thûm**	สาม ทุ่ม
10 p.m.	= sìi **thûm**	สี่ ทุ่ม
11 p.m.	= hâa **thûm**	ห้า ทุ่ม
12 a.m.	= **thîiang khuun**	เที่ยง คืน *midnight*

4. Night

tii ตี *to hit* + number (dark)

12 a.m.	= **thîiang khuun**	เที่ยง คืน *midnight*
1 a.m	= **tii** nùng	ตี หนึ่ง
2 a.m.	= **tii** sɔ̌ɔng	ตี สอง
3 a.m.	= **tii** sǎam	ตี สาม
4 a.m.	= **tii** sìi	ตี สี่
5 a.m.	= **tii** hâa	ตี ห้า

Chapter 17

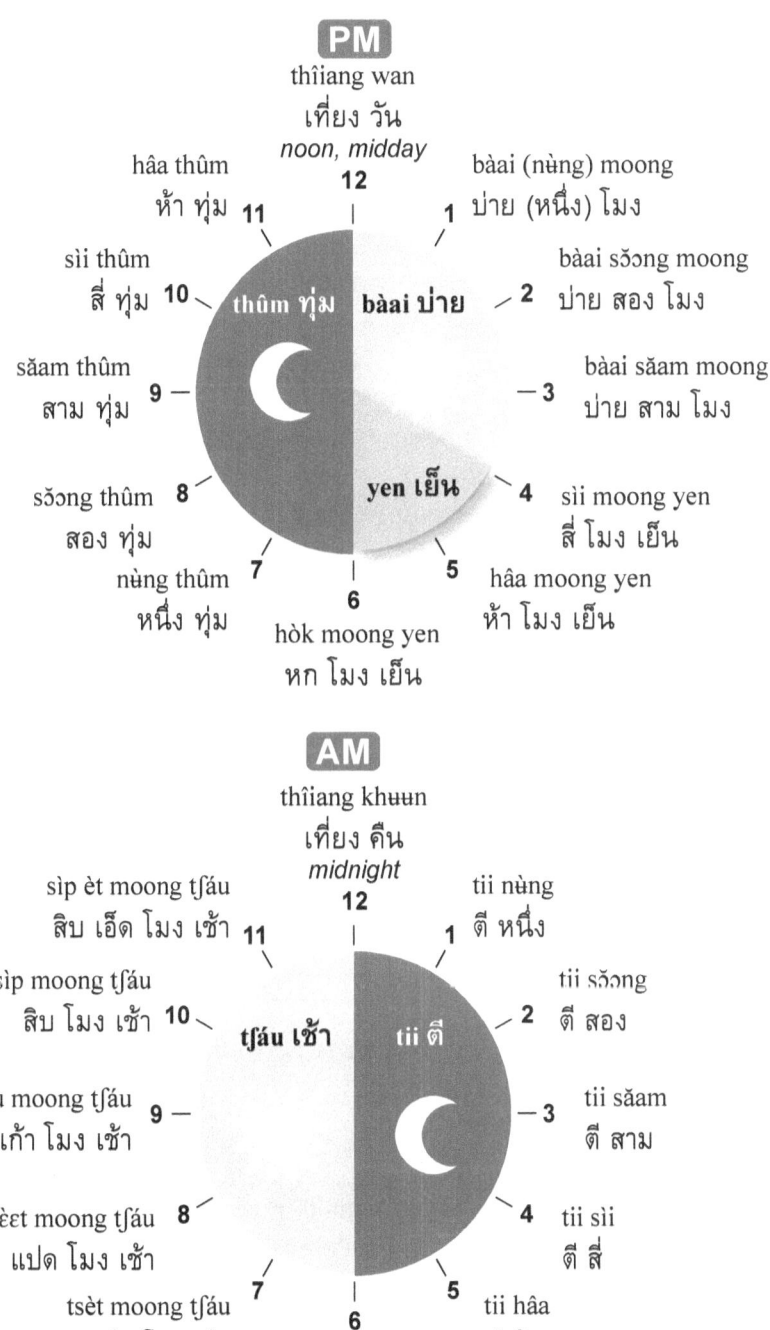

Chapter 17

C) Asking time in Thai

mûua-rai เมื่อไร *when* and **kìi-moong** กี่ โมง *what time* (literally how much hour)

Examples:

> **1** khun tsà pai *mûua-rai* คุณ จะ ไป เม่อื ไร
> you will go *when* – When are you going?

> **2** khun tsà pai *kìi-moong* คุณ จะ ไป กี่ โมง
> you will go *what-hour*
> What time are you going?

> **3** khun tsà pai *phrûng-níi* mái คุณ จะ ไป พรุ่ง นี้ ไหม
> you will go *tomorrow* "question"
> Are you going tomorrow?

> **4** khun tsà pai *phrûng-níi kìi-moong*
> คุณ จะ ไป พรุ่ง นี้ กี่ โมง
> you will go *tomorrow what-hour*
> What time are you going tomorrow?

> **5** tɔɔn-níi *kìi-moong* lέεu ตอน นี้ กี่ โมง แล้ว
> at-this *what-hour* already
> What time is it now?

D) When referring to days, we usually place **wan** วัน *day* before the week days. So, Wednesday becomes *day Wednesday*, **wan phút** วัน พุธ (literally day Mercury)

Examples:

wan-tsan	วัน จันทร์	*Monday*
wan-angkhaan	วัน อังคาร	*Tuesday*
wan-phút	วัน พุธ	*Wednesday*
wan-phárúhàt	วัน พฤหัส	*Thursday*
wan-sùk	วัน ศุกร์	*Friday*
wan-său	วัน เสาร์	*Saturday*
wan-aathít	วัน อาทิตย์	*Sunday*

The names of the weekdays are borrowed from Bali/Sanskrit oriented languages.

One particular feature of the week days is that **wan-sau-aathít** วัน เสาร์ อาทิตย์ *day-Saturday-Sunday* is commonly used to also express the English meaning *weekend*.

Another way to express the resting day or holiday is to use the expression **wan-yùt** วัน หยุด *holiday, a day off* (literally day-stop). **yùt** หยุด means *to stop*.

E) Months and dates

1. When you learn the names of the months in Thai, you do not need to remember how many days there are in one particular month.

    There are two main suffixes which are attached to the name of the month, **khom** คม and **yon** ยน. They are actually included in the name of the month and are not usually left out.

    khom คม denotes 31 days and **yon** ยน denotes 30 days.

Examples:

mókkàraa-khom	มกรา คม	*January*
kumphaa-phan	กุมภา พันธ์	*February*
miinaa-khom	มีนา คม	*March*
mee-săa-yon	เมษา ยน	*April*
phrútsàphaa-khom	พฤษภา คม	*May*
míthùnaa-yon	มิถุนา ยน	*June*
kàrákàdaa-khom	กรกฎา คม	*July*
sĭnghăa-khom	สิงหา คม	*August*
kanyaa-yon	กันยา ยน	*September*
tùlaa-khom	ตุลา คม	*October*
phrútsàtsìkaa-yon	พฤศจิกา ยน	*November*
thanwaa-khom	ธันวา คม	*December*

- Naturally, we need one more suffix; it is **phan** พันธ์ for February.

2. If you have forgotten the name of the month, you may use numbers; there will be no problem at all.

Examples:

duuan nùng	เดือน หนึ่ง	month 1 = *January*
duuan sɔ̆ɔng	เดือน สอง	month 2 = *February*
duuan săam	เดือน สาม	month 3 = *March*
duuan sìi	เดือน สี่	month 4 = *April*
etc.		

Many Asian languages such as Chinese and Cambodian use this kind of classification. However, Thais normally like to use the proper name of the month.

F) **tŭua-thîau-diau** ตั๋ว เที่ยว เดียว *one-way ticket* **tŭua-pai-klàp** ตั๋ว ไป กลับ *return ticket*

Chapter 17   229

Examples:

 tʃán mii *tŭua-thîau-diau* thâu-nán
ฉัน มี ตั๋ว เที่ยว เดียว เท่า นั้น
I have *ticket trip-one* only – *I have only a one-way ticket.*

 tʃán mii *tŭua-pai-klàp* lέεu ฉัน มี ตั๋ว ไป กลับ แล้ว
I have *ticket-go-return* already
I already have a return ticket.

The terms **tŭua-thîau-diau** ตั๋ว เที่ยว เดียว *one way ticket* and **tŭua-pai-klàp** ตั๋ว ไป กลับ *return ticket* are normally used when booking a trip.

D. New sounds

All *short vowels* at the end of the word constitute a *closed ending*. They are suddenly stopped in the glottis and are kind of "buried" in the mouth in the similar way as the *stop consonant* **k**. That kind of a closed ending is sometimes called "a glottal stop." In English a *glottal stop* is used, for example, in the word **about**. The first vowel sound **a** is stopped in the glottis. We must use the gottal stop since the mouth is open, and the sound is not stopped by the lips or tongue.

There are nine short vowels in Thai.

Short vowels: ì อิ, ǜ อื, ǜ อุ, è เอะ, ɜ̀ เออะ, ò โอะ, ɛ̀ แอะ, à อะ, ɔ̀ เอาะ

Examples:

tó	โต๊ะ	*table*
phrɔ́	เพราะ	*because*
thɜ̀	เถอะ	*particle for emphasis*
arai	อะไร	*what?*
sàbaai	สบาย	*to be fine*

E. Simple advice

As far as expressing clock time in Thai is concerned, there is no other way than to learn to express the clock time as we have outlined in this chapter. It is normally used by all Thais in speaking. In the beginning, it feels somewhat strange, but when you start using it, you will get used to it quite fast.

There is another way to tell the time called the 24 hour clock, which is used in time tables and official situations. It will be explained in the book: *Understanding the Thai Language and Grammar - Take It Further*.

The grammar rules in Thai are very straightforward. For instance, a verb is not needed for a sentence to be complete. "You pretty" suffices for "you are pretty". Each and every word is always in its basic form. For example: verbs are not conjugated, there are no tenses for verbs, there are no plural forms for nouns and no genders or articles like a, an or the. As an illustration of this, in English we would say, "I drove him to the school", but the same in Thai would be, "I drive he school". The context would reveal the tense. Difficulty arises from the fact that there are a vast number of words and synonyms to be used in different situations. As a foreigner you need to learn to use the right word in the right context. You must consider whom you are talking to and where. This requires some sensitivity on your part to the cultural differences in Thai society.

Since the grammar is simple, the choice of words and their order within the sentence become very important. Some words go together while others do not. There are words which have multiple meanings and are used in a grammatical sense in many different ways. If you know how to use these words well, you are well on the way to speak Thai fluently.

F. Take it further

Refer to the book:

Dhyan Manik: *Understanding the Thai Language and Grammar:*

- More about closed end sounds can be found in Chapter 1, section 1.3.2.
- More about the glottal stop can be found in Chapter 1, section 1.3.3.
- More information can be found in the following Chapters:
- Chapter 4: Days, weeks, months and seasons
- Chapter 5: A complete list of Thai numbers
- Chapter 6: 24-hour clock time using **naalíkaa** นาฬิกา o'clock. That is another way to express the clock time in Thai. It is similar to the Western style 24-hour clock time
- Chapter 7: A long list of words related to travelling, places, buildings etc.

Chapter 18

Using classifiers and numbers

tʃán mii mɛɛu mâak-kwàa sǎam tuua
ฉัน มี แมว มาก กว่า สาม ตัว
I have more than three cats.

> **Highlights**
>
> Classifiers, sometimes called count words or measure words, are very important in Thai when counting things.

A. Sentences

Numbers & classifiers

1 **khùuat** ขวด *bottle*
khɔ̌ɔ *nom* sɔ̌ɔng *khùuat* ขอ นม สอง ขวด
ask milk *two bottle* – May I have two bottles of milk?

2 **thûuai** ถ้วย *cup*
mɯ̂a-waan tʃán dɯ̀ɯm *kaafɛɛ sǎam thûuai*
เมื่อวาน ฉัน ดื่ม กาแฟ สาม ถ้วย
yesterday I drink *coffee three cup*
Yesterday, I drank three cups of coffee.

3 **kɛ̂ɛu** แก้ว *glass*
nám-sôm wan-lá *nùng kɛ̂ɛu* dii
น้ำ ส้ม วัน ละ หนึ่ง แก้ว ดี
liquid-orange day-lá *one glass* good
A glass of orange juice once a day is good.

4 **wan** วัน *day*
tʃán tsà yùu thîi nîi yàang-nɔ́ɔi *hâa wan*
ฉัน จะ อยู่ ที่ นี่ อย่าง น้อย ห้า วัน
I will stay place-this like-few *five day*
I am going to stay here at least for five days.

Chapter 18

5. pii ปี *year*
phîi-tʃaai khɔ̌ɔŋ tʃán aayú *sǎam-sìp pii* lɛ́ɛu
พี่ ชาย ของ ฉัน อายุ สาม สิบ ปี แล้ว
older-brother of I age *30 year* already
My older brother is already 30 years old.

6. hɔ̂ŋ ห้อง *rooms*
thîi bâan tʃán mii *hɔ̂ŋ* hòk *hɔ̂ŋ*
ที่ บ้าน ฉัน มี ห้อง หก ห้อง
at home I have *room six room*
There are six rooms in my home.

7. khrûuaŋ เครื่อง *machines*
kháu mii *khɔɔmphíutɤ̂ɤ lǎai khrûuaŋ*
เขา มี คอมพิวเตอร์ หลาย เครื่อง
he have *computer many machine*
He has many computers.

8. khon คน *persons*
tʃán mii *nɔ́ɔŋ-sǎau sǎam khon* ฉัน มี น้อง สาว สาม คน
I have *younger-sister three person*
I have three younger sisters.

9. an อัน *small pieces*
an-nǎi dii thîi-sùt อัน ไหน ดี ที่ สุด
piece-which good that-most – *Which one is the best?*

10. bai ใบ *bags*
kràpǎu *bai níi* nàk kɤɤn-pai กระเป๋า ใบ นี้ หนัก เกิน ไป
bag piece this heavy excess-go – *This bag is too heavy.*

11. khan คัน *cars, bikes...*
kháu mii *rót-khan* mài เขา มี รถ คัน ใหม่
he have *car-vehicle new* – *He has a new car.*

12 **lûuk** ลูก *round things*
tʃán yàak dâai *sôm sìi lûuk* ฉัน อยาก ได้ ส้ม สี่ ลูก
I want get *orange four piece*
I would like to get four oranges.

13 **lêm** เล่ม *books*
tʃán phûŋ sɯ́ɯ *nǎŋsɯ̌ɯ hâa lêm*
ฉัน เพิ่ง ซื้อ หนังสือ ห้า เล่ม
I just buy *book five copy* – *I have just bought five books.*

14 **tuua** ตัว *body of animals*
phɯ̂ɯan tʃán mii *mɛɛw mâak-kwàa sǎam tuua*
เพื่อน ฉัน มี แมว มาก กว่า สาม ตัว
friend I have *cat much-more three body*
My friend has more than three cats.

15 **tʃánít** ชนิด *type of things*
ráan-aahǎan nán mii *aahǎan khɛ̂ɛ sǎam tʃánít*
ร้าน อาหาร นั้น มี อาหาร แค่ สาม ชนิด
shop-food that have but *food only three type*
That restaurant has only three types of food.

Common expressions
(kham thîi tʃái bɔ̀i-bɔ̀i คำ ที่ ใช้ บ่อยๆ)

phûut lên พูด เล่น
speak play – *I am joking.*

mâi kháu-tsai ไม่ เข้า ใจ
no enter-heart – *I do not understand.*

kháu-tsai เข้า ใจ
enter-heart – *I understand.*

sànùk mâak สนุก มาก
fun much – *Lots of fun!*

B. Vocabulary

khùuat	ขวด	bottle (used for anything served in bottles)
khɔ̌ɔ	ขอ	to ask
nom	นม	milk
thûuai	ถ้วย	cup, bowl (used for anything served in cups and bowls)
mûua-waan	เมื่อวาน	yesterday
dəəm	เดิม	to drink
kɛ̂ɛu	แก้ว	glass (used for anything served in a glass: water, beer, juice etc.)
wan-lá	วัน ละ	once a day
nám-sôm	น้ำ ส้ม	orange juice
wan	วัน	day (used for number of days)
tsà	จะ	will
yùu	อยู่	to stay, to live
yàang-nɔ́ɔi	อย่าง น้อย	at least
yàang	อย่าง	as, like, a way of
nɔ́ɔi	น้อย	little, few, not many
pii	ปี	year (used for number of years)
phîi-tʃaai	พี่ ชาย	older brother
phîi	พี่	elder (used for elder brother, sister, friend or colleague...)
tʃaai	ชาย	male, man
khɔ̌ɔng	ของ	of, possessive form
hɔ̂ng	ห้อง	room
thîi	ที่	at
bâan	บ้าน	home, house

khrŵŵang	เครื่อง	machine (used for electrical devices: refrigerators, computers etc.)
khɔɔmphíutəə	คอมพิวเตอร์	computer
lăai	หลาย	several, many
khon	คน	people (used for persons)
nɔ́ɔng-săau	น้อง สาว	younger sister
nɔ́ɔng	น้อง	younger (used for younger sister, brother, friend or colleague...)
săau	สาว	young woman, girl
an-năi	อัน ไหน	which one?
an	อัน	piece (used for small items: parts, bits, portions, slices etc.)
năi	ไหน	which, where?
dii thîi-sùt	ดี ที่ สุด	to be best
thîi-sùt	ที่ สุด	most, maximum
bai	ใบ	leaf, sheet (used for items like bags, glasses, cups, fruits, plates, sheets of paper, eggs etc.)
kràpău	กระเป๋า	bag
nàk	หนัก	to be heavy
kəən-pai	เกิน ไป	too, too much
khan	คัน	stick, rod (used for cars, bikes and some other vehicles, spoons, forks, umbrellas etc.)
rót-khan mài	รถ คัน ใหม่	new car
mài	ใหม่	to be new
lûuk	ลูก	ball, child (used for fruits, balls, round objects, hills, mountains etc.)
yàak-dâai	อยาก ได้	to want, to want to get

sôm	ส้ม	orange, to be acid
lêm	เล่ม	(used for books, knives, candles)
phûng	เพิ่ง	just
sɯ́ɯ	ซื้อ	to buy
năngsɯ̌ɯ	หนังสือ	book
tuua	ตัว	body (used for animals, clothes, chairs, tables, letters, things etc.)
măa	หมา	dog
mâak-kwàa	มาก กว่า	more than
tʃánít	ชนิด	types, kinds, sorts of things
ráan-aahăan	ร้าน อาหาร	restaurant
ráan	ร้าน	shop, store
aahăan	อาหาร	food
nán	นั้น	that
mii khêɛ	มี แค่	to have only, nothing but
khêɛ	แค่	only
phûut lên	พูด เล่น	to joke
phûut	พูด	to speak
lên	เล่น	to play
khâu-tsai	เข้า ใจ	to understand
sànùk mâak	สนุก มาก	lots of fun

C. How the language works

Classifiers are very important components in the Thai language. In order to be able to speak Thai fluently, you need to have some knowledge of classifiers. They are sometimes also called count words or measure words. Some classifiers are also used in a similar way in English. The difference is that all nouns (books, cars, people etc.) in Thai are counted by classifiers. That means simply that the number is always placed before a classifier and not before the main noun.

Let us see some sentences and see how it works.

A) Similar classifiers (Thai vs English)

We use classifiers also in English such as numbers of days, years, bottles, glasses, etc. Some common examples are:

khùuat	ขวด	*bottle, anything served in bottles*
wan	วัน	*day*
pii	ปี	*year*
aathít	อาทิตย์	*week*
khráng	ครั้ง	*number of times*
naathii	นาที	*minute*
kìloo	กิโล	*kilogram*
thûuai	ถ้วย	*cup, anything served in cups*
kɛ̂ɛu	แก้ว	*glass, anything served in glasses*
tsaan	จาน	*plate, anything served on plates*

Examples:

> phǒm yùu thîi nîi hòk *wan* lɛ́ɛu
> ผม อยู่ ที่ นี่ หก วัน แล้ว
> I stay place this six *day* already
> *I have already stayed here for six days.*

- In this sentence, the main noun is also a classifier **wan** วัน *day*.
- The sentence is constructed the similar way in English. The same applies when we talk about weeks, years and number of times.

> **2** phǒm maa thîi nîi hòk *khráng* lέεu
> ผม มา ที่ นี่ หก ครั้ง แล้ว
> I come place this six *time* already
> *I have already been here six times.*

- Here the main noun is also a classifier **khráng** ครั้ง *time*.
- The sentence is constructed in the similar way in English.

> **3** kháu pai sǎam-sìp *naathii* thîi-lέεu
> เขา ไป สาม สิบ นา ที ที่ แล้ว
> he go three-ten *minute* that-already
> *He left thirty minutes ago.*

- Here the classifier **naathii** นาที *minute* is also the main word.
- It is measuring units of time.

> **4** an-níi nàk sìp *kìloo* อัน นี้ หนัก สิบ กิโล
> piece-this weigh ten *kilogram*
> *This one weighs ten kilograms.*

- Here we have used the measure unit of weight, **kìloo** กิโล *kilogram*.

> **5** au *biia* sɔ̌ɔng *kɛ̂ɛu* เอา เบียร์ สอง แก้ว
> take *beer* two *glass* – *I want two glasses of beer, please!*

- Here we have the measure unit of quantities **kɛ̂ɛu** แก้ว *glass*.
- It is used in the similar way as in English.
- The number is placed before the classifier. A classifier in Thai comes usually after the main noun, here **biia** เบียร์ *beer*.

> **6** khɔ̌ɔ *nám-plàu* sǎam *khùuat* ขอ น้ำ เปล่า สาม ขวด
> ask *water-plain* three *bottle*
> Could I have three bottles of water?

- Here we have the measure unit of quantity **khùuat** ขวด *bottle*. It is used for anything that is served in bottles.
- The number is placed before the classifier, here **khùuat** ขวด *bottle* which comes usually after the main noun, here **nám-plàu** น้ำ เปล่า *water*.

B) The classifier can be the same as the main noun

There are a few words for which the main noun serves as a classifier.
Examples:

hɔ̂ng	ห้อง	*room*
roong-riian	โรง เรียน	*school*
roong-rɛɛm	โรง แรม	*hotel*
bɔɔrísàt	บริษัท	*company*
khon	คน	*person, people*

etc.

> **1** bâan tʃán mii *hɔ̂ng* lǎai *hɔ̂ng* บ้าน ฉัน มี ห้อง หลาย ห้อง
> home I have *room* many *room*
> *My home has many rooms.*

- In this sentence, the main noun is also a classifier **hɔ̂ng** ห้อง *room*.

> **1.1** bâan tʃán mii lǎai *hɔ̂ng* บ้าน ฉัน มี หลาย ห้อง
> home I have *many room* – *My home has many rooms.*

- However, in casual speaking the main noun **hɔ̂ng** ห้อง *room* is often dropped. That is perhaps because it is too much of a bother to repeat the same word.

c) Classifiers which are used for many different types of nouns

Examples:

khrûuang	เครื่อง	for *machines, refrigerators, computers, electrical devices...*
bai	ใบ	for *bags, glasses, cups, fruits, plates, sheets of paper*
khan	คัน	for *cars, spoons, forks, umbrellas...*
lûuk	ลูก	for *fruits, children, balls, round objects...*
lêm	เล่ม	for *books, knives, candles...*
tuua	ตัว	for *animals, clothes, chairs...*
yàang	อย่าง	for *types, sorts of things*
tʃánít	ชนิด	for *kinds, sorts of things*

> **1** tʃán sɯ́ɯ *năngsɯ̌ɯ* sɔ̌ɔng lêm lɛ́ɛu-kɔ̂ɔ *thiian* sìp lêm
> ฉัน ซื้อ หนังสือ สอง เล่ม แล้ว ก็ เทียน สิบ เล่ม
> I buy *book* two *copy* then-also *candle* ten *piece*
> *I bought two books and ten candles.*

- Here we have used the classifier **lêm** เล่ม for **năngsɯ̌ɯ** หนังสือ *book* and **thiian** เทียน for *candle*.

- **lêm** เล่ม is also commonly used for *knives* and some sharp objects such as *rods* and *scissors*.

> **2** rót khan nii sǐi dɛɛng mɯ̌an kàp rôm khan nán
> รถ คัน นี้ สี แดง เหมือน กับ ร่ม คัน นั้น
> *car vehicle* this colour red as with *umbrella rod* that
> *This red car has the same colour as that umbrella.*

- Here we have used the classifier **khan** คัน for **rót** รถ *car* and **rôm** ร่ม *umbrella*.
- **khan** คัน is also commonly used for *spoons* and *forks*.

> **3** nai *kràpǎu bai* níi mii khɛ̂ɛ *khùuat* sìp *bai*
> ใน กระเป๋า ใบ นี้ มี แค่ ขวด สิบ ใบ
> in *bag piece* this have only *bottle* ten *piece*
> In this bag there are nothing but ten empty bottles.

- **bai** ใบ can be used for many nouns such as *bags, fruits, eggs, sheets of paper, leaves, tickets, pillows* etc.
- When it is used with **khùuat** ขวด *bottle* which is a classifier (a measure word) in itself, the meaning becomes *empty bottles*.
- **khùuat sìp bai** ขวด สิบ ใบ is *six empty bottles* but **nom sìp khùuat** นม สิบ ขวด is translated into English as *six bottles of milk*.

D) **khon** คน as a classifier

khon คน *person, people* as a classifier is also used in English. For example **tsèt khon** เจ็ดคน is translated into English as *seven people*. The difference is that in Thai we always need to use the classifier **khon** คน when we are referring to people.

Examples:

> mii *nák-riian* nùng rɔ́ɔi *khon* nai roong-riian
> มี นัก เรียน หนึ่ง ร้อย คน ใน โรง เรียน
> have *nák-study* hundred *person* in building-study
> There are one hundred students in the school.

> **2** mii *khruu* sìi *khon* nai roong-rian
> มี ครู สี่ คน ใน โรง เรียน
> have *teacher* four *person* in building-study
> *There are four teachers in the school.*

> **3** *khon* thai tsèt *khon* maa lɛ́ɛu คน ไทย เจ็ด คน มา แล้ว
> *person* Thai seven *person* come already
> *Seven Thais have already arrived.*

- In English, we can place the number before the main noun (one hundred students, four teachers etc.). In Thai, number comes before the classifier.
- **khon** คน *person* is used whenever we refer to people.

E) Using classifiers without a main noun

When the context is clear, Thai people often drop the main noun and use only a classifier.

Examples:

> **1** phŏm mii sǎam *bai* – *bai* níi nàk mâak
> ผม มี สาม ใบ – ใบ นี้ หนัก มาก
> I have three *bag* – *bag* this heavy very
> *I have three bags. This bag is very heavy.*

- Here we have used the classifier **bai** ใบ for **kràpǎu** กระเป๋า *bag* which is understood from the context, and **kràpǎu** กระเป๋า *bag* is dropped.
- Note also that when we use demonstratives such as *this, that, these, those*, we normally use classifiers. Hence, *this bag* is translated into Thai as **kràpǎu bai níi** กระเป๋า ใบ นี้ (literally bag item this).

- **bai** ใบ is commonly used for *bags, glasses, cups, fruits, plates, sheets of paper...*

> **2** tʃɔɔn nâng khâ – *tuua* níi sàbaai
> เชิญ นั่ง ค่ะ – ตัว นี้ สบาย
> invite sit khâ – *body* this comfortable
> *Please sit down. This chair is comfortable.*

- Here we have used the classifier **tuua** ตัว for **kâuîi** เก้าอี้ *chair* which is understood from the context, and **kâuîi** เก้าอี้ *chair* is dropped.

- **tuua** ตัว is commonly used for *chairs, tables, items of clothing, animals, letters...*

> **3** lêm thîi khun hâi tʃán nâa-sŏn-tsai mâak
> เล่ม ที่ คุณ ให้ ฉัน น่า สน ใจ มาก
> *copy* that you give I nâa-interesting-heart very
> *The book you gave to me is very interesting.*

- Here we have used the classifier **lêm** เล่ม for **nǎngsǔu** หนังสือ *book* which is understood from the context, and **nǎngsǔu** หนังสือ *book* is dropped.

- **lêm** เล่ม is commonly used for *books, knives, candles...*

F) What to do if you don't know or remember the classifier?

an อัน is normally used for small objects such as *ashtrays, pieces of different items*.

If you do not know the classifier, **an** อัน may also be used for larger items. It is considered to be a better choice compared to not using a classifier at all.

Examples:

> **1** khɔ̌ɔ *klûuai* sìi *an* ขอ กล้วย สี่ อัน
> ask *banana* four *piece* – *May I have three bananas?*

- You can get by with **an** อัน *small items* even if there is another correct classifier.
- The correct classifier for **klûuai** กล้วย *banana* is either **bai** ใบ or **lûuk** ลูก.
- However, you should not use **an** อัน *small items* for *people* and common *large objects like cars, houses, air planes* etc.

> **2** kháu mii *rót sǎam an* เขา มี รถ สาม อัน
> he have *car three piece* – *He has three cars.*

- This sentence is grammatically correct but it would sound very weird to the Thai ear. In this case, Thais would probably correct you and say that you should use **khan** คัน *vehicle* here.
- Note that there are a large number of classifiers in Thai. Sometimes, even Thais would have a hard time to remember the correct classifier if it is seldom used.

> **3** kháu mii *sǎam rót* เขา มี สาม รถ
> he have *three car* – *He has three cars.*

- This sentence is not correct.
- Generally, one cannot place the number before the main noun; it is grammatically wrong and no Thai, in any circumstances, would say something like in the sentence 3.
- They would understand you but would think that you are a foreigner who has not yet learned to speak Thai correctly.

kháu mii *rót yá* เขา มี รถ เยอะ
he have *car many* – *He has many cars.*

- **yá** เยอะ *many, much* is a handy word since it can be placed after the main noun, and there is no need for any classifier. This is perfectly correct.
- Thais often use this type of construction. It can be used for anything which exists in large quantities, even for people.

kháu mii *rót lăai khan* เขา มี รถ หลาย คัน
he have *car many vehicle* – *He has many cars.*

- There is another word for *many*, **lăai** หลาย *many, several*.
- This word calls upon for the use of a classifier and cannot be used alone in the same way as **yá** เยอะ *many, much*. See the previous sentence 4.

D. New Sounds

Consonant clusters:

A consonant cluster is formed by two consonant sounds. In the English language, there are many more consonant clusters than in Thai. Some common English clusters are: **bl**ue, **pr**actice, **fr**ee, **st**udent, **sp**ine etc. So, English speakers are used to make these type of sounds even though consonant clusters can be made from different consonants in Thai. In English and Thai, consonant clusters are used in a similar way. For example, the cluster **pr** in the Thai word **pr**àp ปรับ *to adjust* and in the English word **pr**actise sound the same.

Consonant clusters in Thai are made from the following consonant combinations:

kw กว, **kr** กร, **kl** กล, **khw** ขว-คว, **khr** ขร-คร, **khl** ขล-คล, **tr** ตร, **pr** ปร, **pl** ปล, **phr** พร, **phl** ผล-พล

We would advise you to learn Thai consonant clusters as they come up. There is no point to try to memorize all the ways to make consonant clusters in Thai. They come naturally as you go on with your studies.

E. Simple advice

The Thai writing system is very complex, and it takes a long time and much serious effort to master it well. Just to give you one example:

phan-rá-yaa ภรรยา is Pali/Sanskrit origin word meaning *wife* in English. It has three syllables.

The original Thai words commonly have only one syllable and are not spelled in this way. In this word we have *four consonant* symbols after each other **ph** ภ + **r** ร + **r** ร + **y** ย. The last symbol is the long vowel sound **aa**. Yet, the actual pronunciation is **phan-rá-yaa.** The word contains sounds as **ph, an, r, a, y** and **aa**. These sounds (**an**) and (**a**) are not spelled but pronounced.

This is the reason why we don't waste time with the complex Thai writing system at the beginning. It is very complicated, and to learn to read and write takes considerable time. The original Thai words and sounds are not that difficult.

F. Take it further

Refer to the book:

Dhyan Manik: *Understanding the Thai Language and Grammar:*

- More about Thai consonant clusters can be found in Chapter 1, section 1.4.1
- More about English consonant clusters used in Thai can be found in Chapter 1, section 1.4.2
- A complete list of Thai numbers can be found in Chapter 5.
- Names of some common animals and insects can be found in Chapter 8.
- A list of Thai classifiers, also called count words or measure words, can be found in Chapter 18.

Chapter 19

Using Thai prefixes to form special meanings

kháu pen khon tsâu-tʃúu
เขา เป็น คน เจ้า ชู้
He is a playboy (casanova).

Chapter 19

> **Highlights**
>
> Prefixes are commonly placed before adjectives, adverbs, verbs and nouns to form special meanings.

A. Sentences

a) General prefixes

1 **khwaam** ความ *matter* turns verbs or adjectives into abstract nouns

1.1 thúk-khon tông phûut *khwaam-tsing*
ทุก คน ต้อง พูด ความ จริง
every-person must speak *matter-truth*
Everybody must speak the truth.

1.2 kháu mii *khwaam-khít* thîi dii เขา มี ความ คิด ที่ ดี
he have *matter-think* that good – *He has a good idea.*

1.3 tʃán mii *khwaam-sùk* mâak-mâak ฉัน มี ความ สุข มากๆ
I have *matter-happy* much-much – *I am very happy.*

2 **kaan** การ *task* normally turns verbs into nouns (English form *-ing*)

2.1 *kaan-àan* sǎmkhan mâak การ อ่าน สำคัญ มาก
task-read important very – *Reading is very important.*

2.2 *kaan-bin* mâi khôi ngâai การ บิน ไม่ ค่อย ง่าย
task-fly no hardly easy – *Flying is not that easy.*

Chapter 19

2.3 *kaan-fùk* tham-hâi khun phûut phaasăa-thai kèng
การ ฝึก ทำ ให้ คุณ พูด ภาษา ไทย เก่ง
task-practise make-give you speak language-Thai talented
Practising makes you an expert in speaking Thai.

2.4 *kaan-hâi* lé *kaan-dâai-ráp* pen sìng sămkhan nai tʃiiwít
การ ให้ และ การ ได้ รับ เป็น สิ่ง สำคัญ ใน ชีวิต
task-give and task-get-receive be thing important in life
Giving and receiving are important aspects in life.

3 **khîi** ขี้ before adjectives often refers to a negative quality

3.1 tʃán *khîi-kìiat* nít-nɔ̀i ฉัน ขี้ เกียจ นิด หน่อย
I *khîi-lazy* small-little – *I am a little lazy.*

3.2 phûuan tʃán *khîi-aai* mâak-mâak เพื่อน ฉัน ขี้อาย มากๆ
friend I *khîi-shy* very-very – *My friend is very shy.*

3.3 kháu *khîi-luum* bɔ̀i-bɔ̀i เขา ขี้ ลืม บ่อยๆ
he *khîi-forget* often-often – *He is often forgetful.*

4 **nâa** น่า *worthy of* indicates a certain condition

4.1 kaan-riian phaasăa-tsiin *nâa-sŏn-tsai*
การ เรียน ภาษา จีน น่า สน ใจ
task-study language-China *nâa-interested-heart*
To study Chinese is interesting.

4.2 tʃán mâi yàak pai – *nâa-kluua*
ฉัน ไม่ อยาก ไป – น่า กลัว
I no want go – *nâa-fear* – *I don't want to go. It is scary.*

4.3 phûu-yĭng khon nán *nâa-mɔɔng* ผู้ หญิง คน นั้น น่า มอง
person-women person that *nâa-look*
That girl is charming.

4.4 aahăan thîi nîi *nâa-arɔ̀i* อาหาร ที่ นี่ น่า อร่อย
food place-this *nâa-delicious* – Food here looks delicious.

5 **tsai** ใจ *heart, mind* indicates emotion

5.1 khon-thai *tsai-kwâang* คน ไทย ใจ กว้าง
person-Thai *heart-wide* – Thai people are generous.

5.2 kháu *tsai-dii* tsing-tsing เขา ใจ ดี จริงๆ
he *heart-good* truly-truly – He is really kind.

5.3 *tsai-yen-yen* ใจ เย็นๆ
heart-cool-cool – Calm down! Take it easy!

b) Prefixes referring to people

6 **khon** คน *person* refers to persons and people

6.1 tʃán tôŋ-kaan *khon-tʃûuai* ฉัน ต้อง การ คน ช่วย
I need-task *person-help* – I need a helper.

6.2 tʃán tʃɔ̂ɔp *khon-dii* ฉัน ชอบ คน ดี
I like *person-good* – I like good people.

6.3 tʃán maa thîi-nîi *khon-diau* ฉัน มา ที่ นี่ คน เดียว
I come place-this *person-one* – I came here alone.

7 **phûu** ผู้ *person* refers to persons and people

7.1 kháu pen *phûu-hâi* เขา เป็น ผู้ ให้
he be *person-give* – He is a giver.

7.2 rau mii *phûu-lên* sìp khon เรา มี ผู้เล่น สิบ คน
we have *person-play* ten person – *We have ten players.*

7.3 tʃán yàak tsà pen *phûu-tsàt-kaan*
ฉัน อยากจะ เป็น ผู้ จัด การ
I want will be *person-arrange-job*
I like to become a manager.

8 **tsâu** เจ้า *person* refers to persons who have special skills

8.1 khrai tʃɔ̂ɔp phûu-tʃaai *tsâu-tʃúu* ใคร ชอบ ผู้ ชาย เจ้า ชู้
who like person-male *tsâu-lover*
Who likes playboys (casanova)?

8.2 kháu pen khon *tsâu-khwaam-khít*
เขา เป็น คน เจ้า ความ คิด
he be person *tsâu-matter-think* – *He is a man with ideas.*

8.3 thîi-nîi khrai pen *tsâu-naai* ที่ นี่ ใคร เป็น เจ้า นาย
place-this who be *person-boss* – *Who is the boss here?*

9 **tʃaau** ชาว *person* indicates profession and nationality

9.1 *tʃaau-naa* tham-ngaan nàk ชาว นา ทำ งาน หนัก
person-farm do-work heavy – *Farmers are hard working.*

9.2 *tʃaau-thai* sùphâap ชาว ไทย สุภาพ
person-Thai polite – *Thai people are polite.*

9.3 *tʃaau-tsiin* kèng ชาว จีน เก่ง
person-China talented – *Chinese people are talented.*

9.4 thîi indiia mii *tʃaau-hinduu* lăai khon
ที่ อินเดีย มี ชาว ฮินดู หลาย คน
at India have many *person-hindu*
In India there are many Hindus.

c) Prefixes to describe a certain *profession*

10 **tʃáng** ช่าง *profession* indicates skills such as technician, mechanic...

10.1 *tʃáng-máai* tông mii fĭi-mɯɯ ช่าง ไม้ ต้อง มี ฝี มือ
mechanic-wood must have skills
A carpenter must have craftsmanship.

10.2 tsà pai hăa *tʃáng-klɔ̂ng* จะ ไป หา ช่าง กล้อง
will go search *mechanic-camera*
I am going to look for a photographer.

10.3 *tʃáng-sɔ̂m* sɔ̂m rót ช่าง ซ่อม ซ่อม รถ
mechanic-repair repair car – *The mechanic repairs cars.*

11 **nák** นัก *profession* indicates certain skill or profession

11.1 tʃǎn yàak pen *nák-khàau* ฉัน อยาก เป็น นัก ข่าว
I want be *person-news* – *I want to become a journalist.*

11.2 piitə̂ə pen *nák-kiilaa* ปีเตอร์ เป็น นัก กีฬา
Peter be *person-sport* – *Peter is an athlete.*

11.3 tʃǎn rúu-tsàk *nák-rɔ́ɔng* lăai khon
ฉัน รู้ จัก นัก ร้อง หลาย คน
I know-will *person-sing* many person
I know many singers.

12 **lûuk** ลูก *subordinate* indicates a certain occupation, category or junior partner

12.1 wan níi rau mii *lûuk-kháa* yɔ́ วัน นี้ เรา มี ลูก ค้า เยอะ
day this we have *partner-business* much
Today, we have many customers.

12.2 kháu mii *lûuk-muu* sɔ̌ɔng khon เขา มี ลูก มือ สอง คน
he have *partner-hand* two person – *He has two helpers.*

12.3 kháu pen *lûuk-nɔ́ɔng* phǒm เขา เป็น ลูก น้อง ผม
he be *partner-minion* (younger person) I
He is my subordinate.

    d) Special prefixes to express passive voice

13 **doon** โดน

13.1 khǎu *doon tsàp* เขา โดน จับ
he *doon catch* – *He was caught.*

13.2 kháu *doon* tamrùuat *tsàp* เขา โดน ตำรวจ จับ
he *doon* police *catch* – *He was arrested by the police.*

14 thùuk ถูก

14.1 kháu *thùuk khǎng* เขา ถูก ฝาก ขัง
he *thùuk jail* – *He was in jail.*

14.2 kháu *thùuk* tamrùuat *khǎng* เขา ถูก ตำรวจ ขัง
he *thùuk* police *jail* – *He was put in jail by the police.*

Common expressions
(kham thîi tɟǎi bɔ̀i-bɔ̀i คำ ที่ ใช้ บ่อยๆ)

mâi-pen-rai ไม่ เป็น ไร
no-be-anything – *Never mind. You are welcome.*

mâi mii panhǎa ไม่ มี ปัญหา
no have problem – *There is no problem.*

mâi mii àrai ไม่ มี อะไร
no have what – *Nothing. There is nothing.*

> àrai-kɔ̂ɔ-dâai อะไร ก็ ได้
> what-also-can – *Anything is fine. Whatever!*

B. Vocabulary

khwaam	ความ	matter
khwaam-tsing	ความ จริง	truth
thúk-khon	ทุก คน	everybody
khwaam-khít	ความ คิด	idea
khwaam-sùk	ความ สุข	happiness
kaan	การ	task (English form -ing)
kaan-àan	การ อ่าน	reading
sămkhan	สำคัญ	important
kaan-bin	การ บิน	flying
khɔ̂i	ค่อย	hardly
ngâai	ง่าย	easy
kaan-fùk	การ ฝึก	practising
fùk	ฝึก	to practise
tham-hâi	ทำ ให้	to make
kèng	เก่ง	to be talented, skilful
kaan-hâi	การ ให้	giving
hâi	ให้	to give
kaan-dâai-ráp	การ ได้ รับ	receiving
dâai	ได้	to get
ráp	รับ	to receive
sìng	สิ่ง	thing, things
nai tʃiiwít	ใน ชีวิต	in life
khîi	ขี้	to waste, to defecate, to crap

Chapter 19

khîi-kìiat	ขี้ เกียจ	to be lazy
kìiat	เกียจ	to be lazy
nít-nɔ̀i	นิด หน่อย	a little
khîi-aai	ขี้ อาย	to be shy
aai	อาย	to be shy
mâak-mâak	มากๆ	very much
khîi-lɯɯm	ขี้ ลืม	to be forgetful
lɯɯm	ลืม	to forget
bɔ̀ɔi-bɔ̀ɔi	บ่อยๆ	very often
nâa	น่า	worthy of
nâa-sŏn-tsai	น่า สน ใจ	to be interesting
sŏn	สน	to be interesting
phaasăa	ภาษา จีน	Chinese (language)
nâa-kluua	น่า กลัว	to be frightening, scary
phûu-yĭng khon nán	ผู้ หญิง คน นั้น	that girl
nâa-mɔɔng	น่า มอง	to be charming, attractive
mɔɔng	มอง	to look at
aahăan	อาหาร	food
nâa-arɔ̀i	น่า อร่อย	to be appetizing, delicious, tasty
tsai	ใจ	heart, mind
kwâang	กว้าง	to be wide, broad
tsai-kwâang	ใจ กว้าง	to be generous, broad-minded
tsai-dii	ใจ ดี	to be kind, generous
tsing-tsing	จริงๆ	really, honestly
tsai-yen-yen	ใจ เย็นๆ	calm down, take it easy
tsai-yen	ใจ เย็น	to be calm
tsai	ใจ	heart

Chapter 19

yen	เย็น	to be cool
khon	คน	person
khon-tʃûuai	คน ช่วย	helper
tông-kaan	ต้อง การ	to want, to need
tʃɔ̂ɔp	ชอบ	to like
khon-dii	คน ดี	good person
maa	มา	to come
khon-diiau	คน เดียว	alone
phûu	ผู้	person
phûu-hâi	ผู้ ให้	donor, giver, supplier
phûu-lên	ผู้ เล่น	player
sìp khon	สิบ คน	ten persons
phûu-tsàt-kaan	ผู้ จัด การ	manager
tsàt-kaan	จัด การ	to manage
tsàt	จัด	to prepare, to arrange
kaan	การ	task, work
tsâu	เจ้า	person
tsâu-khwaam-khít	เจ้า ความ คิด	man with ideas
khwaam-khít	ความ คิด	idea, thought
khrai	ใคร	who?
phûu-tʃaai	ผู้ ชาย	male
tsâu-tʃúu	เจ้า ชู้	playboy, casanova
tʃaau	ชาว	person
tʃaau-naa	ชาว นา	farmer
naa	นา	farm, field
tham-ngaan nàk	ทำ งาน หนัก	to work hard
tʃaau-thai	ชาว ไทย	Thai people
tʃaau-tsiin	ชาว จีน	Chinese people
tʃaau-hinduu	ชาว ฮินดู	Hindus

tʃáng	ช่าง	technician, mechanic
tʃáng-máai	ช่าง ไม้	carpenter
máai	ไม้	wood, timber, stick
fĭi-mɯɯ	ฝี มือ	skill, craftsmanship
tʃáng-klɔ̂ng	ช่าง กล้อง	photographer
klɔ̂ng	กล้อง	camera
tʃáng-sɔ̂m	ช่าง ซ่อม	mechanic, repairman
sɔ̂m rót	ซ่อม รถ	to repair cars
nák	นัก	indicates certain skill
nák-khàau	นัก ข่าว	journalist
khàau	ข่าว	news
nák-kiilaa	นัก กีฬา	sportsman, athlete
kiilaa	กีฬา	sport, game
nák-rɔ́ɔng	นัก ร้อง	singer
rɔ́ɔng	ร้อง	to sing, to cry, to complain
lûuk	ลูก	subordinate, junior partner
lûuk-kháa	ลูก ค้า	customer
lûuk-mɯɯ	ลูก มือ	helper
sɔ̌ɔng khon	สอง คน	two people
lûuk-nɔ́ɔng	ลูก น้อง	subordinate
doon	โดน	expressing passive voice
thùuk	ถูก	expressing passive voice
tsàp	จับ	to catch
tamrùuat	ตำรวจ	police
khăng	ขัง	to imprison, jail
tìt-khúk	ติด คุก	to imprison
tìt	ติด	to be stuck
khúk	คุก	jail, prison
dâai	ได้	can, to be able to

angkrìt	อังกฤษ	English
tὲɛ	แต่	but
kèng	เก่ง	to be talented, skilled

C. How the language works

In order to speak Thai well, you need to understand how the prefixes are used in Thai. In Thai, there are several prefixes, which are used either before verbs, adjectives, adverbs or nouns to change the meaning. Note that we do not give an exact word to word translation for every prefix since the meaning is very much determined by the compound construction, and to translate the prefix alone is not always easy.

A) Commonly used general prefixes

1. **khwaam**	ความ	*matter*
2. **kaan**	การ	*task*
3. **khîi**	ขี้	*usually has some negative connotation*
4. **nâa**	น่า	*worthy of*
5. **tsai**	ใจ	*heart, mind prefix indicates emotion*

We take these first since they are perhaps the most common prefixes in Thai. They are commonly placed before verbs or adjectives.

1   **khwaam** ความ *matter* normally converts verbs or adjectives into abstract nouns.

Examples:

khwaam-rúu	ความ รู้	*knowledge*
khwaam-khít	ความ คิด	*idea*
khwaam-făn	ความ ฝัน	*dream*
khwaam-tsing	ความ จริง	*truth*

Chapter 19

Sentences:

> **1.1** rau tông mii *khwaam-rúu* เรา ต้อง มี ความ รู้
> we must have *matter-know* – *We must have knowledge.*

- Here we have converted the verb **rúu** จริง *to know* into a noun **khwaam-rúu** ความ จริง *knowledge*.

> **1.2** *khwaam-rák* lέ *khwaam-tsing* pen sìng thîi sămkhan nai tʃiiwít
> ความ รัก และ ความ จริง เป็น สิ่ง ที่ สำคัญ ใน ชีวิต
> *matter-love* and *matter-truth* be thing that important in life
> *Love and truth are important aspects in life.*

- Here we have converted the verb **rák** รัก *to love* into a noun **khwaam-rák** ความ รัก *love* and an adjective **tsing** จริง *true* into a noun **khwaam-tsing** ความ จริง *truth*.

2 **kaan** การ *task, work* normally converts verbs into nouns.

Examples:

kaan-hâi	การ ให้	*giving*
kaan-dâai	การ ได้	*getting*
kaan-khàp	การ ขับ	*driving*
kaan-phûut	การ พูด	*speaking*

This kind of construction is called "a gerund" in English (verb + -ing).

Sentences:

> **2.1** *kaan-khàp* rót dooi mâi mii bai-anúyâat antàraai
> การ ขับ รถ โดย ไม่ มี ใบ อนุญาต อันตราย
> *task-drive* car by no have item-permit dangerous
> *Driving a car without a licence is dangerous.*

- Here we have converted the verb **khàp** ขับ *to drive* into a noun **kaan-khàp** การ ขับ *driving*.
- Note, however, that in spoken Thai, the prefix **kaan** การ *task* is often dropped in this context.

> **2.2** *kaan-phûut* dii tɛ̀ɛ baang-khráng yùu ngîiap-ngîiap dii-kwàa
> การ พูด ดี แต่ บาง ครั้ง อยู่ เงียบๆ ดี กว่า
> *task-speak* good but some-time stay quiet-quiet good-more
> *Speaking is good, but sometimes to be quiet is better.*

- Here we have converted the verb **phûut** พูด *to speak* into a noun **kaan-phûut** การ พูด *speaking*.
- In spoken Thai, the prefix **kaan** การ *task* is often dropped in this context.

3 The prefix **khîi** ขี้ can be used with adjectives, nouns and verbs.

Examples:

khîi-bòn	ขี้ บ่น	*to be complaining*
khîi-kìiat	ขี้ เกียจ	*to be lazy*
khîi-mau	ขี้ เมา	*to be an alcoholic*
khîi-aai	ขี้ อาย	*to be shy*
khîi-lên	ขี้ เล่น to	*to be playful*
khîi-hŭng	ขี้ หึง	*to be jealous*
khîi-luum	ขี้ ลืม to	*to be forgetful*

khîi ขี้ as a prefix usually has some negative connotation, particularly when placed before *verbs* and *adjectives*. **khîi** ขี้ alone as a verb means simply *to defecate, to crap, to shit*.

Sentences:

 kháu *khîi-kìiat* nít-nɔ̀i เขา ขี้ เกียจ นิด หน่อย
he *khîi-lazy* small-little – *He is a bit lazy.*

- Here we have placed **khîi** ขี้ before the adjective **kìiat** เกียจ *lazy*. In English, **khîi-kìiat** ขี้ เกียจ means *to be lazy.*
- We use **khîi** ขี้ for word to word translation here since it is not easy to give a direct English translation.

 tʃán *khîi-lɯɯm* mâak-mâak
ฉัน ขี้ ลืม มากๆ
I *khîi-forget* very-very
I am very forgetful. / I forget everything.

- Here we have placed **khîi** ขี้ before the verb **lɯɯm** ลืม *to forget*. In English, **khîi-lɯɯm** ขี้ เกียจ means *to be forgetful.*

Note that as a noun **khîi** ขี้ means *shit, waste, residue.* It can be used together with other nouns to create new meanings:

Examples:

khîi phɯ̂ŋ	ขี้ ผึ้ง	*beeswax, wax*
khîi hǔu	ขี้ หู	*earwax*
khîi taa	ขี้ ตา	*gum in the eyes*
khîi lép	ขี้ เล็บ	*dirt in the nails*

 nâa น่า *worthy of* is a prefix used to make verbs or adjectives be "worthy of something".

Examples:

nâa-rák	น่า รัก	*to be cute, to be loveable*
nâa-mɔɔng	น่า มอง	*to be attractive, to be charming*
nâa-àan	น่า อ่าน	*to be enjoyable to read*

nâa-yùu	น่า อยู่	*to be pleasant to stay, to be liveable*
nâa-kluua	น่า กลัว	*to be frightening, to be scary*
nâa-bùua	น่า เบื่อ	*to be boring*
nâa-sŏn-tsai	น่า สน ใจ	*to be interesting*
nâa-tsà	น่า จะ	*should*

nâa น่า *worthy of* is a lovely prefix. It is not easy to translate directly into English. You will understand the meaning from the following examples:

> **4.1** krung-thêep *nâa-yùu* กรุงเทพ น่า อยู่
> Bangkok *nâa-live – Bangkok is a nice place to live.*

- When **nâa** น่า is placed before a verb, it turns a verb to into an adjective. Here we have placed **nâa** น่า before the verb **yùu** อยู่ *to stay, to live.* **nâa-yùu** น่า อยู่ can be translated into English as *liveable.*
- Note that we use **nâa** น่า for word to word translation here since it is not easy to give a direct translation into English.

> **4.2** thîi níi *nâa-bùua* tsang ที่ นี่ น่า เบื่อ จัง
> place-this *nâa-boring* very – *It is very boring here.*

- When **nâa** น่า is placed before an adjective, it gives an adjective extra colour and emphasis.
- Here we have placed **nâa** น่า before the adjective **bùua** เบื่อ *boring.* It can be left out as well.

> **4.3** phŏm *nâa-tsà* pai tɔɔn-níi ผม น่า จะ ไป ตอน นี้
> I *should-will* go at-this – *I should go now.*

- When **nâa** น่า is placed before the tense marker **tsà** จะ *will,* the meaning becomes *should.*

Note:

There is another word in Thai which is pronounced exactly the same as **nâa** หน้า *worthy of,* but it has a different spelling and meaning; it is also used grammatically differently.

Examples:

nâa	หน้า	*season, next, front*
nâa-fǒn	หน้า ฝน	*rainy season*
nâa-nǎau	หน้า หนาว	*winter*
nâa-rɔ́ɔn	หน้า ร้อน	*summer*
khráng-nâa	ครั้ง หน้า	*next time*
pii-nâa	ปี หน้า	*next year*
nâa-naa	หน้า นา	*farming season*
pràtuu-nâa	ประตู หน้า	*front door*

Note also that **naa** นา *field, farm* is pronounced with the middle tone. **tham-naa** ทำ นา *to farm* is literally translated into English as *to do farming.*

 tsai ใจ *heart, mind* prefix indicates emotion

Examples:
Prefix

tsai-dii	ใจ ดี	*to be kind, to be generous*
tsai-khěng	ใจ แข็ง	*to be strong-minded*
tsai-nɔ́ɔi	ใจ น้อย	*to be easily offended*
tsai-rɔ́ɔn	ใจ ร้อน	*to be hot-tempered*
tsai-khɛ̂ɛp	ใจ แคบ	*to be narrow-minded*

Suffix

dii-tsai	ดี ใจ	*to be happy, to be pleased*
mân-tsai	มั่น ใจ	*to be confident*

Chapter 19

nɛ̂ɛ-tsai	แน่ ใจ	to be certain, to be sure
tsing-tsai	จริง ใจ	to be sincere, to be honest
phɔɔ-tsai	พอ ใจ	to be satisfied

tsai ใจ *heart, mind* is very important in Thai. It is used constantly together with other words as a prefix and also as suffix to form special meanings. It is normally placed before or after adjectives that express the state of mind or emotion.

Sentences:

> **5.1** khon-thai *tsai-kwâang* คน ไทย ใจ กว้าง
> person-Thai *heart-wide* – *Thai people are generous.*

- Here we have placed **tsai** กว้าง *mind, heart* before the adjective **kwâang** กว้าง *wide, broad.*
- **tsai-kwâang** ใจ กว้าง is translated into English as *broad-minded, generous.*

> **5.2** kháu *tsai-dii* tsing-tsing เขา ใจ ดี จริงๆ
> he *heart-good* truly-truly – *He is really kind.*

- Here we have placed **tsai** กว้าง *mind, heart* before the adjective **dii** ดี *good.*
- **tsai-dii** ใจ ดี is translated into English as *to be kind, generous, good-hearted.*

> **5.3** kháu *dii-tsai* tsing-tsing เขา ดี ใจ จริงๆ
> he *good-heart* truly-truly – *He is really happy.*

- Here we have placed **tsai** กว้าง *mind, heart* after the adjective **dii** ดี *good.*
- **dii-tsai** ดี ใจ is translated into English as *happy, glad, pleased.*

Chapter 19

> **5.4** *tsai-yen-yen* ใจ เย็นๆ
> heart-cool-cool – *Calm down! Take it easy!*

tsai-yen-yen ใจ เย็นๆ is an idiomatic expression. Thai people use it when they want tell the other to *calm down.* It is normally used with friends only.

B) Prefixes referring to people

- 6. **khon**   คน   prefix for *person, people*
- 7. **phûu**   ผู้   prefix for *person, people*
- 8. **tsâu**   เจ้า   *person;* prefix to show ownership, to be good at something or to show continuity
- 9. **tʃaau**   ชาว   prefix for *persons*

khon คน *person* is used as a prefix and a classifier. As a prefix, **khon** คน *person* can be placed before adjectives and adverbs.

Examples:

khon-kɛ̀ɛ	คน แก่	*old person*
khon-diiau	คน เดียว	*alone*
khon-dii	คน ดี	*good person*
khon-ruuai	คน รวย	*rich person*
khon-ùun	คน อื่น	*another person*
khon-thai	คน ไทย	*Thai person*
khon-khâi	คน ไข้	*sick person*
khon-khǎai	คน ขาย	*seller, shopkeeper*
khon-bâa	คน บ้า	*madman*

Sentences:

> **6.1** khun maa *khon-diiau* tʃâi-mái khá
> คุณ มา คน เดียว ใช่ ไหม คะ
> you come *person-only* yes-"question" khá
> *Did you come alone?*

- Here we have placed **khon** คน *person* before the adverb **diiau** เดียว *only, sole*. The meaning in English is *alone*.

> **6.2** *khon-khăai* săam khon pai phák-phɔ̀ɔn
> คน ขาย สาม คน ไป พัก ผ่อน
> *person-sell* three person go rest-relax
> *Three shopkeepers went for a break.*

- Here we have placed **khon** คน *person* before the verb **khăai** ขาย *to sell*. The meaning in English is *seller, shopkeeper*.

- Note that in the phrase **săam khon** สาม คน, **khon** คน *person* is used as a classifier. See the previous Chapter 18 for more about classifiers.

7 **phûu** ผู้ prefix for *person, people*

    phûu ผู้ *person* is normally placed before verbs, nouns and adjectives in order to make nouns which are related to people.

Examples:

phûu-yĭng	ผู้ หญิง	*woman, female*
phûu-tʃaai	ผู้ ชาย	*man, male*
phûu-yài	ผู้ ใหญ่	*adult, grown up*
phûu-tʃûuai	ผู้ ช่วย	*helper, assistant*
phûu-tʃom	ผู้ ชม	*audience*

phûu ผู้ *person* is used somewhat differently compared to **khon** คน *person*. Sometimes the prefixes **phûu** ผู้ and **khon** คน are interchangeable.

Chapter 19

You must learn the difference by using the language. However, one major difference is that **khon** คน can be used as a prefix and also as a classifier. On the other hand, **phûu** ผู้ is normally used as a prefix only. So, we could say **khon** คน has wider usage, and **phûu** ผู้ more specific.

Sentences:

> **7.1** phǒm tông-kaan *phûu-tʃûuai* ผม ต้อง การ ผู้ ช่วย
> I need-task *person-help* – *I need a helper.*

- Here we have placed **phûu** ผู้ *person* before the verb **tʃûuai** ช่วย *to help*. The meaning becomes **phûu-tʃûuai** ผู้ ช่วย a *helper*.
- In this sentence, we also could have used **khon** คน *person* instead of **phûu** ผู้ *person*, and the meaning would not be much different.

> **7.2** *phûu-yǐng* thúk-khon tʃɔ̂ɔp tèng-nâa
> ผู้ หญิง ทุก คน ชอบ แต่ง หน้า
> *person-female* every-person like beautify-face
> *Every woman likes to use makeup.*

- Here **phûu** ผู้ *person* is placed before the noun **yǐng** *female*. **phûu-yǐng** ผู้ หญิง is translated into English as a *woman*.
- **khon** คน *person* is used here as a classifier, **thúk-khon** ทุก คน *everybody*.

> **7.3** rau mii *phûu-lên* sìp khon เรา มี ผู้ เล่น สิบ คน
> we have *person-play* ten person – *We have ten players.*

- Here **phûu** ผู้ *person* is placed before the verb **lên** เล่น *to play*. **phûu-lên** ผู้ เล่น is translated into English as a *player*.
- **khon** คน *person* is used here as a classifier, **sìp khon** สิบ คน *ten people*.

- Many times, **phûu** ผู้ *person* and **khon** คน *person* are used in the same sentence but in a different grammatical function.

8 **tsâu** เจ้า *person* is a prefix to show ownership, to be good at something or to show continuity.

Examples:

tsâu-tʃúu	เจ้า ชู้	*casanova, flirty*
tsâu khɔ̌ɔng	เจ้า ของ	*owner*
tsâu-bâan	เจ้า บ้าน	*homeowner*
tsâu-khwaam-khít	เจ้า ความ คิด	*person with ideas*

It is not very easy to translate **tsâu** เจ้า *person* directly into English. You need to learn it by using the language.

Sentences:

> **8.1** kháu tsâu-tʃúu tsing-tsing เขา เจ้า ชู้ จริงๆ
> he person-lover really-really – *He is really a casanova.*

- Here we have placed **tsâu** เจ้า *person* before the noun **tʃúu** ชู้ *lover, affair*. **tsâu-tʃúu** เจ้า ชู้ is translated into English as *casanova* or *to be flirty*.

> **8.2** thîi-nîi khrai pen *tsâu-naai* ที่ นี่ ใคร เป็น เจ้า นาย
> this-place who be *person-boss* – *Who is the boss here?*

- Here we have placed **tsâu** เจ้า *person* before the noun **khɔ̌ɔng** ของ *possession, things, stuff*. **tsâu-khɔ̌ɔng** เจ้า ของ is translated into English as an *owner*.

Chapter 19

> **8.3** piitə̂ə pen khon *tsâu-khwaam-khít*
> ปีเตอร์ เป็น คน เจ้า ความ คิด
> Peter be person *tsâu-matter-think*
> *Peter is a man with ideas.*

- Here we have placed **tsâu** เจ้า *person* before the noun **khwaam-khít** ความ คิด *idea, thought*. **tsâu-khwaam-khít** เจ้า ความ คิด can be translated into English as a *man with ideas*.

9 **tʃaau** ชาว prefix for *persons*

- **tʃaau** ชาว *person* also refers to persons but is used differently compared to **phûu** ผู้ *person*.
- **tʃaau** ชาว *person* refers to larger groups or entities of people such as nationalities, religions, professions, etc. However, in most cases, it can be replaced by **khon** คน *person*.
- **tʃaau** ชาว *person* is more formal than **khon** คน *person*.
- **tʃaau** ชาว prefix for *persons* indicates profession, nationality, etc.

Sentences:

> **9.1** *tʃaau-naa* tham ngaan nàk ชาว นา ทำ งาน หนัก
> *person-farm* do work heavy – *Farmers are hard working.*

- Here we have placed **tʃaau** ชาว *person* before the noun **naa** นา *field, farm*. **tʃaau-naa** ชาว นา is translated into English as a *farmer*.

> **9.2** *tʃaau-thai* sùphâap ชาว ไทย สุภาพ
> *person-Thai* polite – *Thai people are polite.*

- Here we have placed **tʃaau** ชาว *person* before the adjective **thai** ไทย *Thai*. **tʃaau-thai** ชาว ไทย is translated into English is a *Thai, a Thai person.*

- **khon-thai** คน ไทย *Thai* is actually a more common expression in speaking.

tʃaau-tsiin kèng ชาว จีน เก่ง
person-China talented – Chinese people are talented.

- Here we have placed **tʃaau** ชาว *person* before the adjective **tsiin** จีน *Chinese*. **tʃaau-tsiin** ชาว จีน is translated into English as a *Chinese person*.

- **khon-tsiin** คน จีน a *Chinese person* is actually a more common expression in speaking.

thîi indiia mii *tʃaau-hinduu* lăai khon
ที่ อินเดีย มี ชาว ฮินดู หลาย คน
at India have person-hindu many person
In India there are many Hindus.

Here we have placed **tʃaau** ชาว *person* before the adjective **hinduu** ฮินดู *Hindu*. **tʃaau-hinduu** ชาว ฮินดู is translated into English as a *Hindu* (a person who practises Hinduism).

- **khon-hinduu** คน ฮินดู *Hindu* is actually a more common expression in speaking.

C) Prefixes to describe a certain *profession*

   10. **tʃáng** ช่าง *mechanic*

   11. **nák** นัก *person* also indicates a certain profession with some skills

   12. **lûuk** ลูก prefix indicates a certain occupation, category or a junior partner

What is the difference between **tʃáng** ช่าง and **nák** นัก?

Chapter 19

 tʃáng ช่าง *mechanic*

Examples:

tʃáng-klɔ̂ng	ช่าง กล้อง	*photographer*
tʃáng-sɔ̂m-rót	ช่าง ซ่อม รถ	*car mechanic*
tʃáng-máai	ช่าง ไม้	*carpenter*

The prefix **tʃáng** ช่าง can be translated into English as a *mechanic*, *technician* or *engineer*. It indicates a certain profession with some skills.

Sentences:

 tʃáng-klɔ̂ng thàai-rûup   ช่าง กล้อง ถ่าย รูป
mechanic-camera take-picture
A photographer takes pictures.

- Here we have placed **tʃáng** ช่าง *mechanic* before the noun **klɔ̂ng** *camera*. **tʃáng-klɔ̂ng** ช่าง กล้อง is translated into English as a *photographer*.

 phǒm tông-kaan *tʃáng-sɔ̂m-rót*
ผม ต้อง การ ช่าง ซ่อม รถ
I need-task *mechanic-repair-car* – *I need a car mechanic.*

- Here we have placed **tʃáng** ช่าง *mechanic* before the verb **sɔ̂m-rót** ซ่อม รถ *to repair cars*. **tʃáng-sɔ̂m-rót** ช่าง ซ่อม รถ is translated into English as a *car mechanic*.

 tʃáng-máai tông mii fĩi-mɯɯ   ช่าง ไม้ ต้อง มี ฝี มือ
mechanic-wood must have skills
A carpenter must have craftsmanship.

- Here we have placed **tʃáng** ช่าง *mechanic* before the noun **máai** ไม้ *wood, timber*. **tʃáng-máai** ช่าง ไม้ is translated into English as a *carpenter*.

11 **nák** นัก *person* also indicates a certain profession with some skills.

nák นัก can be placed before verbs, adjectives and nouns. The meaning is doing something, usually a profession.

Examples:

nák-rɔ́ɔng	นัก ร้อง	*singer*
nák-sàdɛɛng	นัก แสดง	*actor, performer*
nák-bin	นัก บิน	*pilot*
nák-kiilaa	นัก กีฬา	*sportsman, athlete*

It is not easy to translate **nák** นัก directly into English. So, you need to learn it by using the language.

Generally, we may say that if you can't call somebody **tʃáng** ช่าง a *mechanic*, then **nák** นัก is perhaps a good choice. Also, **tʃáng** ช่าง *mechanic* has to do more with learned skills while **nák** นัก is more general and can also refer to a natural talent or to intellectual capacities.

Sentences:

11.1 phûɯan tʃán pen *nák-sàdɛɛng* เพื่อน ฉัน เป็น นัก แสดง
friend I be *person-play* – *My friend is an actor.*

- Here we have placed **nák** นัก *person* before the verb **sàdɛɛng** แสดง *to play, to perform*. **nák-sàdɛɛng** นัก แสดง is translated into English as an *actor, performer*.

11.2 *nák-bin* wái-tsai dâai นัก บิน ไว้ ใจ ได้
person-fly store-heart can – *Pilots can be trusted.*

- Here we have placed **nák** นัก *person* before the verb **bin** บิน *to fly*. **nák-bin** นัก บิน is translated into English as a *pilot*.

> **11.3** kháu pen *nák-kiilaa* thîi kèng tsang
> เขา เป็น นัก กีฬา ที่ เก่ง จัง
> he be *person-sport* that talented very
> *He is a very good sportsman!*

- Here we have placed **nák** นัก *person* before the noun **kilaa** บิน *sport, game*. **nák-kiilaa** นัก กีฬา is translated into English as a *sportsman, athlete*.

12 **lûuk** ลูก as a prefix

lûuk ลูก prefix indicates a certain occupation, category or a junior partner. **lûuk** ลูก can also be used as a prefix for things other than people.

Examples:

lûuk-kháa	ลูก ค้า	*customer*
lûuk-mɯɯ	ลูก มือ	*helper, assistant*
lûuk-tʃín	ลูก ชิ้น	*meatball*
lûuk-pɯɯn	ลูก ปืน	*bullet*
lûuk-máai	ลูก ไม้	*trickery, lace*

Sentences:

> **12.1** wan níi rau mii *lûuk-kháa* yɔ́ วัน นี้ เรา มี ลูก ค้า เยอะ
> day this we have *partner-business* much
> *Today, we have many customers.*

- Here we have placed **lûuk** ลูก before the verb **kháa** ค้า *to trade, to do business*. **lûuk-kháa** ลูก ค้า is translated into English as a *customer*.

> **12.2** kháu mii *lûuk-muu* sɔ̌ɔng khon เขา มี ลูก มือ สอง คน
> he have *person-hand* two person – *He has two helpers.*

- Here we have placed **lûuk** ลูก before the noun **muu** มือ *hand*. **lûuk-muu** ลูก มือ is translated into English as a *helper, assistant*.

> **12.3** kháu pen *lûuk-nɔ́ɔng* phǒm เขา เป็น ลูก น้อง ผม
> he be *person-minion* (younger person) I
> *He is my subordinate.*

- Here we have placed **lûuk** ลูก before the noun **nɔ́ɔng** น้อง *younger person, minion*. **lûuk-nɔ́ɔng** ลูก น้อง is translated into English as a *subordinate*.

> **12.4** khun tʃɔ̂ɔp kin *lûuk-tʃín* mái คุณ ชอบ กิน ลูก ชิ้น ไหม
> you like eat *ball-piece* "question"
> *Do you like to eat meatballs?*

- **lûuk** ลูก can be used with things. Then it is used to refer to round objects.
- Here we have placed **lûuk** ลูก before the noun **tʃín** น้อง *piece, fraction*. **lûuk-tʃín** ลูก ชิ้น is translated into English as *meatballs*.
- **lûuk** ลูก is a multifunctional word and has many meanings. It goes beyond the scope of this book to include a complete review of usages.

13 Special prefixes to express passive voice

In English, we place the word *by* before the agent who carried out the action. In Thai, we may use either **doon** โดน or **thùuk** ถูก.

| **doon** | โดน | *to hit* |
| **thùuk** | ถูก | *to touch* |

Chapter 19

Thais often prefer to express types of negative activity such as *being robbed, arrested, raped, injured,* etc. with the passive voice. In these situations, the subject usually does not have any control of the situation.

Note that **doon** โดน and **thùuk** ถูก can also be grammatically understood as helping verbs. We have decided to place them under the prefixes category since they may be used in a similar way as some other prefixes. They are normally interchangeable.

In other contexts, **doon** โดน also means *to touch* or *to hit* and **thùuk** ถูก means *to touch, to be correct, right, cheap* or *inexpensive.*

Sentences:

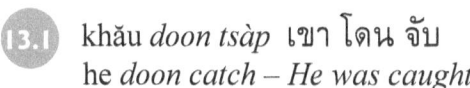

khǎu *doon tsàp*   เขา โดน จับ
he *doon catch – He was caught.*

- This is the passive voice without an agent carrying out the action.
- The prefix **doon** โดน is placed before the main verb **tsàp** จับ *to catch.*

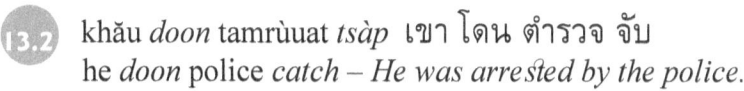

khǎu *doon* tamrùuat *tsàp*   เขา โดน ตำรวจ จับ
he *doon* police *catch – He was arrested by the police.*

- Here, the agent, **tamrùuat** ตำรวจ *police,* has carried out the action.
- The prefix **doon** โดน is placed before the agent, and the main verb **tsàp** จับ *to catch* is placed at the end of the sentence.

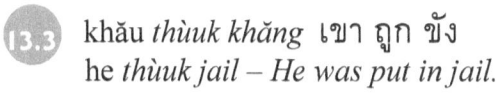

khǎu *thùuk khǎng*   เขา ถูก ขัง
he *thùuk jail – He was put in jail.*

- We may use **thùuk** ถูก instead of **doon** โดน and the meaning is the same.
- This is the passive voice without an agent carrying out the action.

- The prefix **thùuk** ถูก is placed before the main verb **fàak-khăng** ฝาก ขัง *to put in jail*.

 khău *thùuk tamrùuat khăng* เขา ถูก ตำรวจ ขัง
he *thùuk police jail* – He was put in jail by the police.

- We may use **thùuk** ถูก instead of **doon** โดน and the meaning is the same.
- Here, the agent, **tamrùuat** ตำรวจ *police*, has carried out the action.
- The prefix **thùuk** ถูก is placed before the agent, and the main verb **khăng** ขัง *to put in jail* is placed at the end of the sentence.

D. New sounds

In this section, we review once more all consonant sounds used in Thai.

1. Complete list of consonant sounds

We have now introduced all the Thai consonant sounds and vowel sounds. Note, however, that in the Thai script there are forty-two consonants symbols, but only 20 actual sounds. Note also that the initial consonant sounds are normally pronounced differently at the end of the syllable or word.

Consonant sounds:

We shall mark with **bold** those sounds which may cause some problems to English speakers.

Initial sounds:
b, **p**, ph, d, **t**, th, s, f, **ts**, **tʃ**, **k**, kh, y, w, m, n, **l**, **r**, **ng**, h

Stop end sounds:
p, ph, b = **p**
d, t, th, s, ts, tʃ = **t**
k, kh = **k**

p is stopped by the *lips*, **t** is stopped by the tip or the blade of tongue behind the *upper teeth* and **k** is stopped in the *glottis* (glottal stop). These sounds are not released; therefore, not any puff of air is coming out of your mouth when you produce these end sounds. Similar sounds in English are normally released with a slight puff of air.

Sonorant end sounds:

m = m
n = n
l = n
r = n
y = i
w = u
ng = ng

Sonorant end sounds differ from the stop end sounds; they are not stopped but can be continued without any effort. They are produced in the similar way in Thai and in English.

E. Simple advice

We may say that the Thai language is very innovative and flexible as far as speaking is concerned but very conservative as far as writing is concerned. For example, the tones of some words are changing over time, but writing in the Thai script normally remains the same. To change spelling of any language is very difficult. In English, it has been tried without much success. However, it is not entirely impossible. Lao, which has a similar writing system as Thai, has simplified its writing system. Also, the French revised completely the Vietnamese writing system. It is now written with western letters; before it was written with Chinese characters.

Now, you may wonder why it is like that? Well, the Thai language is very ancient and has a long history. It has developed over time from many sources. It has often kept the original spelling of the foreign word but modified the sound to suit the Thai way to speak. This is very much true with the words which have been borrowed from Bali/Sanskrit origin languages. Actually, the same is true with the English language. English has borrowed a major part of its vocabulary from French, Latin, Germanic and some other foreign languages. Therefore, spelling in English is not logical.

F: Take it further

Refer to the book:

Dhyan Manik: *Understanding the Thai Language and Grammar:*

- More about Thai end sounds can be found in Chapter 1, section 1.3.
- A list of commonly used prefixes can be found in Chapter 19.
- Passive voice as a prefix can be found in Chapter 19, section 19.4.
- **tsai** ใจ heart as a prefix can be found in Chapter 20, section 20.1.
- **tsai** ใจ heart as a suffix can be found in Chapter 20, section 20.2.

Chapter 20

Connecting words, phrases and sentences

phŏm khít wâa théeksîi khan níi sĭia-lέεu
ผม คิด ว่า แท็กซี่ คัน นี้ เสีย แล้ว
I think this taxi is broken.

Highlights

lé	และ	and
léɛu-kɔ̂ɔ	แล้ว ก็	and, and then
léɛu	แล้ว	then, after that
kɔ̂ɔ-ləəi	ก็ เลย	therefore, so, as a result
tɛ̀ɛ	แต่	but
wâa	ว่า	that
phrɔ́-wâa	เพราะ ว่า	because
rɯ̌ɯ	หรือ	or
thâa	ถ้า	if
tɔɔn-thîi	ตอน ที่	when
nɔ̂ɔk-tsàak	นอก จาก	except, apart from
etc.		

A. Sentences

1. tʃiiang-mài sànùk *lé* yen-sàbaai dûuai
เชียงใหม่ สนุก และ เย็น สบาย ด้วย
Chiang Mai fun *and* cool-fine also
Chiang Mai is fun and also nice and cool.

2. tʃán kamlang dɯ̀ɯm kaafɛɛ – *léɛu-kɔ̂ɔ* khui kàp phɯ̂ɯan tʃán yùu
ฉัน กำลัง ดื่ม กาแฟ – แล้ว ก็ คุย กับ เพื่อน ฉัน อยู่
I kamlang drink coffee – *then-also* chat together friend I be
I am drinking coffee and chatting with my friend.

(3) tʃán tsà kin-khâau kɔ̀ɔn – *lɛ́ɛu* pai tham-ngaan
ฉัน จะ กิน ข้าว ก่อน – แล้ว ไป ทำ งาน
I will eat-rice first – *then* go do-work
I am going to eat first, and then I will go to work.

(4) rót-bát mâi maa – rau *kɔ̂ɔ-lǝǝi* nâng thɛ́ɛksîi
รถ บัส ไม่ มา – เรา ก็ เลย นั่ง แท็กซี่
car-mail no come – we *also-so* sit taxi
The bus did not come. Therefore, we took a taxi.

(5) khâu-tsai lɛ́ɛu – *tɛ̀ɛ* phǒm mâi hěn-dûuai
เข้า ใจ แล้ว – แต่ ผม ไม่ เห็น ด้วย
enter-heart already – *but* I no see-with
I understand now, but I don't agree with you.

(6) tʃán khít *wâa* thɛ́ɛksîi khan níi sǐia-lɛ́ɛu
ฉัน คิด ว่า แท็กซี่ คัน นี้ เสีย แล้ว
I think *that* taxi this spoil-already
I think this taxi is broken.

(7) kháu tham-ngaan thîi paarîit – *phrɔ́-wâa* sànùk
เขา ทำ งาน ที่ ปารีส – เพราะ ว่า สนุก
he do-work at Paris – *because-that* fun
He works in Paris, because it is fun.

(8) khun yàak yùu thîi níi *rǔɯ* pai thîau
คุณ อยาก อยู่ ที่ นี่ หรือ ไป เที่ยว
you want stay place this *or* go trip
Do you like to stay here or go out?

(9) *thâa* mâi sàbaai tʃán tsà yùu thîi bâan
ถ้า ไม่ สบาย ฉัน จะ อยู่ ที่ บ้าน
if no well I will stay at home
If I don't feel good, I'll stay at home.

10. tʃán nɔɔn lɛ́ɛu – tɔɔn-thîi kháu maa
ฉัน นอน แล้ว – ตอน ที่ เขา มา
I sleep already – *at-that* he come
I was already sleeping when he came.

11. phŏm tʃɔ̂ɔp kin thúk yàang *nɔ̂ɔk-tsàak* núua-sàt
ผม ชอบ กิน ทุก อย่าง นอก จาก เนื้อ สัตว์
I like eat every-kind *outside-from* meat-animal
I like to eat everything except meat.

Common expressions
(kham thîi tʃái bɔ̀i-bɔ̀i คำ ที่ ใช้ บ่อยๆ)

khɔ̌ɔ-thôot ขอ โทษ
ask-pardon – *Excuse me! Sorry!*

arai-ná อะไร นะ
what-ná – *What? What did you say?*

khun yàak dùum arai คุณ อยาก ดื่ม อะไร
you want drink what – *What would you like to drink?*

tʃôok-dii-ná โชค ดี นะ
luck-good-ná – *Cheers! Good luck!*

B. Vocabulary

lɛ́	และ	and
sànùk	สนุก	to be fun
yen	เย็น	to be cool
dûuai	ด้วย	also, with
lɛ́ɛu-kɔ̂ɔ	แล้ว ก็	and, and then
kamlang	กำลัง	action in progress

Chapter 20

khui	คุย	to chat
kàp	กับ	together
phûuan	เพื่อน	friend
yùu	อยู่	state exists
lɛ́ɛu	แล้ว	then, after that
kin-khâau	กิน ข้าว	to eat
kɔ̀ɔn	ก่อน	first
tham-ngaan	ทำ งาน	to work
rót-bàt	รถ บัส	bus
kɔ̂ɔ-lǝǝi	ก็ เลย	so, therefore, as a result
nâng thɛ́ɛksîi	นั่ง แท็กซี่	to take a taxi
tɛ̀ɛ	แต่	but
hěn-dûuai	เห็น ด้วย	to agree
hěn	เห็น	to see
dûuai	ด้วย	with, also, as well
wâa	ว่า	that
sǐia-lɛ́ɛu	เสีย แล้ว	to be broken
sǐia	เสีย	to be spoiled
tɛ̀ɛ-wâa	แต่ ว่า	but
phrɔ́	เพราะ	because that
phrɔ́-wâa	เพราะ ว่า	because
paarîit	ปารีส	Paris
rǔɯ	หรือ	or
tʃɔ̂ɔp	ชอบ	to like
yùu	อยู่	to stay, to live
pai thîau	ไป เที่ยว	to go out
thâa	ถ้า	if
mâi sàbaai	ไม่ สบาย	not well

thîi bâan	ที่ บ้าน	at home
tɔɔn-thîi	ตอน ที่	when
nɔɔn	นอน	to sleep
lɛ́ɛu	แล้ว	already
nɔ̂ɔk-tsàak	นอก จาก	except, besides, apart from
thúk-yàang	ทุก อย่าง	everything
nɯ́ɯa-sàt	เนื้อ สัตว์	meat
tʃôok-dii-ná	โชค ดี นะ	Cheers! Good luck! Take care!

C. How the language works

When you are ready for more complicated sentences, then you need to know how to connect words, phrases and independent clauses or sentences together.

We have chosen the most common conjunction words to play with.

They are:

lɛ́	และ	and
lɛ́ɛu-kɔ̂ɔ	แล้ว ก็	and, and then
lɛ́ɛu	แล้ว	then, after that
kɔ̂ɔ-ləəi	ก็ เลย	therefore, so, as a result
wâa	ว่า	that
tɛ̀ɛ	แต่	but
tɛ̀ɛ-wâa	แต่ ว่า	but
phrɔ́	เพราะ	because
phrɔ́-wâa	เพราะ ว่า	because
rɯ̌ɯ	หรือ	or
thâa	ถ้า	if

Chapter 20

hàak	หาก	*if*
tɔɔn-thîi	ตอนที่	*when*
nɔ̂ɔk-tsàak	นอกจาก	*except, besides, apart from*

These conjunction words are normally used to connect words, phrases and sentences or independent clauses.

1. And, and then, then

And, and then are very common conjunction words. We introduce here three words normally used in Thai. They are:

lɛ́	และ	*and*
lɛ́ɛu-kɔ̂ɔ	แล้ว ก็	*and, and then*
lɛ́ɛu	แล้ว	*and then, after that*

Examples:

> **1.1** tʃán kamlang dùɯm kaafɛɛ – *lɛ́ɛu-kɔ̂ɔ* (*lɛ́*) khui kàp phɯ̂ɯan tʃán yùu
> ฉัน กำลัง ดื่ม กาแฟ – แล้ว ก็ (และ) คุย กับ เพื่อน ฉัน อยู่
> I kamlang drink coffee – *then-also* (and) chat friend I be
> *I am drinking coffee and chatting with my friend.*

- These two words, **lɛ́ɛu-kɔ̂ɔ** แล้ว ก็ *and, and then* and **lɛ́** และ *and*, can be used interchangeably to connect two clauses: *drinking coffee* and *chatting with a friend*.

- **lɛ́ɛu-kɔ̂ɔ** แล้ว ก็ is a friendlier style. It is normally used in speaking. **lɛ́** และ sounds a bit official; therefore, it is often used in writing and formal situations.

> **1.2** tʃán sɯ́ɯ klûuai sǎam wǐi lɛ́ (*lɛ́ɛu-kɔ̂ɔ*) ʔɛppôŋ hòk lûuk
> ฉัน ซื้อ กล้วย สาม หวี และ (แล้ว ก็) แอปเปิ้ล หก ลูก
> I buy banana three cluster and (*then-also*) apple six piece
> *I bought three bunches of bananas and six apples.*

- Here these two words, **lɛ́** และ *and* and **lɛ́ɛu-kɔ̂ɔ** แล้ว ก็ *and, and then* are connecting two nouns: *three clusters of bananas* and *six apples*.

- **lɛ́** และ can replace **lɛ́ɛu-kɔ̂ɔ** แล้ว ก็ in most of the situations. It sounds more official, however.

> **1.3** kháu sùphâap lɛ́ɛu-kɔ̂ɔ (lɛ́) nâa-rák dûuai
> เขา สุภาพ แล้ว ก็ (และ) น่า รัก ด้วย
> she polite and *then-also* (and) nâa-love also
> *She is polite and also cute.*

- Here these two words, **lɛ́ɛu-kɔ̂ɔ** แล้ว ก็ *and, and then* and **lɛ́** และ *and* are connecting two adjectives: **sùphâap** สุภาพ *polite* and **nâa-rák** *cute*.

- Both are grammatically correct, but **lɛ́** และ *and* sounds more official.

> **1.4** tʃán tsà kin-khâau kɔ̀ɔn – *lɛ́ɛu-kɔ̂ɔ* (lɛ́ɛu) pai tham-ngaan
> ฉัน จะ กิน ข้าว ก่อน – แล้ว ไป ทำ งาน
> I will eat-rice first – *then-also* (then) go do-work
> *I am going to eat first, and then (after that) I will go to work.*

- Here these two words, **lɛ́ɛu-kɔ̂ɔ** แล้ว ก็ *and, and then* and **lɛ́ɛu** แล้ว *then*, are connecting two independent clauses. The meaning is *I am going to do something first, and after that I will do something else*.

- We could drop **kɔ̂ɔ** ก็ *also* and use only **lɛ́ɛu** แล้ว *then*. The meaning would be the same.

- However, **lɛ́ɛu-kɔ̂ɔ** แล้ว ก็ *and, and then* is a very handy term since it can be used in many different situations. It is, therefore, often preferred in speaking.

- **lɛ́** และ *and* cannot be used in this structure since the meaning here is *then, and then, after that* and not simple *and*.

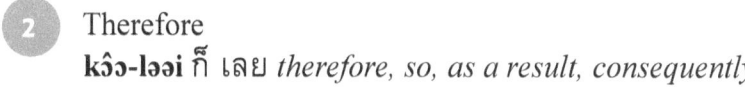 Therefore

kɔ̂ɔ-ləəi ก็ เลย *therefore, so, as a result, consequently*

Examples:

 rót-bàt mâi maa – rau *kɔ̂ɔ-ləəi* nâng théeksîi
รถ บัส ไม่ มา – เรา ก็ เลย นั่ง แท็กซี่
car-bus no come – we *also-so* sit taxi
The bus did not come; therefore, we took a taxi.

- The compound construction **kɔ̂ɔ-ləəi** ก็ เลย *therefore, so, as a result* is normally used to connect two independent clauses.
- **kɔ̂ɔ-ləəi** ก็ เลย is best understood as one word which is usually translated into English as *therefore, so, as a result, consequently, hence etc...*
- Note that Thais *sit* in a taxi while the English take a taxi; the meaning is the same.

 fǒn tòk nàk – *kɔ̂ɔ-ləəi* mâi pai
ฝน ตก หนัก – ก็ เลย ไม่ ไป
rain-fall heavy – *also-so* no go
It was raining a lot. So, we didn't go.

- Often English speakers prefer to use *so* instead of *therefore* or *as a result*. **kɔ̂ɔ-ləəi** ก็ เลย *therefore, so, as a result* is commonly used in Thai in speaking.
- Note that **ləəi** เลย is commonly used as an intensifier in Thai. It can be translated into English in several different ways; all depends on the context. In the negative sentence, the meaning is *not at all*. In an other context, the meaning can be *to pass, to go through, for sure* etc.

Examples:

mâi tʃɔ̂ɔp ləəi	ไม่ ชอบ เลย	I don't like it *at all*.
kháu kèng tsang ləəi	เขา เก่ง จัง เลย	He is talented *for sure*.
phàan pai ləəi	ผ่าน ไป เลย	*Go ahead!*

3 That, but, because

wâa	ว่า	*that*
tɛ̀ɛ	แต่	*but*
tɛ̀ɛ-wâa	แต่ ว่า	*but*
phrɔ́	เพราะ	*because*
phrɔ́-wâa	เพราะ ว่า	*because that*

Examples:

> **3.1** tʃán khít *wâa* théeksîi khan níi sĭia-lɛ́ɛu
> ฉัน คิด ว่า แท็กซี่ คัน นี้ เสีย แล้ว
> I think *that* taxi vehicle this spoil-already
> *I think that this taxi is broken.*

- **wâa** ว่า *that* is a very common conjunction word in Thai. If you listen to two Thais having a coffee break discussion, you will many times hear phrases like: **tʃán khít wâa**... ฉัน คิด ว่า *I think that...* **kháu bɔ̀ɔk wâa** เขา บอก ว่า *he told that...* etc.

> **3.2** khâu-tsai lɛ́ɛu – *tɛ̀ɛ* (tɛ̀ɛ-wâa) phŏm mâi hĕn-dûuai
> เข้า ใจ แล้ว – แต่ (แต่ ว่า) ผม ไม่ เห็น ด้วย
> enter-heart already – *but* (but-that) I no see-with
> *I understand now, but I don't agree.*

- **tɛ̀ɛ** แต่ *but* is used in Thai in the similar way as *but* in English.
- We may replace **tɛ̀ɛ** แต่ *but* with **tɛ̀ɛ-wâa** แต่ ว่า *but*; the meaning is the same. However, the colour of the sentence is slightly different.

Chapter 20

> **3.3** kháu tham-ngaan thîi paarîit–*phrɔ́* (phrɔ́-wâa) sànùk
> เขา ทำ งาน ที่ ปารีส – เพราะ (เพราะ ว่า) สนุก
> he do-work at Paris – *because* (because-that) fun
> *He works in Paris, because it is fun.*

- **phrɔ́** เพราะ *because* is used in Thai in the similar way as *because* in English.
- We may replace **phrɔ́** เพราะ *because* with **phrɔ́-wâa** เพราะ ว่า *because*; the meaning is the same. However, the colour of the sentence is slightly different.

4 Or, if

rǔu	หรือ	*or*
rǔu-wâa	หรือ ว่า	*or*
thâa	ถ้า	*if*
hàak	หาก	*if*

Examples:

> **4.1** khun yàak yùu thîi nîi – *rǔu* (rǔu-wâa) pai thîau
> คุณ อยาก อยู่ ที่ นี่ – หรือ (หรือ ว่า) ไป เที่ยว
> you want stay place this – *or* (or-that) go trip
> *Do you like to stay here or go out?*

- **rǔu** หรือ *or* is used in Thai in the similar way as *or* in English.
- We may replace **rǔu** หรือ *or* with **rǔu-wâa** หรือ ว่า *or*; the meaning is the same, however. The colour of the sentence is slightly different.

> **4.2** *thâa* (hàak) mâi sàbaai – tʃán tsà yùu thîi bâan
> ถ้า (หาก) ไม่ สบาย – ฉัน จะ อยู่ ที่ บ้าน
> *if* (if) no well – I will stay at home
> *If I don't feel good, I'll stay at home.*

- **thâa** ถ้า *if* is used in Thai in the similar way as *if* in English.
- We may replace **thâa** ถ้า *if* with **hàak** หาก *if*; the meaning is the same, however. **hàak** หาก *if* is seldom used; it may sound somewhat official.

5. When, while
tɔɔn-thîi ตอน ที่

> **5.1** tʃán nɔɔn lɛ́ɛu – *tɔɔn-thîi* kháu maa
> ฉัน นอน แล้ว – ตอน ที่ เขา มา
> I sleep already – *at-that* he come
> *I was already sleeping when he came.*

> **5.2** *tɔɔn-thîi* kháu maa – tʃán nɔɔn lɛ́ɛu
> ตอน ที่ เขา มา – ฉัน นอน แล้ว
> *at-that* he come – I sleep already
> *When he came, I was already sleeping.*

- **tɔɔn-thîi** ตอน ที่ *when* is used in Thai in the similar way as *when* in English.
- We may place **tɔɔn-thîi** ตอน ที่ *when* between two independent clauses (sentence 5.1) or at the beginning of the two clauses (sentence 5.2); it all depends on the emphasis.

6. Except, apart from

In Thai, we normally use **nɔ̂ɔk-tsàak** นอก จาก *except* in order to express the English meaning *apart from, except*.

It can be translated into English in several different ways. Depending on the context the translation could also be: *except for, besides, other than, apart from, not including...*

Examples:

> **6.1** phŏm tʃɔ̂ɔp kin thúk yàang – *nɔ̂ɔk-tsàak* núua-sàt
> ผม ชอบ กิน ทุก อย่าง – นอก จาก เนื้อ สัตว์
> I like eat every-kind – *outside-from* meat-animal
> *I like to eat everything except meat.*

- **nɔ̂ɔk-tsàak** นอก จาก *except* is placed here before the noun **núua-sàt** เนื้อ สัตว์ *meat;* that is an exception.

> **6.2** *nɔ̂ɔk-tsàak* rót-tìt – krungthêep kɔ̂ɔ nâa-yùu
> นอก จาก รถ ติด – กรุงเทพ ก็ น่า อยู่
> *outside-from* car-stuck – Bangkok also nâa-live
> *Besides traffic jams, Bangkok is a nice place to live.*

- Here **nɔ̂ɔk-tsàak** นอก จาก *except* is placed before the word **rót-tìt** รถ ติด *traffic jam*; that is an exception.

> **6.3** sùuan-yài tʃán mâi yàak pai thîau mâak – *nɔ̂ɔk-tsàak* pai tʃiiang-mài – *phrɔ́-wâa* sànùk tàlɔ̀ɔt
>
> ส่วน ใหญ่ ฉัน ไม่ อยาก ไป เที่ยว มาก – นอก จาก ไป เชียง ใหม่ – เพราะ ว่า สนุก ตลอด
>
> part-big I no want go travel much – *outside-from* go Chiang Mai – *because-that* fun always
>
> *Generally, I don't like to travel much except going to Chiang Mai is always fun.*

- Here **nɔ̂ɔk-tsàak** นอก จาก *except* is placed before the phrase **pai tʃiiang-mài** ไป เชียง ใหม่ *to go to Chiang Mai*; that is an exception.

D. New sounds

As an English speaker, you are well advised to make some extra effort to get vowel sounds right in Thai. English vowels are pronounced in different ways by several distinct accents. Yet, people understand each other. Thai vowels must be pronounced clearly (either short or long), and not be blurred by anything else.

In this section we shall review again all vowel sounds used in Thai. All vowel combinations are made out of 18 pure vowel sounds. The pure vowel sounds are:

Open ending:

1. Pure long vowels: aa อา, ii อี, uu อู, **ee** เอ, ɛɛ แอ, **oo** โอ, ɔɔ ออ, əə เออ, **ʉʉ** อือ
2. Special vowels: am อำ, au เอา, ai ใอ, ไอ
3. Long diphthongs: iia เอีย, **ʉʉa** เอือ, uua อัว
4. Short vowel combinations: iu อิว, ui อุย, eu เอ็ว, ai อัย
5. Long vowel combinations: eeu เอว, əəi เอย, ooi โอย, ɛɛu แอว, aai อาย, aau อาว, ɔɔi ออย, iiau เอียว, **ʉʉai** เอือย, uuai อวย

Closed ending:

1. Pure short vowels: à อะ, ì อิ, ù อุ, è เอะ, ɛ̀ แอะ, ò โอะ, ɔ̀ เอาะ, ə̀ เออะ, **ʉ̀** อึ
2. Short diphthongs: ìa เอียะ, **ʉ̀a** เอือะ, ùa อัวะ

Note that we have marked those vowel sounds with **bold** which may cause some problems for English speakers.

E. Simple advice

If you had to learn only three conjunction words, they should be:

lέεu-kɔ̂ɔ แล้ว ก็ *and, and then*, **phrɔ́-wâa** เพราะ ว่า *because* and **tὲε-wâa** แต่ ว่า *but*.

lέεu-kɔ̂ɔ แล้ว ก็ *and, and then* is a very handy expression since it can be used in many different situations. It has a number of meanings such as *and, then, and then, after that.* Hence, it is often preferred in speaking. **lέεu** แล้ว and **kɔ̂ɔ** ก็ can also be used separately alone as conjunction words, but the usage is somewhat more specific or restricted.

tὲε-wâa แต่ ว่า *but* is a simple conjunction word; it is used in the similar manner as the English word *but*. **tὲε-wâa** แต่ ว่า *but* and **tὲε** แต่ *but* are usually interchangeable.

phrɔ́-wâa เพราะ ว่า *because* is also a simple conjunction word; it is used in the similar manner as the English word *because*. **phrɔ́-wâa** เพราะ ว่า *because* and **phrɔ́** เพราะ *because* are normally interchangeable.

In addition, Thai people love to use the conjunction word **wâa** ว่า *that* in many different situations together with a number of words. There are a few verbs after which **wâa** ว่า *that* is normally placed.

Here are some common examples:

bɔ̀ɔk wâa	บอก ว่า	*tell that*
phûut wâa	พูด ว่า	*say that*
khít wâa	ฉัน คิด ว่า	*think that*
rúu-sὺk wâa	รู้ สึก ว่า	*believe that*
wăng wâa	หวัง ว่า	*hope that*
khâu-tsai wâa	เข้า ใจ ว่า	*understand that*
tsam-dâai wâa	จำ ได้ ว่า	*remember that*

t͡ʃûɯa wâa	เชื่อ ว่า	*believe that*
dâai-yin wâa	ได้ ยิน ว่า	*hear that*

Well, perhaps we also should mention **lɛ́** และ *and*. Note, however, that **lɛ́ɛu-kɔ̂ɔ** แล้ว ก็ *and, and then* can almost always be used instead of **lɛ́** และ *and* in speaking.

F. Take it further

Refer to the book:

Dhyan Manik: *Understanding the Thai Language and Grammar*

- More about Thai end sounds can be found in Chapter 1, section 1.3.
- A more extensive list of conjunction words can be found in Chapter 16. Conjunction words are used to connect words, phrases and sentences.

Chapter 21

Tones of the Thai language

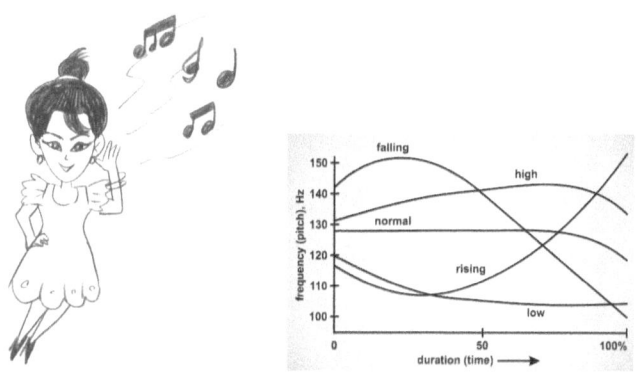

Tone Chart of "Jackson Gandour" (1976)

> **Highlights**
>
> Normal tone   (*sim* ซิม no tone mark)
>
> Low tone   (*sìng* สิ่ง tone mark pointing down)
>
> Falling tone   (*sîng* ซิ่ง mark as a hat)
>
> High tone   (*sím* ซิ้ม tone mark pointing up)
>
> Rising tone   (*sǐng* สิง mark as a hat upside down)

A. Tones with short and long vowels

i อิ

sim	ซิม	*sim card*
sìng	สิ่ง	*thing*
sîng	ซิ่ง	*fast*
sím	ซิ้ม	*aunt*
sǐng	สิง	*to be possessed*

ii อี

pii	ปี	*year*
pìi	ปี่	*flute*
pîi	ปี้	*elder brother (northern dialect)*
píi	ปี๊	*(only a sound, no meaning)*
pǐi	ปี๋	*fully*

ù อุ

rum	รุม	to crowd around
tùm	ตุ่ม	pimple, water jar
lûm	ลุ่ม	lowland
rúng	รุ้ง	rainbow
lŭm	หลุม	hole

uu อู

puu	ปู	crab
pùu	ปู่	grandfather
phûu	ผู้	person
búu	ปู๊	military, fight
phŭu	ผู	(only a sound, no meaning)

è เอะ

tʃen	เช็น	(only a sound, no meaning)
tsèn	เจ่น	(only a sound, no meaning)
tʃên	เช่น	as, for example
tséng	เจ๊ง	to go broke
tsĕng	เจ๋ง	smart

ee เอ

tsee	เจ	vegetarian
tsèe	เจ่	(only a sound, no meaning)
tsêe	เจ้	elder sister
tsée	เจ๊	elder sister
tʃĕe	เฉ	to deviate, not straight

ò โอะ

son	ซน	to be naughty
sòng	ส่ง	to send
sôm	ส้ม	acid, orange
sóm	ซ้ม	(only a sound, no meaning)
sŏm	สม	suitable

oo โอ

moong	โมง	hour
mòong	โหม่ง	to head in the ball game
môong	โม่ง	to be gigantic
móong	โม้ง	(only a sound, no meaning)
mŏong	โหมง	(only a sound, no meaning)

à อะ

sang	ซัง	stubble of rice
sàng	สั่ง	to order
sân	สั้น	short
sám	ซ้ำ	to repeat
săng	สังข์	conch shell

aa อา

maa	มา	to come
màa	หม่า	to brew (not used today)
mâa	ม่าห์	ghost (not used today)
máa	ม้า	horse
măa	หมา	dog

au เอา

kau	เกา	to scratch
kàu	เก่า	to be old
khâu	เข้า	to enter
kháu	เคา	he, she
khău	เขา	hill, mountain

aau อาว

khaau	คาว	smelly (fishy smelly)
khàau	ข่าว	news
khâau	ข้าว	rice
kháau	ค้าว	(only a sound, no meaning)
khău	ขาว	white

ai ใอ ไอ

sai	ไซ	fish trap
sài	ใส่	to put on, to wear
sâi	ไส้	intestine
sái	ไช้	which, whatever
săi	ใส	clear

aai อาย

saai	ทราย	sand
sàai	ส่าย	to swing
sâai	ส้าย	(only a sound, no meaning)
sáai	ซ้าย	left side
săai	สาย	line

> **Common expressions**
> (kham thîi chái bòi-bòi คำ ที่ ใช้ บ่อยๆ)
>
> khít òok rʉ́-yang คิด ออก รึ ยัง
> think out or-not yet – *Have you figured it out?*
>
> rɔɔ dǐiau ná รอ เดี๋ยว นะ
> wait moment ná – *Wait a moment!*
>
> khít òok lɛ́ɛu คิด ออก แล้ว
> think out already – *Yes, I have!*
>
> yàak-rúu-yàak-hěn อยาก รู้ อยาก เห็น
> want-know-want-see – *I am curious.*

B. Vocabulary

khít òok	คิด ออก	to figure out
rɔɔ	รอ	to wait
dǐiau	เดี๋ยว	moment
yàak rúu	อยาก รู้	to want to know
yàak hěn	อยาก เห็น	to want to see
yàak-rúu-yàak-hěn	อยาก รู้อ ยาก เห็น	to be curious

C. How the language works

In order to speak correct Thai, *you do not need to know the tone rules,* but it is good to have some practical knowledge of how tones are used in Thai. Similarly, when you sing you do not need to know the note, but you should sing in tune.

There are five tones in the Thai language: **middle**, **low**, **falling**, **high** and **rising**. The middle tone is sometimes also called the medium, common or level tone.

Normally, foreigners learn tones from transliterations and also by listening.

When a word is written only with Roman letters, and the tone marks are omitted from the transliteration, you cannot know the correct tone, and often the meaning of the word, unless you see the word in a particular context. For instance, try to figure out the right tone for the following transliterated script.

mai	ไมล์	*mile* (middle tone)
mai	ใหม่	*new* (low tone)
mai	ไม่	*not* (falling tone)
mai	ไหม	question word in speaking (high tone)
mai	ไหม	*silk* (rising tone)

There is no way to know the tone unless you know the Thai word. For Thai people, the above five words represent five different sounds. Thais do not separate pronunciation from tones. If you know the Thai script, then you would know the meaning and the tone of these words.

When tone marks are left out from the transliterated text, it is impossible to figure out the meaning of the word or the tone in isolation. The good news is however that when you use the word in the sentence, the meaning can be understood in the absence of the right tone since the meaning can be figured out from the context.

For Thais a different tone means a different pronunciation and naturally a different sound. So, you cannot ignore tones of the Thai language totally even though you could somehow get by using only one tone, the middle tone.

Chapter 21

If you want to learn the tone rules of the Thai script, you need to know the basics of the Thai writing system. The tones in the Thai language are determined by the initial consonant, the end sound, the length of the vowel, and by Thai tone marks which are different from the tone marks used in transliterations.

If you know the tone rules, you can figure out the right tone from the Thai script.

The tone of a syllable or a word in Thai is determined by:

1. The class of the initial consonant
2. The end sound and length of the vowel
3. The tone marks
4. Tone regulators (symbols อ and ห are used as tone regulators)

Note that very few people (Thai or foreign) know the tone rules of the written Thai words since they are quite complicated. Thais know the correct tone of written words since they have learned it naturally.

Here we have indicated the tone marks in transliterations. Hence, there is not any problem to figure out the correct tone and the meaning.

mai	ไมล์	*mile* (middle tone)
mài	ใหม่	*new* (low tone)
mâi	ไม่	*not* (falling tone)
mái	ไหม	*question word in speaking* (high tone)
măi	ไหม	*silk* (rising tone)

Sometimes there is a mismatch between the Thai spelling and tone. One example is a *question word* **mái** ไหม which is pronounced with the *high tone.* **măi** ไหม *silk* is written exactly the same in the Thai script but pronounced with a different tone, *rising tone*. There are only a few words like this.

D. New sounds

We have already learned all Thai sounds in Chapters 1–20.

We recommend, however, that you also learn all the five tones properly.

When you master all the sounds and all five tones properly, you can learn the tones of new words basically in three different ways.

1. By listening to native Thai people or audio files.
2. By reading the transliterated text with special tone marks.
3. By reading the Thai script for which you need to know the basics of the Thai writing system and the tone rules. It should be noted that this is not very easy since you need to know the theory of the Thai writing system. Thais have learned the tones naturally and use them intuitively; they do not need to think about the complex tone rules. After all when you speak, you do not have time to think about tone rules.

   When a word is written only with Roman letters, and the tone marks are omitted from the transliteration, you cannot know the correct tone and often neither know the meaning of the word. The difficulty arises from the fact that many words would be transliterated the same.

E. Simple advice

Do not worry too much about tones in the beginning. They will come naturally without too much effort on your part.

Thais do not usually call the tones by the same name as we westerners do. If you ask the average Thai about the name of the tone, you may not get a satisfactory reply. Thai people know the tones, but are not concerned about what they are called. They are born into the habit. They do not care about the theory of tones which may have been thought at school. Similarly, if you ask an average native English speaker "how to make the future perfect tense", you may be looked upon as asking a stupid question. So, you need to use your ears while attempting to get the right tone from your Thai friends.

Even though tones are a very important part of the Thai language, correct pronunciation and usage of the right word in the right situation are important as well. The right tone does not help if the word is not pronounced correctly.

On the other hand, if you only use the normal tone for all words, pronounce them right (consonants and vowels) and use the right word in the right situation, you may often be understood; then, you are speaking Thai in your own way and not exactly like a Thai.

F. Take it further

After you have learned the most important aspects of the Thai language from this book, there are several ways how to proceed.

You may also wish to review the book Dhyan Manik: *Understanding the Thai Language and Grammar – Take It Further* (ISBN 978-952-6651-46-0) in order to gain some more knowledge about how to use the Thai language while you communicate with Thai people.

If your main focus is to learn to speak and improve your speaking skills, then concentrate on that and forget about reading and writing altogether. If you decide to learn the theory of the Thai writing system, which usually includes reading and writing, then go for that. Note, however, that the task is vast and that hinders you from learning to speak and communicate fluently with Thai people. The fact is that you have only so much energy at one time; you need to be clear about your priorities. That way you will save much time and won't hit your head against the wall.

It may take several years to reach the level at which you are able to read a Thai newspaper or write an official letter. Most foreigners never get there. Writing an essay or an official letter can prove to be difficult even in your own language. That is why we have editors who are experts in languages. So, what about your Thai? Well, to learn to send a text message in Thai to your friend can't be that difficult since the focus is on understanding and not being absolutely correct grammatically.

Note, however, that most language schools in Thailand begin with teaching the Thai script, consonant and vowel symbols. Instead, in this book we have concentrated only on sounds and how to put words together, since you need to know all Thai sounds in order to speak Thai fluently. Reading and writing well is a totally different project.

Check also the website *www.thaibooks.net* for more information.

Bibliography

Becker, Benjawan Poomsan. Thai for Beginners.
   Paiboon Publishing, California, 1995.

Becker, Benjawan Poomsan. Thai for Intermediate
   Learners. Paiboon Publishing, California, 1998.

Becker, Benjawan Poomsan. Thai for Advanced Learners.
   Paiboon Publishing, California, 2000.

Burusphat Somsonge. Reading and Writing Thai.
   Institute of Language and Culture for Rural Development,
   Mahidol University, Bangkok, 2006.

Dhyan, Manik. 22 Secrets of Learning Thai – Complete Guide to
   Sounds, Tones and Thai Writing System, Dolphin Books, 2014.

Dhyan, Manik. Learning Thai with hâi ให้. Dolphin Books, 2016.

Dhyan, Manik. Learning Thai with dâai ได้ Book I.
   Dolphin Books, 2017.

Dhyan, Manik. Learning Thai with dâai ได้ Book II.
   Dolphin Books, 2018.

Dhyan, Manik. Understanding the Thai Language and
   Grammar – Take It Further. Dolphin Books, 2020

Higbie, James & Thinsan Snea. Thai Reference Grammar:
   The Structure of Spoken Thai. Orchid Press, Bangkok, 2003.

James, Helen. Thai Reference Grammar.
   D.K. Editions & Suk's Editions, Bangkok, 2001.

Kanchanawan, Nitaya & Eynon, Matthew J. Learning Thai (A
   Unique and Practical Approach). Odeon Store, Bangkok, 2005.

Ponmanee, Sriwilai. Speaking Thai for Advanced Learner. Thai
   Studies Center, Chiang Mai Universtity, Chiang Mai, 2001.

Smyth, David. Thai: An Essential Grammar.
   Routledge, London and New York, 2002.

Smyth, David. Teach Yourself Thai.
   Hodder Headline, London, 2003.

22 Secrets of Learning Thai

– Complete Guide to Sounds, Tones and Thai Writing System

Twenty-two Secrets of Learning Thai teaches you all the sounds used in spoken and written Thai. It includes 20 consonant sounds, 18 pure vowel sounds, all special vowels and vowel combinations. It points out the main obstacles for learners, for example which Thai sounds are most difficult for an English speaker to produce. It then gives you handy tips to help overcome these difficulties. Much care has been taken to describe each sound in phonetic as well as in practical terms so that everyone should be able to grasp the correct way to produce Thai sounds.

The book has been designed so that it can be used by all levels of Thai learners. It contains a special exercise section, which teaches you in a step by step manner how to learn to read Thai script. At the same time all the Thai tone rules are taught in theory and practice. The student will get to know the most common Thai consonant symbols as well as rare symbols mostly borrowed from Indic languages, Pali and Sanskrit.

The book includes two audio CDs which feature more than 500 words spoken by native speakers to give you examples of how the words are produced in practice. In addition to individual words, the audio CDs feature many of the most common expressions used by Thai people in everyday conversation.

This book is suitable for self-study and can also be used as an aid in the classroom. It contains a vast number of tips to assist you in learning Thai and understanding some of the crucial cultural aspects of the language.

This book and CDs will set you on the road to confident Thai language learning.

22 Secrets of Learning Thai

– *Learning Thai with hâi* ให้

hâi ให้, along with words like dâai ได้, lέεu แล้ว and kɔ̂ɔ ก็, is one of the most important words in the Thai language.

When speaking Thai, it is important to understand the correct usage of the verb hâi ให้ in everyday speech.

One simple way to use the verb hâi ให้ is *to give something to someone*. It is used in a similar manner as the English verb *to give*.

In addition, hâi ให้ is used as a causative verb which has several different meanings depending on the situation, and the way it is spoken. It can be translated into English as *to let, to allow, to make* and even *to order* or *to force someone to do something*.

In some situations hâi ให้ is better translated into English as the preposition *for*, as in *for you, for me* etc. It is also often used in idiomatic phrases where it carries no meaning itself but denotes only the sense of a command.

Thais use the verb hâi ให้ in an intuitive way in a variety of situations in order to express feelings, wishes, commands and nuances of meaning while communicating with each other every day.

If you learn this word well, you will be rewarded.

22 Secrets of Learning Thai

– Learning Thai with dâai ได้

Book I, Secrets 1–14

Whether you are a beginner or an advanced learner, you certainly want to learn to speak Thai fluently. This book will take you a long way towards your goal.

dâai ได้ is one of the most common words in Thai. It is a multifunctional helping verb and is used by Thais in several different ways. It has many distinct meanings depending on where it is placed in a sentence and which other words are used with it. With this book you won't just learn how to use dâai ได้ but will also acquire a deeper knowledge of the Thai language in general.

Included are:
- complete and informative written examples
- audio spoken by native speakers
- highlights and explanations of dâai's ได้ usage
- sections of simple and easy to understand advice
- useful hints and tips on dâai ได้ and the spoken Thai language

Furthermore, you will get to see the language "through the eyes of dâai ได้". Study this book and you will be rewarded; your Thai friends will be amazed at your deep understanding of the subtleties of their language.

22 Secrets of Learning Thai

– *Learning Thai Tenses with dâai* ได้

Book II, Secrets 15–22

Whether you are a beginner or an advanced learner, you will surely want to learn to speak Thai fluently. In order to do this, it is vital to use time words and tense markers correctly.

The English term *tense* is also a handy way to talk about past, present and future activities in Thai, even though there are no tenses as such in the Thai language. When compared to English, Thai tenses are expressed very differently.

It is often said that **dâai** ได้ denotes a past tense. However, it would be better not to think of **dâai** ได้ as the past tense marker since it can also be used to refer to present or future events.

To help you speak Thai fluently the Book II includes:
- complete and informative written examples
- audio spoken by native speakers
- highlights and explanations of **dâai**'s ได้ usage
- sections of simple and easy to understand advice
- useful hints and tips on **dâai** ได้ and the spoken Thai language

Books I and II complement each other. However, each book has a different focus. In Book I, Secrets 1–14, we introduced **dâai** ได้ and explained where it should be placed in sentences. **dâai** ได้ has several grammatical functions; hence, it also has several meanings depending on the context. In Book II, Secrets 15–22, we focus on tenses.

Have fun while you study them both; then, you will understand how Thais express themselves in everyday life!

Learning Thai Quicly and Easily

– Understanding the Thai Language and Grammar – Take It Further

Table of Contents

Chapter 1. Introduction to sounds and Thai transliteration
 1.1 Thai consonant sounds
 1.2 Thai vowel sounds
 1.3 End sounds
 1.4 Consonant clusters

Chapter 2. Original Thai words compared to foreign origin words
 2.1 Common original Thai words
 2.2 Common Chinese words
 2.3 Common Khmer words
 2.4 Common Pali/Sanskrit words
 2.5 Common English words

Chapter 3. Personal pronouns, family members and body parts
 3.1 Personal pronouns
 3.2 Family members and relatives
 3.3 Body parts

Chapter 4. Days, weeks, months and seasons
 4.1 Days of the week
 4.2 Months
 4.3 Seasons

Chapter 5. Thai numbers
 5.1 Cardinal numbers
 5.2 Ordinal numbers

Chapter 6. 24-hour clock using naalíkaa นาฬิกา o'clock
 6.1 Morning time
 6.2 Afternoon time
 6.3 Evening time
 6.4 Night time
 6.5 Expressing minutes

Chapter 7. Travelling, places, buildings and countries of the world
   7.1   Travelling and directions
   7.2   Buildings and places
   7.3   Countries of the world

Chapter 8. Names of some common animals and insects

Chapter 9. Foods, drinks and spices
   9.1   Some common Thai foods
   9.2   Vegetables, nuts etc.
   9.3   Fruits
   9.4   Drinks
   9.5   Desserts
   9.6   Spices

Chapter 10. Health & personal items
   10.1   Some common health vocabulary
   10.2   Not feeling well
   10.3   Some common diseases
   10.4   To heal illnesses
   10.5   Personal items

Chapter 11. Adjectives
   11.1   General adjectives
   11.2   Adjectives normally related to people and feelings (to be happy, sad, smart etc.)
   11.3   Adjectives describing quality, often used for things (foods, buildings etc.)
   11.4   Colours as adjectives

Chapter 12. Adverbs
   12.1   How? (adverbs of manner)
   12.2   When? (adverbs of time)
   12.3   How often? (adverbs of frequency)
   12.4   How many? (adverbs of quantity)
   12.5   How much? To what degree? (adverbs of degree)
   12.6   How certain? (adverbs of certainty)
   12.7   Where? What place? (adverbs of place)

Chapter 13. Verbs
   13.1   Adjectives as state verbs + **lɛ́ɛu** แล้ว already

13.2 Other common state verbs + **lέεu** แล้ว already
13.3 Long term action verbs + **lέεu** แล้ว already
13.4 Short term action verbs + **lέεu** แล้ว already

Chapter 14. Thai question words
 14.1 Question words at the end of the sentence only
 14.2 Question words at the end or at the beginning of the sentence

Chapter 15. Prepositions
 15.1 Simple prepositions
 15.2 Prepositions of location
 15.3 Time prepositions

Chapter 16. Conjunction words

Chapter 17. Summary of the Thai tenses
 17.1 Basic sentence
 17.2 Talking about when
 17.3 Talking about how often
 17.4 Talking about the time indicators
 17.5 Talking about the present tense markers
 17.6 Talking about the past tense markers
 17.7 Talking about the future tense marker
 17.8 Talking about the duration of time and point of time

Chapter 18. Classifiers
 18.1 Similar classifiers (Thai vs English)
 18.2 A classifier as the main noun
 18.3 Classifiers with specific meaning
 18.4 Classifiers used for differnt types of nouns

Chapter 19. Prefixes
 19.1 Commonly used general prefixes
 19.2 Prefixes referring to people
 19.3 Prefixes to describe a certain profession
 19.4 Passive voice

Chapter 20. tsai ใจ heart, mind as a prefix or a suffix
 20.1 **tsai** ใจ heart as a prefix
 20.2 **tsai** ใจ heart as a suffix

22 Secrets of Learning Thai books:

- Complete Guide to Sounds, Tones and Thai Writing System (2014)
- Learning Thai with hâi ให้ (2016)
- Learning Thai with dâai ได้ Book I
  Secrets 1–14 (2018)
- Learning Thai Tenses with dâai ได้ Book II
  Secrets 15–22 (2018)
- Learning Thai and Thai Tenses with lɛ́ɛu แล้ว (coming 2020)
- Learning Thai with kɔ̂ɔ ก็ (coming 2021)

Learning Thai Quickly and Easily:

- Learning Thai with Original Thai Words (2019)

- Understanding the Thai Language and Grammar – Take It Further (coming early 2020)

- Learning Thai with English Words (coming 2021)

- Learning Thai with Foreign Words –
  Pali, Sanskrit, Khmer, Chinese... (coming 2022)

Audio spoken in MP3 format by native speakers can be loaded from the following address:

www.thaibooks.net

Thai voices: Ms. Duangmon Loprakhong
              Ms. Waree Singhanart
              Mr. Watit Pumyoo

English voice: Ms. Jiraporn Buasuk

Publisher:

Dolphin BOOKS
www.dolphinbooks.org
info@dolphinbooks.org

www.thaibooks.net
www.facebook.com/22Secrets

www.ingramcontent.com/pod-product-compliance
Lightning Source LLC
LaVergne TN
LVHW091712070526
838199LV00050B/2363